GREAT MYTHS ABOUT ATHEISM

GREAT MYTHS ABOUT ATHEISM

Russell Blackford and Udo Schüklenk

WILEY Blackwell

This edition first published 2013

Wiley-Blackwell is an imprint of John Wiley & Sons, formed by the merger of Wiley's global Scientific, Technical and Medical business with Blackwell Publishing.

Registered Office
John Wiley & Sons Ltd, The Atrium, Southern Gate, Chichester, West Sussex, PO19 8SQ, UK

Editorial Offices
350 Main Street, Malden, MA 02148-5020, USA
9600 Garsington Road, Oxford, OX4 2DQ, UK
The Atrium, Southern Gate, Chichester, West Sussex, PO19 8SQ, UK

For details of our global editorial offices, for customer services, and for information about how to apply for permission to reuse the copyright material in this book please see our website at www.wiley.com/wiley-blackwell.

Library of Congress Cataloging-in-Publication Data
Blackford, Russell, 1954-
50 great myths about atheism / Russell Blackford, Udo Schüklenk. – 1 [edition].
pages cm
Includes bibliographical references and index.
ISBN 978-0-470-67404-8 (cloth : alk. paper) – ISBN 978-0-470-67405-5 (pbk. : alk. paper)
1. Atheism – Miscellanea. I. Title. II. Title: Fifty great myths about atheism.
BL2747.3.B575 2013
211′.8 – dc22

2013006626

A catalogue record for this book is available from the British Library.

Cover design by Simon Levy, www.simonlevy.co.uk

Typeset in 11/13.5pt Sabon by Laserwords Private Limited, Chennai, India

Impression number M:space copyright year (e.g. 1 2012)

Printed in Singapore by Ho Printing Singapore Pte Ltd

Contents

Acknowledgments

We wish to acknowledge assistance from Ophelia Benson, Jenny Blackford, Robert Brookey, Jerry Coyne, Darragh Hare, Tauriq Moosa, Antonio Marturano, Nikoo Najand, Graham Oppy, Jacques Rousseau, Grania Spingies, Naomi Stekelenburg, and Peter Sy. All offered us their favorite myths about atheism, and some went beyond this with other valued assistance or advice. In particular, Professors Coyne and Oppy gave valued comments on an earlier draft of the chapter entitled "The Rise of Modern Atheism."

The following Queen's University students provided us with valuable research assistance at different times during this project: Monica Joshi, Geoff Mason, Brendan McCreary, Nikoo Najand, Matthew Pike, and Eamon Quinn.

We also thank the originator of the Jesus and Mo cartoons featured in this volume for his generous permission to use his wonderful art work.

We owe a particular debt of gratitude to our copy-editor Jenny Roberts, whose rigor, skill, and eye for detail saved us from numerous infelicities and errors (we take full responsibility for those that remain).

Last but by no means least, Jeff Dean, our then editor at Wiley-Blackwell, approached us with the idea for this book. In a way it owes its very existence to him.

Introduction

Atheism is responsible for Stalin, Hitler, and Pol Pot's genocides.
Atheists have no values.
Atheism is just another religion.

No doubt you will have heard such statements about atheism and atheists, in this or some closely related form or shape. All of them are false, just like many others. And yet they have managed to persist remarkably well over time.

The attacks on atheism are often driven by strong emotions, perhaps because atheism threatens values associated with religion (at least in the minds of the attackers). Thus atheists receive a barrage of questions such as the following:

> Without god, what is left of morality? Without god, what purpose is there in man's life? If we do not believe in god, how can we be certain of anything? If god does not exist, whom can we turn to in a time of crisis? If there is no afterlife, who will reward virtue and punish injustice? Without god, how can we resist the onslaught of atheistic communism? If god does not exist, what becomes of the worth and dignity of each person? Without god, how can man achieve happiness? (Smith, 1979, p. 6)

There is an old saying about propaganda – probably not a myth (Macdonald, 2007, p. 38) – that a falsehood repeated often enough will eventually be taken as truth. This is, of course, likely to be true if those who propagate such falsehoods also control large segments of the mass media. A good

50 Great Myths About Atheism, First Edition. Russell Blackford and Udo Schüklenk.

example of this circulated in the United States even as we were writing this book. The myth was created that Barack Obama, the US President no less, was not born in the United States and so was illegitimately president of the country, since only natural-born citizens of the United States may serve in that role. The story was repeated time and again in mass media outlets such as Fox News, by wannabe presidential contenders and others with a vested interest in undermining Obama's presidency. Eventually President Obama was forced, in an act unprecedented in US history, to publish his long birth certificate to prove that he was really born in Hawaii, as he had always said.

At the height of this myth-generating campaign, according to one opinion poll, a majority of registered Republican voters in the South of the country declared a belief either that Mr Obama was not born in the United States (28%) or that they did not know what to believe (30%) (Schlesinger, 2009). Even if you give the 30% the benefit of the doubt, about one in three to four registered Republicans in the South bought into the myth. This tells you something about the power that myths hold over a susceptible public.

What is Atheism?

But what is atheism anyway? That is a fair point to raise, and is not without its share of controversy. We will return to certain aspects in the first batch of myths we examine, but here's an overview of our approach.

Even atheists, and the various organizations they have formed, often argue about what the proper atheistic view should be regarding the existence of gods, including the traditional God of Christianity, Islam, and Judaism. Some argue that an atheist is simply a person who does not believe in God. Others claim that an atheist must think that there is incontrovertible proof that God does not exist. Some atheists think that there is nothing that they have to prove at all. They insist that those claiming the existence of a particular god, or a set of gods, need to demonstrate the truth of their claims. Then there are humanists, secularists, and agnostics, and others with their own labels.

People may choose their labels, and we don't wish to insist that all people who lack theistic belief self-identify with the label "atheist." Some claim to be "agnostic" because they say they have suspended judgment on the issue of God, or a god, or a pantheon of gods. They may point out that this fits with the etymology of the word "agnostic": a denial of *gnosis*, or knowledge. It is not our desire that they renounce their use of this word, but many of the myths apply to them as much as to others who prefer to call themselves "atheists."

Religious adherents and apologists often have their own ideas about what they are attacking. For example, Alister McGrath (2004, pp. 174–175) claims that if you include as an atheist anyone who does not believe in the existence of any god then this is too watered down. Indeed, he describes it as a desperate redefinition to build up the appearance of a substantial atheist demographic. We should, however, note that what attracted McGrath to atheism as a young man was what he saw as its proposal to eradicate religion and to change the world in a "totalizing" way (2004, p. 177). A reading of his book *The Twilight of Atheism* makes it clear that he associates atheism closely with the all-encompassing Marxist-Leninist communism that he embraced in his youth. McGrath's equation of atheism with totalitarianism is exactly one of the myths that we expose and challenge.

Writing over 30 years ago, and not at a time when atheists should have been feeling any desperation of the sort that McGrath mentions, George H. Smith adopted a very broad view of atheism as simply "the absence of religious belief." According to this approach, any person who does not believe in the existence of any god or gods is literally an atheist (Smith, 1979, p. 7). For the purpose of this book we take a similar approach. Not coincidentally this maps nicely on the ancient Greek origin of the word "atheist": the Greek *atheos* means "godless." The epistemological controversies among those who call themselves atheists, as well as their differences about sensible strategies to achieve their political objectives, are interesting, but they are not the subject matter of this book. Accordingly we will not concern you with the details of these controversies, but do feel free to read up on them (Cimino and Smith, 2007).

If this wide definition bothers you, let us add that we are not primarily interested in, for example, children who have not yet had the opportunity to consider religious questions carefully and come to a conclusion. The myths we discuss are, by and large, aimed at more explicit forms of atheism – the atheism of somebody who is familiar with the idea of a god, but has rejected (or been unable to accept) theistic belief after consideration. We are, in other words, concerned with autonomous, thinking individuals. Of course, there are arguments among moral philosophers about the question of what constitutes a truly autonomous individual, but for the purposes of this book we are addressing people capable of making their own informed choices with regard to whether or not they are atheists or believe in a deity of some kind (Dworkin, 1988).

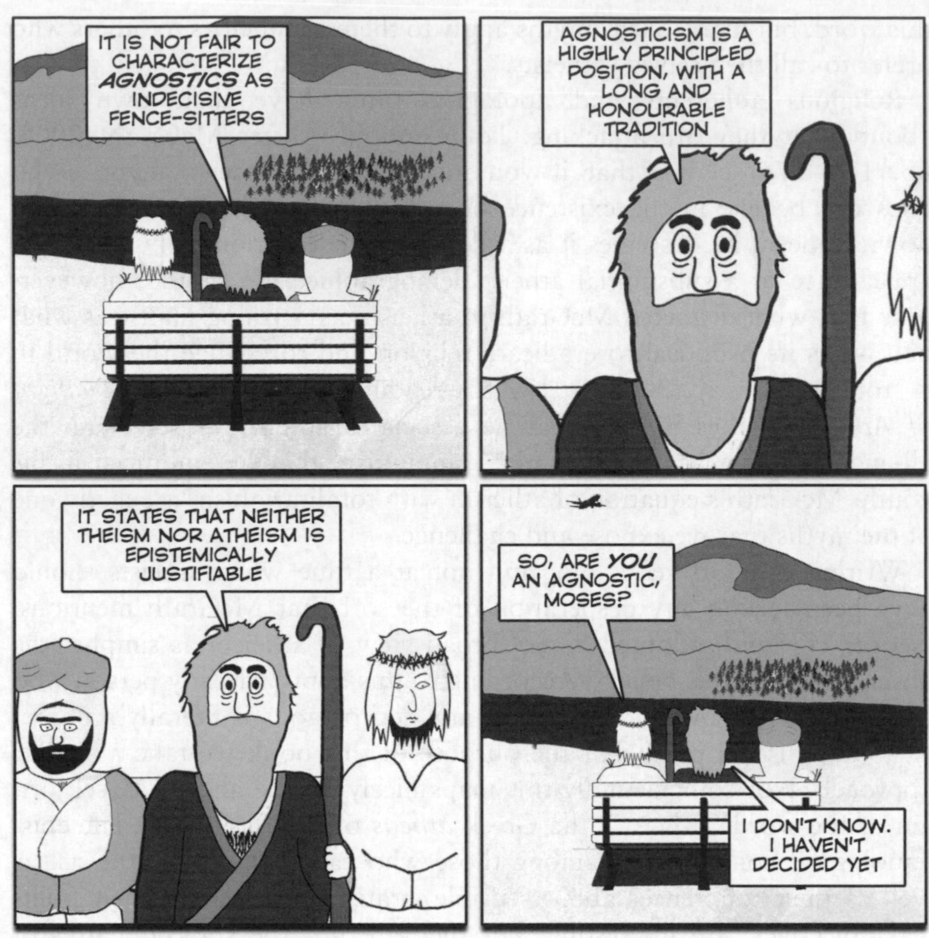

Credited to Jesus and Mo, www.jesusandmo.net

Why Bother About Myths?

We decided that it might be valuable to investigate popular myths about atheists and atheism to see whether there is something more substantial to them that keeps them alive, other than ignorance or mischief making by those who perpetuate them. Belief in some of these myths has had outright harmful consequences for people known to be or believed to be atheists. Atheists have been persecuted, tortured, and even killed for their rejection of monotheistic or other religious ideologies.

Consider one fairly recent example reported from the USA. Damon Fowler was a student at Bastrop High School in Louisiana. When he discovered that his public school planned to include a prayer as part of its graduation ceremony he contacted the school's superintendent in order to alert him to the fact that the planned prayer would be unconstitutional. He requested that the prayer part of the program be cancelled. The superintendent initially agreed, but then the story leaked. Fowler was ostracized in his community, one of his teachers publicly demeaned him, students and anonymous others threatened to beat him up or even kill him. Your life can be threatened today in the USA just because you insist that your constitutional rights not be trampled upon in a public school (Christina, 2011).

A recent sociological survey from the USA shows that atheists constitute the most disliked among marginalized groups, including African Americans, gay people, Muslims, and recent migrants. In fact, most US Americans define themselves as good people against the other, in this case the other being your friendly neighborhood atheist (Edgell *et al.*, 2006). While the laws are not enforced, it is nonetheless true that in some US states atheists are prohibited from holding elected office, and reportedly no less than 40% of the country's citizens refuse to vote for an atheist (R.M., 2012).

Drawing the Lines

It is difficult to discern clear dividing lines between some of the myths. It is not unusual for several of them to be thrown together in the pot of myths, stirred and – *voila!* – a new myth is born. For instance, there is a myth that atheists have no moral core: that we are all wreckers, egoists, or the worst kind of nihilists. There are also myths claiming that atheists are more prone to commit all sorts of heinous crimes. Well stirred in the pot, these two myths give birth to the myth that atheists have no moral core and are, for that reason, more likely to end up committing crimes.

As an example, consider the following quote from a sociological survey. One of the study participants went on the record as follows: "I would say . . . the prisons aren't filled with conservative Republican Christians. The prisons are probably filled with people who don't have any kind of a spiritual or religious core" (Edgell *et al.* 2006, p. 228). This claim is, in fact, untrue. Such claims are slanders against atheists.

Which leads us to an important point. During the months we have spent working on this book, we have often asked ourselves where to draw the line between a myth and a legitimate disagreement with our own views. We have thought about this carefully in choosing and examining the 50 myths that follow. In each case, we are convinced that something is being claimed that is, if not straightforwardly false, at least seriously and demonstrably misleading. We will try, in each case, to explain why that is.

Even in one or two cases where the myth might be literally true, we identify what we consider misleading, as with the claim that atheists don't recognize the sanctity of human life. Well, perhaps we don't, or many of us don't, but the implicit idea that human life possesses "sanctity" needs to be teased out and challenged, as do the implications of the myth for atheists' moral conduct and our view of our fellow humans. There are good reasons to treat each other with kindness and respect, but does ordinary human morality really need such a grandiose idea as *sanctity* to do its work? In such cases, we will make clear what we think is misleading, allowing the reader to be the judge. In all cases, we don't expect to confuse our readers about what we consider straightforward factual errors and what are "merely" tendentious, simplistic, unfair claims.

Related to this, we intend to give the various myths as good a run as we can. If there is a grain of truth in a particular myth, or a point that seems to us arguable, we will honestly identify it. We want to encourage more fairness to atheists, but in doing so we intend to be fair ourselves.

Do These Myths Actually Exist?

Now, you might harbor quietly (or even not so quietly) the suspicion that we could be making these myths up, and that nobody is actually foolish enough to hold some of the views we will be examining. In other words, how can you be sure that we are not creating straw men to attack at our leisure? Well, we have gone to some trouble with this. In most cases, we will provide specific examples of what we are talking about. The usual format, with only minor variations for convenience, will involve referencing examples at the beginning of each myth.

No one should leave this book thinking we are attacking imaginary positions.

How Did We Decide What Myths are Worth Investigating?

In many ways the myths chose themselves – they all seem prominent in the arguments and publications of atheism's critics. We also consulted widely, though informally, with our network of contacts, looking to see what myths they had most often encountered.

But there was nothing scientific about this, and we cannot claim that we were able to conduct representative surveys of people's most favored or most widely held myths about atheism and atheists across the globe. In the end, we chose those myths that we have come across most frequently since we became involved in debates about God. We invite readers to send us their favored myths – perhaps we can use them in future editions of this book.

Are We Picking Easy Targets?

We foresee an inevitable criticism of this book, and it is one that is impossible to prove uncontroversially false. Critics will almost certainly argue that we have chosen "easy targets," that is, we have chosen views or myths that are only held by unreasonable religious people, while ignoring sensible religious views that would have been more difficult to address. It is a variety of the criticism that we have addressed in Myth 35, as well as elsewhere in this book.

One reason why it is difficult to show that this criticism is false is that it resembles people moving the goalposts during a soccer game. Each time we prove a particular myth to be false someone will say, "but you have not shown this – slightly different – variety of the criticism to be wrong, too," or "but you have not addressed the interpretation put forward by theologian X," and so on and so forth. It is, of course, impossible to cover every scrap of argument that was ever uttered by a religious apologist, or even every scrap offered by academic religious apologists. There are simply too many of them out there. What we have done is to ensure that leading religious apologists are referenced generously and honestly throughout this book. It is also worth making another point: apologists who might genuinely be academically weak – they shall remain anonymous here – but who are demonstrably culturally very influential in religious circles are considered fair game by us. No doubt some readers will claim that these are the "wrong" apologists, or that they are "weak" apologists, and that others were not cited by us because we were unable to address their compelling arguments, and so on. Our invitation to readers would be to pass these "better" arguments on to us. Perhaps we can cover your favorites in a further book or a future edition of this one. For now, we boldly predict that others will then deem your favorite apologists the "weak" ones.

Have We Defeated Theism?

We should not beat around the bush about this: are we claiming to have defeated theism? No, that would be wishful thinking. We confront many misconceptions about atheism throughout this book, but does atheism logically follow from that? That certainly is not the case. After all, as mentioned earlier, we have not debunked every possible argument put about by religious apologists, so we cannot claim to have proved all theist views of the world wrong, and equally we cannot claim to have proved that atheism is right. What we have done is debunk a fairly significant chunk of popular myths about atheism.

In the long final chapter entitled "The Rise of Modern Atheism," we go a bit further. This chapter does not claim to defeat theism once and for all, but we allow ourselves to be more opinionated. It should provide a reasonably clear outline of our thinking, while offering readers some useful entry points into the long-standing philosophical debate between theists and atheists. It would take an entire book, or maybe several of them, to present our positive case for rejecting all kinds of religion. Meanwhile, we provide some historical perspective on the rise of atheism, examine why the traditional arguments for the existence of God turned out so inconclusive when philosophers subjected them to scrutiny, and offer some deeper thoughts on the relationship between religion and science. Enough is said, we think, to convey the reasonableness of atheism and suggest the problems with religious alternatives.

1

What is Atheism?

Myth 1 Atheism is Just Another Type of Religion

There is a legitimate argument to be had about what it is to call something a religion. Before we go deeper into that question, however, let us begin with someone who thinks that atheism is just another religion. The perfect place to start looking for pretty much anything these days, is – no doubt you expected this – the internet. One blogger has this to say: "I think it's fair to say that atheism is just another religion, given how certain atheists seem to be about their case. When you debate an atheist it is very much like debating a religious person. They are almost fanatical about their stance."

In case you would rather have it from a more established source, here is a quote from the Anglican Archbishop of Sydney, Peter Jensen: "Atheism is every bit of a religious commitment as Christianity itself" (Godfrey, 2010). Or try Jamaica's Reverend Earlmont Williams:

> At the end of the day, expressing no belief in any god, and holding that to be absolute, is basically placing that non-belief on a pedestal, very much like Christians locate their God on the "highest plain". In essence, atheism itself is unwittingly given divine status. (Williams, 2012)

Sometimes the idea appears in a more restricted form. Consider the popular book *I Don't Believe in Atheists*, by Christopher Hedges (2008), which was issued in a softcover edition with the title *When Atheism Becomes Religion: America's New Fundamentalists*. Hedges claims throughout that

50 Great Myths About Atheism, First Edition. Russell Blackford and Udo Schüklenk.

atheism is a kind of religion, though he seems unsure whether this applies to all atheism or only to the views of a small group of high-profile contemporary atheists, among them Sam Harris and the late Christopher Hitchens. At one point, he blames much in the way of modern Western thought for bequeathing us a "godless religion," naming such historical figures as Descartes, Locke, Hume, Voltaire, Kant, Diderot, Rousseau, and Paine (Hedges, 2008, p. 17). Never mind that the majority of these were, in fact, not atheists at all. More often, his emphasis is on the creation of a surrogate religion by the contemporary atheists whom he most despises (e.g., Hedges, 2008, pp. 17–18).

But what is meant by a "religion"? For something to be a religion, does it have to be a comprehensive worldview, a system of rituals and canons of conduct, or something else? If it was sufficient for a comprehensive worldview to be called a religion, then many detailed ideologies would have to be considered religions. Arguably a religion needs to be based on belief in some kind of entity or force with supernatural powers.

Michael Martin is one thinker who has wrestled with the problem, pointing out that we could understand religion in different ways (Martin, 2007, pp. 217–220). We could understand it in terms of such indicators as belief in supernatural beings, the identification of sacred objects and the practice of rituals involving them, and an associated moral code. Alternatively, we can understand religion in terms of the questions that it asks and answers, such as those about the fundamental characteristics of human beings and nonhuman reality. On the latter approach, any sufficiently comprehensive and integrated worldview – one with metaphysical, ethical, and epistemological components – might count as a religion.

In fact, the concept of religion itself is by no means unproblematic. There does not seem to be an uncontroversial definition for the purposes of scholarly fields such as anthropology, or for the purposes of the law. William James, in his classic discussion of religious experience, doubted that an exact definition was possible (James, 1982 [1902], pp. 26–52). We might question whether what we know as religion is a single phenomenon at all. Frieder Otto Wolf has recently suggested that the concept of religion is "most deeply imbued and tainted by Euro-centrism and naïve assumptions derived from an often unilaterally simplified Christian tradition." He adds:

> It is, indeed, doubtful that there is any meaningful common denominator between the "everyday magical practices" of an indigenous tribe, Judaic obeisance to the commandments of God to be found in the Tora [sic], the practice of Sunni Islam based on the Qur'an, of Sufi mysticism, of Jainism, of Shintoism, or of Buddhism. (Wolf, 2009, p. 250)

To make matters even more complicated, the oldest societies did not specifically distinguish a religious sphere. In such societies, various spirits and gods were seamlessly continuous with the observed phenomena of nature. Such societies' "religious" beliefs and rituals were tightly interwoven into everyday thought and action, and were not clearly distinguished from nonreligious spheres of activity (Wright, 2009, pp. 17–20).

So is the question, "Just what is a religion?" unanswerable? The concept had better have some content, or scholarly discussions of the phenomenon of religion will lack boundaries; the courts will be unable to decide cases in which they need to work out whether, for example, Scientology is a religion for tax purposes; and claims that atheism is a religion will be simply meaningless. It appears to us that the situation is not hopeless and that some meaning can be given to the "atheism is a religion" claim.

Consider the approach taken by Charles Taylor in his monumental study of the historical secularization of Western societies, *A Secular Age*. Writing mainly of the Abrahamic traditions, Taylor explains religion in terms of belief in an agency or power that transcends the immanent order – by which he means the operations of the natural world. For Taylor, religion relates to "the beyond," to an otherworldly order of things, but not in just any way. He posits three specific dimensions. First, religion asserts that there is some higher good or ultimate end beyond ordinary human flourishing. Second, it includes the possibility of personal transformation, to ensure that the higher good is achieved. This, in turn, involves the existence of a transformative and transcendent power. Third, the religious account of our possible transformation involves a sense of human life extending beyond "this life" (Taylor, 2007).

Taylor's analysis is easily applied to Christianity, where the crucial transformation involves salvation through Jesus Christ (however exactly this is explained by different theological systems). Most of the dimensions described by him are also recognizable in the well-known religions of ancient and modern times. Generally, we think, Taylor's key ideas match rather well with ordinary people's understanding of what "a religion" looks like. A religion typically involves an otherworldly order of things and a related dimension to human lives; an ultimate good that transcends worldly kinds of flourishing; the possibility of spiritual transformation, such as the Christian idea of salvation; and the existence of transcendent and transformative powers, such as the Abrahamic God.

Atheism is not a religion on any of these approaches. For example, it is not a comprehensive worldview, a way of life, or a system of rituals and conduct. As we discussed in our Introduction, it is no more than an informed lack of belief in any god(s) or at most a positive belief that no god(s) exist. Atheism is compatible with many views of the world. George H. Smith complains, we think rightly, that atheism is not a "way of life," a "world outlook," or a "total view of life," any more than a failure to believe in magic elves is any of these things. While some philosophical positions are atheistic, atheism in itself does not entail any specific system of thought but can be incorporated into many (Smith, 1979, pp. 21–22).

We sympathize, therefore, when Walter Sinnott-Armstrong writes, "most atheists and agnostics do not make their stance on religion central to their lives in the same way as many evangelical Christians do – and should, in their view." We also know the feeling when he adds: "Except when I am writing books like this, the only time my thoughts turn to religion or God is when religious people raise such issues, such as by confronting me personally or basing public policies on religion" (Sinnott-Armstrong, 2009, p. xvii).

Arguably, some religions, such as Theravada Buddhism, are atheistic, in that they do not necessarily posit the existence of gods (see Martin, 2007, pp. 224–227). However, they do involve spiritual transformations and elements that are easily regarded as otherworldly or supernatural. By contrast, atheism as such – an informed lack of belief in any God or gods – contains no such elements. It is possible, therefore, that someone could adhere to a religion such as Theravada Buddhism while being an atheist, but atheism itself is not a religion.

Myth 2 But the Courts Recognize Atheism as a Religion

From time to time the courts have faced the issue of what counts as a religion, or rather, "What, for legal purposes, is a religion?" Like academic scholars, they have struggled to produce an uncontroversial definition. Unsurprisingly, much of the existing case law emphasizes teachings that relate to an otherworldly or supernatural order. On this approach, atheism is not a religion.

Nonetheless, some courts have treated atheism like a religion for certain purposes, and this has led to claims that they consider atheism to be a religion. We will illustrate our take on the issue by means of judgments rendered by the influential United States Supreme Court. One oft-cited case is *Torcaso v. Watkins* (367 U.S. 48 (1961)), involving Roy Torcaso, an atheist whose post as a notary public in Maryland had been revoked because of his refusal to declare a belief in God. Here it was held that the state of Maryland could not require a declaration of belief in God for a person to be able to hold public office. The court reasoned that such a requirement was contrary to the Establishment Clause in the US

Constitution, which forbids the government from establishing a religion. For the purposes of American constitutional law, forbidden government action in breach of the Establishment Clause includes any requirement that advantages the religious against the nonreligious, as was clearly done by Maryland's requirement of belief in God for anyone wishing to become a notary public.

In a footnote, Justice Black listed "Secular Humanism" among "religions" that do not teach the existence of God. However, secular humanism, at least in some of its forms, is a far more comprehensive belief system than mere atheism. Even if secular humanism were a religion, it would not entail the same about atheism. Furthermore, Justice Black's comment was not part of his reasoning necessary for deciding the case, and is thus regarded as *obiter dicta*, rather than as law binding on lower courts (this is noted by Cherry and Matsumura, 1998/9). The important point is that the court did not rule that Mr Torcaso's atheism was itself a religion.

Years later, the United States Court of Appeals for the Ninth Circuit ruled explicitly in the case of *Peloza v. Capistrano Unified School District* (37 F.3d 517 (9th Cir. 1994)), that "evolutionism" and "secular humanism" are not religions for the purposes of the Establishment Clause. Accordingly, Mr Peloza, a high school biology teacher, was unable to demonstrate that he was required to teach a religion when his duties required that he teach evolutionary biology to his students. The Supreme Court refused to hear an appeal in this case, which thus stands as good law in the United States.

Nonetheless, there are cases (see Davis, 2005) in which atheism has been given some of the same legal protection as religion, and this might even be construed as treating atheism as a religion – at least for certain purposes. One such case is *Kaufman v. McCaughtry* (419 F.3d 678 (7th Cir. 2005)), which involved the rights of an inmate, James Kaufman, within the Wisconsin prison system.

Mr Kaufman invoked the courts to pursue a number of grievances about his treatment by prison officials. One of these was that his First Amendment rights were violated by a refusal to allow him to form a study group for atheist inmates. He intended that the group would study such matters as religious doctrines and practices, apparently from an atheistic perspective. The United States Court of Appeals for the Seventh Circuit upheld his claim in this regard, and was thus prepared to treat Kaufman's atheistic view of the world as his religion for the relevant purpose. He was allowed to exercise his "religion" in the sense of forming and conducting the study group.

Such cases suggest that the current myth is at least partly true. For some purposes, in some situations, the US courts will give nonreligious viewpoints the same protection as religious ones. In that limited sense, they may treat even atheism as a religion. It does not follow, however, that the US courts are foolish enough to treat nonbelief as another form of belief. Consider *Wallace v. Jaffree* (472 U.S. 38 (1985)). This case involved a one-minute period of silence in public schools for prayer or meditation. The court made clear that the constitution requires not only equal treatment between different kinds of religious belief, but also equal treatment between belief and nonbelief. It clearly distinguished the right to choose any religious faith, Christian or otherwise, from the right to choose no faith at all (472 U.S. 38, 52–54 (1985)).

The same ideas can be found in other Supreme Court cases, such as *Engel v. Vitale* (370 U.S. 421, 435 (1962)) and *County of Allegheny v. American Civil Liberties Union Greater Pittsburgh Chapter* (492 U.S. 573, 610 (1989)). A more recent case was *McCreary County v. American Civil Liberties Union* (545 U.S. 844 (2005)), which involved official displays of the Ten Commandments. Throughout this developing body of jurisprudence, the United States Supreme Court has been clear that the First Amendment rules out any favoring of religion over irreligion, as well as any favoring of one religion over another. Irreligion is not thought of here as just another form of religion, even though it receives constitutional protection.

In short, the US courts treat nonbelief with the same protection that they give to belief, at least where relevant. It does not follow, however, that atheism is a religion for legal purposes, even in the United States. Indeed, it would normally fall under the concept of "irreligion" – something that is not to be subordinated to "religion." In any event, whatever the stance of the American courts it does not follow that the courts of other countries will take the same approach.

Once again, the crucial conceptual point we wish to make is this: a lack of belief is not simply *the same* as a form of belief. Atheism requires no more than a lack of belief in any God or gods, and this distinguishes it from typical religions, with their rich creeds, doctrines, rituals, and other practices.

Myth 3 Atheists Believe in God but are in Denial

This claim overlaps to some extent with the myth that atheists hate God, because in order to hate God you also need to believe that God exists. We must be careful here with regard to what we take this myth to mean.

If we take it to mean that there are self-professed atheists (people who claim to be atheists) who secretly believe in a god, then it is plausible enough, if trivial. Surely there will be people out there who claim to be atheists when really they believe in a god of a kind, just as there have been Christian ministers who were actually atheists. Most historically prominent of the latter, perhaps, was the seventeenth century cleric Jean Meslier (see Meslier, 2009 [1729]). For more modern examples, consult the stories of Dan Barker (2008) and John W. Loftus (2012a).

Michael Martin (1996) evaluates, and argues against, a strong version of the myth, namely the claim that no atheists exist (a proposition put forward in Van Til, 1969). As Martin points out, even if some phenomenon, such as morality or the efficacy of logic, could only be explained on a theistic basis it would not follow that atheists actually believe in the existence of God.

Some Christian apologists have speculated about what might motivate professed atheists to be not really atheistic in their worldviews. One good example is a YouTube video that you should be able to access on the internet if you feel so inclined. The narrator aims to demonstrate that we all really believe in God, but that atheists remain in denial for their own nefarious purposes (Lawley, 2009).

Dinesh D'Souza's book *What's So Great About Christianity* provides us with an example as good as any of a high-handed approach by a Christian apologist with pretensions to moral expertise. D'Souza claims that atheism's appeal is being able to escape from moral requirements, since atheists do not believe in Hell or divine judgment (D'Souza, 2007, pp. 268–270). This might, in turn, motivate some of us to deny what is supposedly obvious, namely the existence of God. Ironically enough, D'Souza has himself been in some disgrace among many of his conservative Christian colleagues over his own apparent lapses from a strict Christian sexual morality. This led to his resignation as President of The King's College in New York in October 2012. So it goes.

But why should fear of an afterlife lead to atheism? There are also theistic positions that reject the idea of divine judgment and particularly that of Hell. Why not be motivated to adopt one of those positions, especially if the existence of God is so obvious? If belief were simply volitional – if we could decide at will what to believe, and could adopt whatever beliefs seemed "nicest" or most convenient – we would probably move to some kind of liberal religious position that teaches a doctrine of universal salvation. On such an account, everyone ends up in Heaven, with sins forgiven by a loving God. Compared to this, atheism would surely come a distant second.

The fact is, however, that atheists have many other reasons to reject religious claims. Some atheists do indeed reject many moral strictures that have been favored by Christian churches, but this is usually based on the perception that the strictures lack rational justification.

In his 2007 encyclical letter *Spe Salvi*, Pope Benedict XVI acknowledges a distinctively moral element in modern atheism:

> The atheism of the nineteenth and twentieth centuries is – in its origins and aims – a type of moralism: a protest against the injustices of the world and of world history. A world marked by so much injustice, innocent suffering, and cynicism of power cannot be the work of a good God. A God with responsibility for such a world would not be a just God, much less a good God. It is for the sake of morality that this God has to be contested. (Benedict, 2007)

D'Souza, too, acknowledges that one factor motivating atheism is incomprehension at the suffering and other evils in the world, which cannot be reconciled in any straightforward way with the existence of a benevolent and all-powerful deity (D'Souza, 2007, pp. 271–276). Atheists do, of course, deny many religious claims – for example, Aikin and Talisse offer a long list of claims that atheists reject (Aikin and Talisse, 2011, pp. 48–49) – but that does not mean that we are in denial.

One way of making the claim in this myth is to suggest that belief in God is biologically determined or neurologically based. The grain of truth here may be that there are aspects of human psychology that lead us to attribute agency to inanimate things, and this may feed into religion (e.g., Guthrie, 2007, pp. 291–296). However, even if there are aspects of human psychology that incline toward belief in gods, they cannot be determinative. That should not be surprising, since we are quite capable of understanding that inanimate things are not actually animate. The notion that some aspect of our psychology makes theism inevitable becomes implausible when we consider the sheer number of atheists in the world – surely they are not *all* "really" theists! According to Phil Zuckerman, conservative estimates are that there exist between 500 million to 750 million atheists worldwide (Zuckerman, 2007).

Traditional religious institutions have experienced significant declines in both membership and church attendance. For instance, in Britain a decline in the rate of affiliation with traditional religious institutions has not been countered by a rising rate of membership in nontraditional institutions (Bruce, 2001), and 50 years of polling reveals that an actual decline in religious beliefs shadows the drop in participation.

A 2011 survey shows seemingly contradictory results. When asked in a survey "What is your religion?" 61% of people in England and Wales ticked a religious box (53.48% Christian and 7.22% Other), while 39% ticked "No religion." One could easily interpret this as indicative of Britain remaining a predominantly religious country. However, the same survey asked this follow-up question: "Are you religious?" Only 29% of the same people surveyed said "yes," while 65% answered "no." Much hinges, then, on how one interprets religious identification, when those who identify with a religion indicate in a strong majority that they do not consider themselves religious (British Humanist Association, 2011).

Credited to Jesus and Mo, www.jesusandmo.net

In line with these findings, Georges Rey and Adele Mercier have argued that most so-called theists in the West, at some level, do not really believe in God (Rey, 2007; Mercier, 2009). They claim that anyone who has been exposed to a typical Anglo-European secondary school education will hold a quasi-atheist position. This is one in which an individual may express religious beliefs, but is actually self-deceived. At some psychological level, that is, such individuals do not regard their religious beliefs as true. Even if Rey and Mercier have overstated the case, the theism of many self-declared believers does not go as deep as critics of atheism like to think it does.

Many of us do not believe in the existence of any being that resembles the Abrahamic God or the polytheistic gods of, say, Greek and Norse mythology. We see no good evidence that such beings exist, or that any other beings that could be called "gods" are more than fictional characters. On the contrary, we think that the evidence points the other way. Why not take our word for this? If most or all atheists really believed in God, one might question whether it was a good investment of time by so many prominent theists from St Anselm and St Thomas Aquinas to Leibniz, and through to the present day, to engage in a time-consuming and futile quest to prove God's existence.

Myth 4 Atheists are Certain There is No God

We wonder whether the myth of the dogmatically confident atheist is a deliberate attempt by religious apologists to suggest that atheists are somehow overreaching in their claims. This allegedly dogmatic stance can then be juxtaposed with a liberal, kind-hearted, less-oppressive-than-usual religion.

Eric Reitan, for instance, claims that the form of religion which he advocates is based on hope – a hope that there is a good, transcendent being who somehow redeems all the horrors of the world. He acknowledges that religious groups throughout history have, in fact, claimed certainty: they have "attempted to preserve the illusion of certainty by remorselessly persecuting every 'heretic' whose differing beliefs might threaten that illusion." Nonetheless, he reports that most of the religious people *he* knows accept that they do not possess knowledge, but only hope, and that their beliefs are not beyond dispute (Reitan, 2009, p. 211). By contrast, so he asserts, it is atheists, or at least some of them, who claim certainty (Reitan, 2009, pp. 211–212). This certainty is of concern, epistemologically, because atheists are unable to prove, logically or otherwise, that the God of major monotheistic religions does not actually exist.

What should we make of this argument? First, it should be conceded in fairness that not all religions have been persecutory, though the Abrahamic monotheisms have been more so than most (e.g. Blackford, 2012, pp. 20–33). We should also take note of Reitan's suggestion that human beings have a hunger for certainty, something that is useful in practical situations (such as knowing whether there are rabid wolves in the forest). He adds that this relates poorly to issues concerning the ultimate nature of the universe (Reitan, 2009, p. 211). That may well be so, but it does not detract from the fact that many religious organizations and leaders have historically claimed certainty about such things to the point of imposing their beliefs and canons of conduct through exercises of violence and power. If you are doubtful about this claim, consider Karlheinz Deschner's magisterial study *Kriminalgeschichte des Christentums*. Deschner, a German historian, dedicated his nine-volume magnum opus to writing the criminal history of Christian churches (Deschner, 1986–2008). The suggestion that religion is open to uncertainty, while atheism is the opposite, distorts humanity's historical experience with both.

Perhaps we need harp no further on the dogmatism that is often shown by religious believers and their leaders – but what about atheists? Given the minimalistic definition adopted for the purposes of this book, atheists are simply people who lack belief in any god or gods. We atheists need not even make a positive claim that no gods exist, let alone that our claim is objectively justified in some way. Some atheists do make a stronger claim: they claim that no gods exist and that this is a conclusion sufficiently supported by argument and evidence to count as knowledge. Even that, however, is not the same as a claim to certainty – that is, a belief that is, or should be, held without doubt. The nature of scientific, naturalistic inquiry precludes any such certainty. Falsification still reigns supreme, and scientific findings are always regarded as provisional.

Even where an atheist claims knowledge, that is no more than a claim that a certain belief is *justified* and *true* (and, perhaps, that it tracks the evidence in an appropriate way), not that it is established beyond all doubt. Atheism is not based on a claim to certainty, and there are actually very few things about which we can be certain. Nonetheless, there are many things that we can be *confident* about: for example, very few living people believe in the existence of Zeus; most of us are quite confident that he does not exist, even though there is no absolute certainty of it. We can also be confident about many well-established scientific findings, such as the basics of evolutionary theory and the heliocentric picture of the solar system.

A qualification that should be added here, however, is that some particular conceptions of God may turn out to be self-contradictory or otherwise too vague or incoherent to be true. Where that can be demonstrated to be the case to the satisfaction of a particular atheist, he or she may, indeed, feel certain that this particular god does not exist. But that can apply to any set of claims that is vague, incoherent, or just plain internally inconsistent.

While atheists do not generally claim certainty with regard to the (non) existence of gods or God, some atheists are clearly pretty confident and forthright, and may even be sure of their positions beyond any kind of doubt that they consider reasonable. But even this does not make them dangerous in the way that Reitan suggests when he discusses the work of Richard Dawkins and Christopher Hitchens. It is worth dwelling on Reitan's accusation for a moment to see just how far the myth about atheism and certainty can be taken: "And in a different world, under different conditions, the false certainty that fuels the rabid atheism of Dawkins and Hitchens and Harris might have inspired a crusade against religion far more bloody than the crusade of words they now pursue" (Reitan, 2009, p. 212).

The rhetoric here is both unfair and irresponsible. There is neither a historical case nor current-day evidence to support this sort of excited hand-waving. Reitan insinuates a relationship between his targets ("Dawkins and Hitchens and Harris") and such ideas as disease ("rabid"), violence, and fanaticism. Never mind, that these people have never called for persecution of religion or the imposition of their own views on the world. By means of a metaphor of religious warfare ("crusade"), Reitan suggests that forthright, confident criticism of religion is akin to the acts of invasion and slaughter Christianity has become notorious for (Riley-Smith, 1999). This is not merely the inadvertent use of lazy metaphors. Rather, Reitan piles on this language, suggesting on the same page that Hitchens's book *God is Not Great* is drenched in "aggressive self-righteousness," and that this is caused by the aforementioned false certainty, which also leads to "battle lines being drawn," "joyous delight in stomping all over what others find sacred," "grinding" others' reverent feelings "underfoot," and such overt acts as the destruction of Afghanistan's giant Buddha statues by the Taliban (Reitan, 2009, p. 212).

As a matter of fact, neither Dawkins nor Hitchens nor Harris has recommended any actual stomping, grinding, or destruction of statues. But the impression is created that they are driven by a false certainty which motivates them to behave with Talibanesque fanaticism. All these particular atheists have done is set out their arguments in books, speeches, and the like, doubtless wording them in trenchant, sometimes humorous, ways, but never resorting to force or proposing the use of force. Whatever iconoclasm they have displayed has been metaphorical. There is no evidence to conclude that certain atheists are particularly radical or prone to incite violence. Generally, we are peaceful people, and most of us are painfully aware of our own epistemic limitations.

Myth 5 Atheists Hate or are Angry with God

This common myth appears in a news story by Miles Godfrey, covering a number of attacks on atheism by church leaders in Australia. Here, the Anglican Archbishop of Sydney, Peter Jensen, has this to say on the supposed atheistic hatred of God: "as we can see by the sheer passion and virulence of the atheist – they seem to hate the Christian God." He then elaborates his views in even stronger terms: atheism, he says:

> represents the latest version of the human assault on God, born out of resentment that we do not in fact rule the world and that God calls on us to submit our lives to him.... It is a form of idolatry in which we worship ourselves. (Godfrey, 2010)

Well, do atheists hate, or are we angry with, God?

Let us start with a pretty obvious point: atheists cannot be angry with God, and we cannot even resent God, as Archbishop Jensen claims we do, because we do not believe God actually exists. How could you hate or resent something you do not think exists? That would be a pretty pointless activity. The claim that we are angry with God can be seen as wishful thinking.

It might suit Jensen and like-minded religious figureheads if we were not sincere or serious in our view that God does not exist. Robert T. Lee is one critic of atheists who makes this quite explicit. He argues that atheists "think since they deny the existence of God, they cannot hate Him. But it's really the other way around: they know He exists, that's why they hate Him" (Lee, 2004). It goes without saying, perhaps, that this kind of logic is question-begging. From an atheistic viewpoint, the various gods worshiped by Christians and others are essentially fictional or mythological characters. Why hate them?

Of course, that does not prevent atheists from viewing the Abrahamic God, as depicted for example in various books of the Bible, as a most unattractive character. It is easy to see this being as loving vengeance and warfare, as being prurient in its obsession with matters of sex, and as especially repulsive in its demands for endless praise and worship, and in its requirement of blood sacrifice before forgiving sins. For that reason, many atheists are glad not to live in a world that contains this being. Such a world is clearly not the same as one created and ruled by a truly benevolent deity. Unfortunately, we appear not to be living in *that* world either.

Thus there is a religious cottage industry devoted to explaining (away) the evil that exists in our world despite the presence of a benevolent God, who supposedly created it. Theologians call this the theodicy problem (often referred to as the Problem of Evil). How can it be that there is so much evil existing in a world they believe has been created by an all-powerful, all-knowing, and benevolent deity? The obvious answer is that there simply is no such deity.

Atheists tend to find the religious answers to such questions contrived or unsatisfying. That is not, however, the same as hating an actual being – God. Nor do atheists tend to hate historical or legendary figures, such as Jesus, any more than other such figures about whom little is known with certainty. Some atheists are critical of the moral character of Jesus as depicted in the traditionally accepted Gospels (e.g., Tooley, 2009), but that should not be confused with hatred.

More generally, there is a tendency for religious apologists to blur the distinction between harsh criticism and expressions of hatred. For example, Alister McGrath comments, not exactly in a charitable spirit, on Richard Dawkins: "Dawkins preaches to his god-hating choirs, who are clearly expected to relish his rhetorical salvoes, and raise their hands in adulation" (McGrath and Collicutt McGrath, 2007, p. x). Similarly, Patrick Madrid and Kenneth Hensley write, referring to atheists, "They hate the idea of God, and thus, they hate the idea that some people would believe in Him" (Madrid and Hensley, 2010, p.12). A recent article by Alvin Plantinga provides a rather worrying example:

> As everyone knows, there has been a recent spate of books attacking Christian belief and religion in general. Some of these books are little more than screeds, long on vituperation but short on reasoning, long on name-calling but short on competence, long on righteous indignation but short on good sense; for the most part they are driven by hatred rather than logic. (Plantinga, 2008)

What is disconcerting here is that many such accusations of "hatred" do not even specify hatred of a supernatural (or imaginary) being. This kind of language is problematic, because it is only a small step away from characterizing your opponents as motivated by hatred to calling for their speech to be suppressed and for stigmatizing them as enemies of the social order. Indeed, this is the objective of a long-running campaign fought vigorously by the Organization of Islamic Cooperation. This organization has campaigned for the recognition by the United Nations Human Rights Council that the defamation of religion constitutes a human rights violation. Had the Islamic countries in the Council succeeded with what in effect would have justified censorship of criticism of religion in the name of human rights, countries such as Pakistan with its draconian blasphemy laws could have legitimately claimed that their laws are human rights-compliant (Reuters, 2011). Though the campaign seemed to falter in 2011, it revives with each new controversy involving "blasphemous" acts.

Interestingly, and not surprisingly perhaps, surveys suggest that religious believers are often angry with the God they believe in. A study undertaken

Credited to Jesus and Mo, www.jesusandmo.net

by Julie Exline and colleagues found that between one-third and two-thirds of religious people surveyed in the USA conceded being angry with their respective gods. The reason most frequently mentioned is that they feel let down by God, usually in the aftermath of a major health scare or other personal tragedy that he did not prevent (Exline *et al.*, 2011).

It is perhaps worth noting that *even if* atheists really were angry with God that would tell us nothing with regard to the question of whether or not atheism is true or false. This myth really is a curiously *ad hominem* kind of argument.

Myth 6 Atheism is a Rebellion Against God's Authority

As George H. Smith mentions, atheists are often accused of being in some sort of neurotic rebellion, especially if the atheist concerned is young. Smith notes, however, that atheists cannot win once this approach is taken – a middle-aged atheist can be accused of such things as "the frustration of daily routine, the bitterness of failure, or . . . alienation from oneself and one's fellow man." If the atheist is old, the accusation can relate to "the disillusionment, cynicism and loneliness that sometimes accompany one's later years" (Smith, 1979, p. 24). All of this is question-begging since neither youth nor old age is evidence of any kind of neurotic response to the God question. Speculations about states of mind get us nowhere.

Still, they keep coming. Dinesh D'Souza, for instance, claims that the real reason why people reject theism is that it excuses what he regards as sexual immorality – people become atheists because they do not wish to imagine God's judgment for their sins of adultery and general lechery. For D'Souza, contemporary atheism is "a pelvic revolt against God," and "The orgasm has become today's secular sacrament." He adds that atheism is needed to pave the way for women to have abortions, since, so he thinks, unhooking sexuality from traditional moral restraints will produce numerous unwanted pregnancies. Thus abortion is "atheism's second sacrament." He suggests that it must produce terrible guilt for any woman who is morally healthy to "kill her own unborn child," and that atheism is needed to obviate that guilt (D'Souza, 2007, pp. 268–270). A similar line of reasoning is developed at length by philosopher-theologian James Spiegel, in his not-so-subtly titled book *The Making of an Atheist: How Immorality Leads to Unbelief* (2010).

D'Souza and Spiegel must assume the truth of their beliefs in order to sustain this line of argument, and in that sense they are begging the question at hand. For example, a straightforward secular ethical argument in favor of abortion rights could deny most of what D'Souza takes as a given, namely that the abortion of a fetus is equivalent to the killing of an actual child (Warren, 1998). Once that proposition is denied, it is far from clear that women undertaking an abortion would have good reason to feel terrible guilt – that is, moral guilt beyond what is projected on them by Christian apologists such as D'Souza. Most abortions take place before the fetus is sufficiently developed to experience pain, so the guilt cannot be based on sympathy toward another living, sentient being.

Doubtless there is more to say here, particularly about the actual emotions experienced by women who have abortions (often these are feelings of relief). However, D'Souza cannot simply rely on emotional responses to abortion that may be shared by some of his readers. These will most certainly not be shared by others.

If guided by reason, compassion will side in most instances with a woman who needs an abortion, and will oppose laws that attempt to prevent women having abortions. It is, in fact, the antiabortion position that lacks compassion: it neglects the interests of a pregnant woman who does not wish to be a mother – and may have very good reasons for her preference. In some cases, we are talking about rape victims. In others, the woman may actually be a frightened teenager whose future prospects will be damaged irreparably if she goes ahead with a pregnancy at this stage of her life. Women face many situations in which they consider the possibility of an abortion, and they usually do not make these decisions lightly. This exposes why many of us reject what D'Souza and other Christian conservatives hold out as Christian morality: it is arbitrary and cruel.

The same can be said about another of D'Souza's examples, euthanasia, by which he seems to have in mind physician-assisted suicide. But how can *this* be described as callous? Euthanasia, etymologically meaning "good death," is usually understood as relating to the suffering of competent patients who often face inevitable death from diseases such as cancer, and – crucially – who themselves have made the determination that their lives are not worth living to them. Some patients may find themselves in awful situations, but they are too debilitated to end their own lives. Is it "compassionate" to require them to live on against their own wishes, knowing the ongoing suffering that they must endure, and no matter what legislative safeguards can be put in place to deter abuses and obviate fears (Schüklenk *et al.*, 2011)?

To many atheists – and others who support carefully regulated access to voluntary euthanasia and assisted suicide – it is the policies of the churches that appear cruel, driven more by supernaturalist concepts that human lives are in the hands of God than by concern for the welfare of human beings who are trapped in awful situations. From that point of view, D'Souza's complaints about callousness and compassion are offensive. It is one thing for Roman Catholicism to insist that there is a redemptive value in human suffering; it is quite another to insist that multicultural societies should abide by such implausible dictates. The religious morality that D'Souza espouses detects a kind of redemption and holiness in suffering, helplessness, and misery. But where is the redemptive value in suffering unnecessarily toward the end of our lives? Your average atheist cannot see it, and for good reason.

Christian apologists often seem led astray by their own sense of righteousness. As a result, they misunderstand the straightforward relationship between the widely accepted value of compassion and the moral standards advocated by many atheist thinkers.

At this stage, it is worth asking the question whether such apologists' claims contain any grain of truth. Perhaps they do point to something true, but in a way that is very different from what they imagine. Far from atheists trying to fool themselves that God does not exist so they can reject certain strictures of traditional morality, they may begin with a strong intuition that those strictures are irrational, arbitrary, and cruel. To be fair, that is evidently not a sufficient reason to believe that God does not exist: we could consistently postulate that God exists while also holding that there is nothing wrong with such things as contraception, abortion, and homosexual conduct. This stance is taken by much of contemporary theology, which rejects conservative Christian views of these and related social matters. However, the problem is more indirect – as long as churches and sects issue moral edicts that appear largely irrational, when judged by secular standards, their credibility is undermined.

For many of us, the moral norms advocated by morally conservative theists do not look like the edicts of a superlatively wise and benevolent being, but more like relics from a less enlightened era. At best, some of them may have made sense as standards of behavior in earlier social circumstances, but they make little or no sense now. Once we reach that point, holy books, traditional teachings, and official pronouncements from religious organizations appear unlikely to be divinely inspired. That, in turn, casts doubt on their authority in other matters such as claims about the existence and character of supernatural beings.

Again, this may not in itself be the strongest reason for atheism, but the appearance that holy books and religious institutions are fallible human constructions converges with many other considerations that we'll be discussing. Taken together, these can, quite reasonably lead to the conclusion that supernatural beings do not exist. The bottom line with this myth is that atheism need not be based on disillusionment, cynicism, loneliness, or even an affirmation of sexual freedom. It is a sincere intellectual position.

Myth 7 Atheists See No Good in Religion

It is true that atheists do not see theistic religions as providing superior normative frameworks in which to live our lives. Nor do we consider it necessary to find guidance in the commands of a supreme being, the decisions of a religious organization or its leaders, or the text of a holy book. That does not mean that we never see any good in religion. Atheists can differ over issues like that.

As mentioned throughout this book, many atheists are philosophical naturalists. As such, they reject the existence of any supernatural agencies or powers, but not, for example, the findings of methodologically sound sociological research. There would be no reason for philosophical naturalists to deny that religion can provide some, or even many, people with a sense of community. Likewise, they can accept findings indicating that strongly religious people find their impending death easier to accept than others, though not necessarily more so than intellectually committed atheists. On these, you might want to refer to our treatment of Myths 18, 48, and 49.

Depending on atheists' moral convictions they might appreciate some of the work religious charities undertake in developing countries. However, atheists might be troubled by this good work being mixed up with religious organizations' attempts to convert impoverished or otherwise vulnerable people to their particular ideologies. The Catholic charities providing health care in certain parts of sub Saharan Africa give us a good example of the darker side of religious aid-giving activities. They really do care for people with AIDS and other illnesses, but that does not prevent them from telling their patients that they should not use condoms. Thus they endanger people's lives and welfare because of God's supposed disapprobation of condom use during sexual intercourse. Or again, what would *you* make of an evangelical charity devoted to helping Iraqi refugees to settle into the USA when it refuses to hire a Muslim because he is of the wrong faith (Turnbull, 2010)?

All too often, when it comes to the good of religion there is a flip-side. Acknowledging this is not denying the good done by religious people, even if for the wrong reasons, and even if done with – from our perspective – ulterior motives. We cannot think of a single instance where religiously motivated activities are unequivocally positive. There is virtually always a "but" – think of the disastrous reign of Mother Teresa in India. Christopher Hitchens's book, *The Missionary Position: Mother Teresa in Theory and Practice*, shows that the good work done there from religious motives was anything but good; or, at a minimum, it could have been much better if Mother Teresa had not been fanatically preoccupied with her own delusions about the wonders of poverty and the redemptive value of human suffering (Hitchens, 1997).

Atheists are not necessarily hostile to all religion, and we need not be hostile to religious people, just as Jews need not be hostile to Hindus, Christians need not be hostile to Jews, and so on (Baggini, 2003, p. 92). People are complex, and there is usually far more to them than their views about otherworldly agencies and powers. We should not judge them solely on that dimension.

Religion can sometimes be all-consuming; it can turn to fanaticism and authoritarianism. But that doesn't make all religious people fanatics and authoritarians, any more than atheists are. By and large, atheists know this and will treat people on their merits as individuals. Shouldn't we all take that attitude?

Myth 8 No Atheist Believes in Anything Supernatural

As an addendum to the previous "myth," it is worth noting that most philosophically minded atheists, including the authors of this book, do not believe in supernatural entities, realms (such as Heaven and Hell), forces, and so on. Some of the same considerations that lead atheists to reject belief in gods may lead them not to believe in, for example, ghosts, evil spirits, astral influences, reincarnation, or any sort of afterlife. As Julian Baggini puts the point, atheism "is usually accompanied by a broader rejection of any supernatural or transcendental reality" (2003, p. 3) In other words, there is a strong tendency for atheists to be philosophical naturalists, people who do not believe in anything supernatural or "spooky."

All that said, we atheists differ among ourselves in many ways. Some do believe in supernatural or scientifically anomalous phenomena of various sorts. We have, for example, met atheists who believe in ghosts or who take astrology seriously. Technically, this is possible, since atheism is merely disbelief in God (the deity of monotheistic religions such as Christianity) and other beings that can reasonably be thought of as gods. Indeed, some well-known religions are atheistic or at least open to atheistic interpretations. Religious adherents who interpret their traditions atheistically may nonetheless make various supernatural or otherworldly claims, such as claims about a cycle of death and spiritual rebirth, without postulating the existence of any intelligent beings that would qualify as gods.

Myth 9 It Makes No Sense for an Atheist to Practice Any Kind of Religion

Is this really a myth, or is it the truth? That depends to a large extent on one's definition of religion (see Myth 1). It is worth noting, however, that some belief systems that are commonly thought of as religions do not involve gods, though they involve supernatural forces or principles, spiritual transformations, canons of conduct, and other features that typify religion. Thus Michael Martin argues that some religions could be atheistic. These include Jainism, Confucianism, and some forms of Buddhism (Martin, 2007, pp. 221–229). It would, however, be a logical error to deduce from this statement that atheism is a religion, and Martin emphasizes that it lacks all plausible religion-making characteristics (2007, pp. 220–221).

Let us have a closer look at Buddhism as a possible example of a godless religion. The original form of Buddhism makes no overt reference to gods. The historical character usually referred to as "Buddha" was a man of noble birth named Siddhartha Gautama, born in the foothills of the Himalayas around 566 BCE. According to traditional accounts, Siddhartha lived the first 29 years of his life in sheltered luxury in the family palace, where he was being groomed to inherit the royal duties from his father. Intellectually and spiritually dissatisfied, he stole out of the palace and renounced society, spending the next six years as a wandering ascetic. One night, he sat down under a fig tree and vowed that he would not get up until he had gained enlightenment. That night he did, indeed, attain enlightenment. The remainder of his life was devoted to helping others obtain it, and this is the basis of the Buddhist religion. Nothing in his teachings, as recorded and handed down to us, was theistic, and enlightenment as understood within these teachings does not involve knowledge of any god or gods.

If all this is granted, theism is not the essence of Buddhism, and there is no reason why a Buddhist could not be an atheist. However, this does not preclude the possibility that most Buddhists are actually theists. Indeed, as Martin discusses, some scholars do not accept that Buddhism was originally atheistic – there is an argument that it took over certain gods and a concept of the Absolute (which should, perhaps, be construed in theistic terms) from Hindu teachings (Martin, 2007, pp. 223–227).

Be that as it may, it appears that Buddhism, and some other religions such as Jainism and Confucianism, are at least open to atheistic interpretations. Accordingly, atheists could accept these religions as long as they believed its various nontheistic spiritual doctrines.

It is also possible to engage for various nonreligious reasons in *the practices* required of its adherents by a traditionally theistic religion. In pagan antiquity, the practice of religion as a form of civic duty was well understood. Thus the ruling classes of ancient Rome regarded the state religious rites as a means to earn divine favor for communal purposes, such as victory against enemy tribes, rather than to meet the citizens' "intimate spiritual needs." Even someone who did not believe in any of the traditional deities might have had reason to take part as a gesture of solidarity with fellow citizens, and the authorities did not object if individuals followed their own cultic practices in addition to the formal rites required by the state (Kirsch, 2004, pp. 93–94; Blackford, 2012, pp. 7, 21–23).

Even in modern circumstances, some atheists may have reasons to take part in the practices of a religion, though not believing in the existence of its god or gods, or accepting any teachings about the supernatural. For example, David Benatar argues that it is perfectly possible for an atheist to abide by religious scriptures' guidance without accepting the religion's god (Benatar 2006). Atheists abiding by scriptural rules will have their own motives and reasons for doing so. In days gone by, they might have done so for no other reason than to escape prosecution by religious authorities. In modern times it is more likely that someone would have cultural reasons for participating in the practices of a theistic religion. For example, some atheistic Jews or Muslims might wish to assert an identity, or solidarity, with other Jews or Muslims. More generally, someone might wish to participate in the religious culture that their friends and family members share.

Other reasons for taking part in religious practices might include the desire to impose a particular discipline on oneself, or the desire to bring up children in accordance with family traditions, or certain ideas of moral right and wrong. In her survey project on the religious views and practices of scientists in elite American universities, Elaine Howard Ecklund found a large percentage of atheists, and she certainly found that scientists tend to be less religious than the general public, but very few were "actively working against religion." Many nonbelievers – atheists and agnostics – were involved with houses of worship and were comfortable with religion, in some cases thinking of it as a moral training ground for their children (Ecklund, 2010, p. 150; see also for a first-hand account, Upshur, 2009).

Myth 10 Atheists Worship False Gods (Satan, Money, Materialism, etc.)

We referred earlier (Myth 5) to a newspaper story by Miles Godfrey that deals with a number of attacks on atheism by church leaders in Australia. According to this report, the Catholic Archbishop of Sydney, Cardinal George Pell, harshly criticized nonbelievers, while the city's Anglican archbishop, Dr Peter Jensen, said in his Good Friday sermon that atheism was "a form of idolatry" (Godfrey, 2010). These attacks are part of a long tradition of associating atheism with venality, the pursuit of material goods, consumerism, the fickleness of mere fashion, and even the worship of Satan.

Let us turn first to the most extreme of these charges: that of Satan worship. In modern times, at least, it is surprisingly difficult to find serious thinkers who make such claims about atheists – and considerably easier to find atheists refuting them. We might draw the conclusion that the existence of this myth is itself a myth. But not so fast, please! It appears that many atheists are confronted by this accusation in their personal lives, and that the myth lives on among many ordinary religious people, even if it is not promulgated by theologians and intellectuals.

See, for example, an interview conducted by Kacey Cornell with Dallas-based atheist Sari Nelson, available online. Nelson complains that people she encounters in her daily life assume that as an atheist she must worship Satan, referring, in particular to an exchange about Satan with one of her co-workers who asked her rhetorically, "But aren't you an atheist?" (Cornell, 2009a). In a further post by Cornell, two days later (Cornell, 2009b), she describes an experience of her own in which a man with whom she was talking responded to her statement that she was an atheist by asking, "So does that mean you worship Satan?"

It is unclear just how common this perception might be in the twenty-first century, but anecdotal evidence suggests that many atheists encounter it. Let us put it to rest, then. Some atheists believe in supernatural forces of one kind or another, but by definition they do not believe in the existence of supernatural beings that could be regarded in any way as gods. Atheists do not believe in the existence of Satan, let alone regard him as a god and worship him (Rowe, 1979). The idea is even less plausible once we think for a moment of Satan's role as God's competitor within certain strains of Christian theism in particular. The idea of believing in and worshiping a literal Satan makes no real sense outside of such a context (compare Cline, n.d.).

Satan worship aside, the themes of idolatry, materialism, and so on, were much to the fore in the contributions by speakers for the affirmative in a 2011 public debate on the topic "Atheists Are Wrong" – again held in Sydney. The written versions of the speeches by Archbishop Jensen, academic theologian Tracey Rowland, and theologian cum journalist Scott Stephens all maintain aspects of this association.

Jensen sees atheists as engaging in idolatry when they understand material processes, such as evolution, as sufficient explanations of the world's varied phenomena (Jensen, 2011). Rowland and Stephens show even more hostility toward atheism, closely associating it with all the evils that they detect in contemporary Western society. Rowland blames atheism for "hollowing out" many aspects of human life to what she calls their "materialist shell," thereby producing such things as brutally manipulative sex, consumerism, status anxiety, and the cult of celebrity (Rowland, 2011).

Likewise, Stephens is scathing. "There are," he says, "few things today more fashionable, more suited to our modern conceit, than atheism." He adds that atheism fits what he calls "our modern predicament" of shallowness, nihilism, and self-indulgence, though at least he doesn't regard atheism as the *cause* of this predicament:

> In a way, I think where atheism fits in our cultural moment it is more incidental than that. Our real problem today is the impoverishment of the modern mind, our inability to think properly about such elevated things as the Good, Beauty, Truth, Law, Love, Life, Death, Humanity, the End or Purpose of things, even Sex itself, without such ideas being debased by an incurious and all-pervasive nihilism. (Stephens, 2011)

What should we make of all this? In fact, atheism does not require the worship of anything. As James Rachels argues (1971), worshiping involves a distinct set of actions with a uniquely theistic character. Rachels distinguishes the positive attitude of awe from worship. Awe need not involve the kinds of beliefs involved in worship: for instance, we might be in awe of the beauty of the Great Barrier Reef without worshiping it. Nor need awe involve any activities – but worship certainly does. According to Rachels, worship involves the aim of submitting oneself to a superior power (hence, not all ceremonies involve worship). The activity of worship is meant to express the way in which a particular belief – namely that one occupies a submissive relation to God – "dominates one's whole way of life" (Rachels, 1971, p. 331).

It is difficult to see how such things as money, materialism, consumerism, and evolution could meet the conditions needed to be objects of worship.

It's very doubtful that anyone *worships* these things, in the full sense of the word. Perhaps, however, such claims can be interpreted less literally. Do atheists put money, material goods, or other "false gods" at the center of their lives? This might, we suppose, be a metaphorical kind of "worship." Furthermore, are atheists somehow to blame for, or complicit in, such aspects of modern culture as its emphasis on fashion, celebrity, and material wealth?

Well, where is the evidence? Quite possibly some atheists are capitalists aiming to increase their wealth. They would not be alone in such a venture. The main contenders for the position of Republican candidate for President of the USA in the 2012 presidential elections, Mitt Romney, Ron Paul, Rick Santorum, Rick Perry and Newt Gingrich, made a point of stressing prominently that they did not see a conflict between worshiping their respective gods and maximizing their own income. The Republican primaries ultimately singled out Romney as the party's candidate – thus choosing a man with enormous personal wealth and annual income. He, in turn, chose Paul Ryan as his running mate and candidate for the Vice Presidency of the USA. Ryan is a conservative Christian who shares atheist Ayn Rand's views when it comes to economic matters.

In any event, you will find many atheists who describe themselves as socialists, or, more likely unorthodox left-of-centre. Their primary concern may be societal well-being rather than individual enrichment. It is true, of course, that contemporary societies place great value on wealth and celebrity, but atheists can hardly be blamed for that – indeed, much of this stems from the culture of the United States, which remains the most religious society in the Western world, with far more theists than atheists among its population.

Furthermore, there is a long history of reverence, if not exactly worship, for the supposed majesty of aristocrats and wealthy people. This certainly predates the critiques of religion set forth by modern atheists (critiques that were unknown before the seventeenth century). It is doubtful that many people's tendencies to be impressed by worldly wealth, status, and power have anything to do with atheism, or that atheists are more culpable in this regard than anyone else. Indeed, churches and their leaders – from medieval popes and bishops to modern-day televangelists – have frequently shown a love of material pomp and possessions exceeding that of any well-known atheist (see Golgowski, 2012). If this is a kind of "idolatry," then so be it, but atheists are hardly to blame.

2

Atheist Living

Myth 11 Atheism Robs Life of Meaning and Purpose

Questions about "meaning" and "purpose" can be unclear, since these words are rather vague in the context of someone's life or of human life itself. In particular, life and individual lives are not signs, such as linguistic expressions, so the word "meaning" cannot be applied to them literally – it must be used in some metaphorical or analogical sense (e.g., Nielsen, 1964; Hepburn, 1965). Many religious thinkers hold that for our lives to be meaningful we need to be immortal in some way, or else our lives would be just as meaningless as those of other animals. According to this line of thought, God soon comes into the equation, as only God is capable of offering us immortality. The existence of God, then, is a logically necessary condition for a meaningful human life (Metz, 2003). If this line of reasoning is correct, it follows that atheists are incapable of living a meaningful life as we reject more than the God premise – most of us reject the immortality premise, too.

There are short and long answers to this challenge. The short answer could be, not entirely flippantly, "Life is what we make of it." There is no deeper, God-given meaning to life, regardless of whether our lives are infinitely long or of limited duration. It is up to us to decide how we wish to live our lives to make life worth living to us. It is this self-directedness that makes life meaningful. Given that most monotheist religions are quite old, harking back to long-overcome cultural mores, it is important to recognize

50 Great Myths About Atheism, First Edition. Russell Blackford and Udo Schüklenk.

their threat to a meaningful, self-directed life. Indeed, the French atheist philosopher Michel Onfray makes such a point with respect to Islam:

> A society applying the principles of the Koran would give us a universal nomad encampment, astir with the distant echo of subterranean spasms and the song of the spheres, dead husks orbiting themselves in celebration of nothingness, emptiness, the meaninglessness of a long-defunct history. (Onfray, 2007, p. 214)

Similar statements would be true of all monotheistic religions. Just because many people yearn for their life to have deep meaning does not prove there is such a thing, at least not a meaning given to it by anyone other than by ourselves. As Daniel Dennett suggests, a life of religious devotion may resemble one of romantic love (2006, pp. 250–255), but the devotee's core claims about the existence of God, immaterial souls, an afterlife, and so on, cannot be substantiated.

If we were created by God, he presumably had a literal purpose in mind for us, as we do if we create a tool such as a knife or a hammer. But this is unsatisfactory – a knife may have a purpose because it was designed and manufactured to perform a certain function, but that is not significant from the viewpoint of the knife. Likewise, if you were created, as in Aldous Huxley's *Brave New World*, for some specific purpose (such as cleaning toilets) that might not be what you want. We do not really want to find out that we were made to serve a purpose established by somebody else (see Baggini, 2003, p. 59).

Perhaps someone could take pleasure in the idea of doing God's will, as some people once took pleasure in the idea of serving the aristocracy, but today this seems demeaning if anything. Or perhaps we can just take it on faith that God has some sort of purpose for us that does not involve serving *his* purposes – but this is getting mysterious, since we do not know what it might be or whether it is actually something that we could embrace even if we knew what it is (Baggini, 2003, p. 59).

As mentioned in our introductory remarks to this myth, the entire complaint that life might not have meaning or purpose is less than clear. Nonetheless, the claim that life lacks "meaning" and "purpose" without God obviously has some intuitive appeal for many people – it resonates with them in some way – and this seems worth exploring further.

Some writers distinguish between what Paul Edwards terms the "cosmic" and "terrestrial" senses of life's being meaningful (Baier, 1957; Edwards, 1966). As Edwards develops the distinction, the former requires the reality of a universal design, such as a plan in the mind of God. The latter applies at the level of an individual life and consists in individuals having significant commitments that imbue their actions with zest. Whether life is meaningful in the cosmic sense depends upon whether there actually is a universal design. However, Edwards denies, we think rightly, that this would entail that anyone's life has meaning in the terrestrial sense. In that sense, he suggests, the actuality of a universal design could give meaning to individuals' lives only if they knew and approved of it and their place in it (Edwards, 1966, p. 132; see also Nielsen, 1964, pp. 184–185). Conversely, he argues that it is possible for an individual's life to have meaning in the terrestrial sense even if life, conceived as the sum of human activity and experience, is not meaningful in the cosmic sense.

We concur with Edwards that it is the terrestrial sense that really matters. The lack of a God and a divine plan in no way entails that our individual lives must lack commitments, values, or the kind of zest that can come from living in accord with them. Importantly, lack of belief in gods of any sort is no impediment to living a life where what you do and experience connects closely with the things you value.

For all that, Eric Reitan is concerned that life for many people would lack meaning if theistic beliefs were untrue. Ultimately, this is an empirical claim. If true, it raises the question whether preserving unfounded beliefs might be worthwhile. Enlightenment philosopher Immanuel Kant's dictum comes to mind here:

> *Enlightenment is the human being's emergence from his self-incurred minority. Minority* is inability to make use of one's own understanding without direction from another. This minority is *self-incurred* when its cause lies not in lack of understanding but in lack of resolution and courage to use it without direction from another. *Sapere aude!* Have courage to make use of your *own* understanding! is thus the motto of enlightenment. (Kant, 1996 [1784], p. 17, italics in original)

Many atheists would suggest that approaching life along these lines provides it with meaning.

Reitan cites an argument put by David Swenson that starts along the following lines. First, a common view of what makes a life happy or meaningful is that it possesses an abundance of good things: "not just material property but friends, meaningful work, exposure to great art, bodily health, adventures that get the blood pumping, and the like" (Reitan, 2009, p. 205). At this point, an element of confusion is already introduced, since Reitan speaks of both a happy life and a meaningful life. He defines neither of these, yet it is obvious that at least for some people they might not be the same thing. For example, a life may be happy in the sense that things go well for the person concerned, but there may then be a separate question as to whether and in what sense this life can be considered meaningful.

Swenson and Reitan do not deny that friendship, art, health, and so on, are genuine goods, or claim that their value should be deprecated, but Reitan observes that "the empirical world of pitiless indifference does not richly bless everyone with these things." On the contrary, he thinks that "most lives would be impoverished" if their richness in these things were the measure. As Reitan reports and develops the argument, possession of these things cannot be the measure of a meaningful life, because this would entail that most people do not live meaningful lives. According to Reitan (2009, p. 205), Swenson says, indeed, that choosing such good things as the end and aim of life does injury to the mass of people who are unable to attain them.

This seems a thoroughly confused line of reasoning. First, how are we doing *injury* to people if we notice that their lives are lacking many good things? Or how are we doing them injury if we pursue these goods for ourselves? Perhaps that might be arguable in the case of pursuit of material property, insofar as this is finite. But if I pursue such things as friendships and meaningful work I do not thereby deprive others of them. These are not scarce goods that are gained only at others' expense. In particular, it is possible for all people to have friendships and other close relationships such as those with parents or children. In the nature of things, there are enough of these to go around in any population – the larger the population the more people there are with whom any one of us might have close relationships.

Something similar can be said about meaningful work: a society might be organized in such a way that many jobs are repetitive, boring, and alienating, but that need not be the case. Nor does the available amount of meaningful work remain constant as populations get larger, and if it does so as a result of technological change this can sometimes open up more space for leisure and contemplation. Equally, my health does not preclude yours: we are not involved in a competition for a finite amount of health. On the contrary, we may find mutual benefit if both of us are healthy, and so able to make social contributions. Exposure to art is another good example: my being exposed to art does not preclude your being exposed to art, and it may be better for both of us if both of us are exposed to it (for example, we can share and discuss the experience).

In short, the sort of goods that Swenson and Reitan discuss are not necessarily the rewards in a zero-sum game. Potentially they are available to most people, though achieving this might require considerable political will. It is quite misleading to talk of pursuing goods such as health, loving relationships, and meaningful work as if this pursuit harms others.

Perhaps the claim about an "injury" to others is meant in a more metaphorical sense – somehow we are misrepresenting the situation of others, not doing justice to the goodness of their lives, if the emphasis is on the importance of such goods as health, loving relationships, and meaningful work. We are implicitly denigrating the people who lack these things. But there is no denigration here. Surely we have every reason to feel compassion for people who find themselves friendless and unloved, trapped in alienating work (or dispirited by unemployment), or suffering from a painful, perhaps life-threatening disease. These may not be complete barriers to living a meaningful life, though someone suffering from all of them at the same time is certainly in a very bad situation. It is merely being realistic to acknowledge that they are the kinds of things that can take the zest from one's life; those in such a situation have already been injured, and it is not *you* who injures them if you comment on their situation. This talk of "injury" is a rhetorical trick that merits exposure and condemnation.

That point made, why should we assume that everyone is leading a meaningful life? If anything, it appears on the face of it that the opposite is true – that at least *some* people are not leading lives that are, in any sense, meaningful. That does not mean, by the way, that their lives could not be happy. Vice versa, a meaningful life may well be deeply unhappy (Kernohan, 2006, p. 6).

Reitan provides another argument along the lines that living as if there is a God is the only way that we can show solidarity with those whose lives are shattered by horror (Reitan, 2009, p. 206). Surely, however, it is not a terribly viable proposition to lead a life on a basis that you have no reason to think is actually *true* in order to show solidarity with those who have it bad. The existence of people who are doing badly in this life is not a reason for us to abandon our intellectual honesty. Arguably a more sensible and honest way to show solidarity with them is to acknowledge that they really do have things bad – and then to try to do something about it. That old Christian favorite of the redemptive value of human suffering should not be proffered here, and nor should the Christian standard bearer for doing nothing, namely sending prayers for help to a nonexistent deity.

Wohlgennant argues that religious believers can live with no fundamental doubts about the meaning of life, because they believe that God knows "the meaning and purpose" of every event: a person "who believes this meaning to be in the keeping of God – even if he cannot know it himself – has not lost it" (Wohlgennant, 1987, p. 37). But how coherent is this?

It may explain why some religious people feel comfort from religion even if they are otherwise disappointed or afflicted or confused, and why they might not be able to understand how atheists can find life "meaningful." We understand how religious explanations of the universe and human experience can be reassuring for many people, even if they are not actually true. Loss of faith might mean loss of what gave believers an assurance that their actions had purpose, that their values were justified, and that they understood something of the universe, including some puzzling aspects of human experience.

However, atheists like us do not perceive the world as a meaningless, frightening place. Atheism does not prevent people from leading lives that they find deeply absorbing and valuable – worthwhile from their own point of view. The atheist's challenge and opportunity lies in a preference for self-directedness, as opposed to the other-directedness that is on offer

Credited to Jesus and Mo, www.jesusandmo.net

from mainstream monotheistic religions. If we actually want purpose in life, we want something that speaks to our own goals, projects, values, and so on. We think it is best if the effort itself is worthwhile for us, and if the goal, should we achieve it, creates something that is of lasting value as understood by us.

Myth 12 Atheism is Depressing

The claim has frequently been made that atheism is depressing. Among others, Dinesh D'Souza espouses this view (2007, p. 274). It is true that atheism offers no false comfort in the face of harsh realities such as aging and death, or the way that cruel people can sometimes prosper. Atheists do not, for example, console themselves that death is followed by a happy immortal life in heaven or that there is a cosmic system of redress whereby the good are rewarded and the evil punished. Thus it is often claimed that atheism fails to offer what theism can, consolation to the suffering.

Furthermore, atheism does not offer a universe that cares for us, or that loves and suffers in the way that we do. Even some atheists have found this a troubling thought. In his essay "A [originally The] Free Man's Worship," Bertrand Russell (2000 [1903]) portrayed the world as bleak, uncaring, and impersonal, while Albert Camus believed that human beings expect the universe to be responsive to our efforts and able to provide us with guidance. However, he said, the universe is, or at least appears to be, totally oblivious to us, governed merely by mathematical laws. His essay "The Myth of Sisyphus" (reprinted in Camus, 1975) evokes a sense of strangeness and bleakness that many people apparently experience when they contemplate an uncaring universe. Camus questions whether life is worthwhile under those conditions. The threat is not merely that we may abandon our values and purposes if the character of the universe in which we find ourselves gives these no support; it is that life itself may be so oppressive that suicide is the preferable option.

It is understandable when some argue that it would be nicer if the universe had been planned by a benevolent higher entity that continues to look after our needs. Thus Louise M. Antony rightly notes that some people feel safer in a universe overseen by a benevolent God. She adds, however, that this is not her own experience:

> The world of my childhood, a world in which the supernatural intruded regularly into daily life, was a frightening world, a world in which *anything* could happen: the sun could stop, the dead could rise, virgins could give birth. Angels were real, but so were demons, and demons could take over your soul. (Antony, 2007, p. 56)

She prefers a world that is governed by the laws of nature, where she knows what she is dealing with (Antony, 2007, p. 57).

More generally, atheism does not offer anyone the guarantee of living a fulfilling and satisfying life, but it does not deny the possibility that a life in this world can be enough. It encourages us to live this life to the full, whatever that may mean to us as individuals. And when loved ones die we can celebrate their lives, rather than concentrating on the comforting myth that they continue in some other world where they will be nothing like the people that they were.

For its part, religion obviously offers comforts; without them, and in the face of so much adversity in so many religious as well as secular people's lives, believers likely would long have recanted their beliefs. However, it is worth keeping in perspective what these comforts involve. For conservative Christians, the possibility of Hell goes along with that of Heaven, and not all are certain that they are destined for the latter. Imagine also the stress that must go with membership in the Jehovah's Witnesses, a religion insisting that only 144,000 of its members will ever make it into Heaven, while other "good people" will continue living an infinite life on earth – somehow (Watchtower Society, 2013). Some Christians believe that they will undergo a period of suffering in Purgatory after death, before Heaven is available to them. There are also the ordinary human fears of the suffering involved in actually dying and the grief in leaving behind loved ones.

As Scott Aikin and Robert Talisse ask, how exactly is it a comforting thought, when you are suffering a serious and painful disease, that there is an all-good, all-powerful, all-knowing God who allows you to suffer? Isn't it doubly tragic if this being, who could stop your suffering, declines to do so (Aikin and Talisse, 2011, p. 146)? It might be that theistic belief does actually comfort people, though Aikin and Talisse question even this, noting that when they are confronted with horrific events – such as massively destructive tsunamis – believers wrestle openly with the Problem of Evil, trying to understand why God allowed these things to happen. Here, belief in God arguably adds to the distress. The best way to comfort others, as Aikin and Talisse suggest, is by giving them such things as support, care, and love (Aikin and Talisse, 2011, p. 147).

How, then, did Camus, whom we mentioned earlier, answer his question about suicide? He thinks that we can live with zest and meaning by affirming our own values. We can, according to Camus, stage a kind of inner revolt against the absurdity of our condition. Our individual lives can then be both meaningful and happy.

Carl Sagan offers an alternative vision. He finds meaning and happiness in seeing our world as it is, with all its love, beauty, and magnificence, as well as the presence of death. For Sagan, there is an attraction in the idea of immortality, "that some thinking, feeling, remembering part of me will continue," but he knows of no reason to suggest that this is "more than wishful thinking." He adds:

> The world is so exquisite, with so much love and moral depth, that there is no reason to deceive ourselves with pretty stories for which there's little good evidence. Far better it seems to me, in our vulnerability, is to look Death in the eye and to be grateful every day for the brief but magnificent opportunity that life provides. (Sagan, 1997, p. 258).

The important thing to realize is that atheists do not have to be miserable or depressed, but it is true that we must find our own meaning and fulfillment, because, unlike in the case of God-belief, meaning is not delivered to us by religion and faith. So, as far as this myth is concerned: atheists are not unavoidably miserable and depressed, but, of course, some individuals atheist might feel misery or depression. The same applies to many Christians and other theists.

Most of us can find genuine happiness in facing the world courageously, and being open to uncertainty as more and more is discovered – with still more always available to learn. We should be open to learning and growing and to all the ordinary things that can make life good, such as love and relationships, art, culture, and the pleasures of the senses. As long as we are not harming others, and we help them when we can, we have the added benefit that we don't need to feel guilty about how we live our lives – we don't have to worry about claims that we are sinners, or about irrational canons of conduct that no one could ever conform to perfectly.

Myth 13 Atheists Have No Sense of Humor

Governor Mike Huckabee, evangelical preacher cum would-be presidential candidate cum Fox News personality, has insisted that "atheists don't have a good sense of humor," because some of us were annoyed about his – possibly – humorous suggestion that atheists deserve special days (akin to religious special days). He volunteered April 1, April Fool's Day, as a possibility (Huckabee, 2012). Yes, very droll! Imagine how hilarious he would find a suggestion to move Christmas to April 1. Surely we'd find Governor Huckabee rolling on the floor laughing.

Mind you, Huckabee isn't alone here. Don Boys, writing on a website appropriately titled "CanadaFreePress: Because without America there is no Free World" (wait, this isn't the humorous bit!) concludes his epic treatment of an atheist critic as follows: "Joseph's letter did produce some lighter moments for me as he proved once again that Atheists don't have a sense of humor. I always knew they had no sense. After all, God says they are fools" (Boys, 2011). Given our humorlessness, not to say foolishness, it is no wonder that Wendy Kaminer can note in *The Atlantic* magazine, "Atheism in America requires a sense of humor, however black, a thick skin, or an active embrace of outsider status; lacking these defenses, you risk being unnerved by the onslaught of religiosity and mired in a sense of victimhood" (Kaminer, 2011).

Many satirists, literary humorists, and stand-up comedians have been atheists – perhaps George Carlin (1937–2008) was the stand-up comedian most famous for his iconoclastic attacks on religious belief, but there have been, and still are, many others. Indeed, conventions devoted to atheist activism and thought frequently include well-known comedians as entertainers. There seems to be a strong affinity between atheism and brash, fearless comedy. So the myth of the humorless atheist is a funny one, funny as in *peculiar*, but it does exist. Then again, perhaps it goes without saying that atheists also complain about Christians suffering from a serious lack of humor (e.g., Fortin, 2009).

The truth of the matter is that you will probably find atheists, Christians, Muslims, and any number of other people holding all sorts of ideological convictions, who lack a good sense of humor. Others in these categories will have as good a sense of humor as you could want. Unsurprisingly, just how you sort them will depend a great deal on your own taste in humor.

Why don't we let you ponder this serious question with a couple of jokes (slightly edited, because we're humorless enough to do that) and leave it there? First, a Christian joke (atheists show a sense of humor, please, if you can):

> An atheist was walking through the woods. "What majestic trees!" he said to himself. "What powerful rivers! What beautiful animals!"
>
> As he was walking alongside the river, he heard a rustling in the bushes behind him. He turned to look. He saw a seven-foot grizzly charge toward him, so he ran as fast as he could up the path. He looked over his shoulder and saw that the bear was closing in on him.
>
> He glanced over his shoulder again, and the bear was even closer. He tripped and fell to the ground. He rolled over to pick himself up, but saw the bear was right on top of him, reaching for him with its left paw, and raising its right paw to strike! At that instant, the atheist cried out, "Oh please, God, help me!"

Time stopped.

The bear froze.

The forest was still.

As a bright light shone upon the atheist, a great Voice came out of the sky. "You deny my existence all these years, teach others I don't exist, and even credit creation to cosmic accident. Do you expect me to help you out of this predicament. Am I to count you as a believer?"

The atheist looked directly into the light. "It would be hypocritical of me to suddenly ask you to treat me as a Christian now, but perhaps you could make the BEAR a Christian?"

"Very well," said the Voice.

The light went out. The sounds of the forest resumed. And the bear dropped its right paw, brought both paws together, bowed its head, and spoke:

"Lord bless this food, which I am about to receive from thy bounty. Through Christ our Lord, amen." (Debunking Atheists, 2008)

And one for the atheists (believers show your sense of humor please, if you can):

An atheist buys an ancient lamp at an auction, takes it home, and begins to polish it. Suddenly, a genie appears, and says, "I'll grant you three wishes, Master."

The atheist says, "I wish I could believe in you." The genie snaps his fingers, and suddenly the atheist believes in him.

The atheist says, "Wow! I wish all atheists would believe this." The genie snaps his fingers again, and suddenly atheists all over the world begin to believe in genies.

"What about your third wish?" asks the genie.

"Well," says the atheist, "I wish for a billion dollars." The genie snaps his fingers for a third time, but nothing happens. "What's wrong?" says the atheist.

The genie shrugs and says, "Just because you believe in me doesn't mean I exist." (No More Hornets, 2007)

It would have been tempting to crack an Islam joke, too, but a few too many Muslims have a habit of killing folks who make fun of their God, or their blessed prophet, so there might be a bit of a humor problem in Islam (Hitchens, 2006; Sjølie, 2010).

As far as we are concerned, atheists have not been shown to lack humor when compared to other people. Perhaps the charge that atheists lack humor has a more serious objective, namely suggesting that atheists are unpleasant people – you know, the kinds of folk you would not go out with to have a good time. Even if it had been shown that we lack a sense of humor, of course, it would have no bearing on the question of whether our stance on the God question is sound, or else comedians would be the true authorities on God's existence.

Myth 14 Atheists Don't Appreciate Some of the Greatest Works of Art

This myth actually appears in two forms. One suggests that atheists would be unable to create great works of art such as religious artists have created, simply because these artists were driven by their religious beliefs. In its absence, they would not have been able to create what they did. Various authors in both the mainstream media (Ravenhill, 2008) and academic journals (Neill and Ridley, 2010) have argued this case. The concern here is not fundamentally about whether or not God exists, or even whether atheists lose out greatly in our appreciation of art, but about the harm we might incur if there were no religious artists left.

For instance, because so much artistic expression is motivated by religious belief, a predominantly secular society might be losing out on future works comparable to Bach's Mass in B Minor. Mark Ravenhill, a British playwright, contends for this position:

> the greatest artists, from Matthias Grünewald in the 15th century to Benjamin Britten in the 20th, had a genuine Christian faith. complicated, questioning, agonised at times, as any intelligent faith should be, but a very real faith all the same. (Ravenhill, 2008)

He concludes that "we should celebrate the Christian legacy in western art and society – and stop the Dawkins army from denying us the possibility of drawing inspiration from faith to create the art of the future" (Ravenhill, 2008).

It is difficult to test the claim that classic works of art produced by religious artists might have been impossible for atheists to produce. Where an artwork actually expresses religious beliefs and feelings, it could not have been created in all sincerity by an atheist, but then again any kind of religious belief will also restrict the feelings and beliefs that its holder can express sincerely. Works of art are produced by artistic minds – and such minds differ very greatly. Given that there are both religious and nonreligious artists, it seems at least doubtful that religious belief provides a substantively more competitive artistic output (Dawkins, 2006, pp. 86–87).

The fact that religious orders financed many works of art – indeed, most during long periods of European history – explains why many of humanity's greatest works of art have been created by religious artists, or by artists who claimed to be religious. Today we have plenty of evidence for the capacity of atheists and agnostics to produce great works of art. Here are the names of just a few of them, from Wikipedia's "List of Atheists" article (as of July 23, 2012): Seamus Heaney (Nobel Prize for Literature), Percy Shelley, George Orwell, Béla Bartók, Dmitri Shostakovich, Stanley Kubrick, Bertrand Russell, Woody Allen, Hector Berlioz – and there are too many others to list here.

The other form of this argument claims that atheists are unable to appreciate religiously motivated works of great art, because we are unable to appreciate the religious component that is constitutive of the work in question. However, appreciation of art is notoriously difficult to measure. There will be many religious people who are unable to appreciate classical music or experience much joy in listening to it, while many atheists might enjoy classical music composed by religious and atheist composers alike. David Pugmire, for instance, argues that "sacred music expresses and evokes emotional attitudes of distinctive kinds. Even people who are irreligious in their beliefs can find themselves moved by it" (Pugmire, 2006). A similar line of reasoning is offered by Alex Neill and Aaron Ridley (2010). One of us, for instance, greatly enjoys gospel music and appreciates the particularly calming impact the Bach/Gounod song "Ave Maria" has on him during stressful times. You do not need to be a Christian to appreciate these as well as other artistic outputs, even if they were originally motivated by religious belief.

A simple thought experiment shows how problematic this myth really is. If atheists are unable to appreciate artistic works produced by theists, how far does this generalize? Are Christians unable to appreciate works produced by atheists and agnostics, or by polytheistic pagans in classical and preclassical times? Are they unable to appreciate works created by, say, Muslims, Buddhists, and Hindus? It is possible, of course, that someone could be blinded to the merit of an artwork by hostility to its creator or by what it was intended to express, but it is simplistic to imagine that this is an insuperable barrier to appreciating art by people with different beliefs about the universe. Much that is expressed in art transcends these sorts of differences, and involves common human experiences, making works such as Homer's *Iliad* and *Odyssey* widely accessible even today, when the gods of ancient Greece are no longer worshiped.

Furthermore, it is possible for people to enter imaginatively into frames of mind and views of the world that are very different from their own. It is foolish to imagine that atheists cannot appreciate, say, the religious poetry of John Donne or Gerard Manley Hopkins, even though it expresses attitudes and thoughts that the atheist disagrees with. Purveyors of this myth greatly underestimate human powers of imagination and sympathy.

Myth 15 There is no Christmas in Atheist Families

The claim is that atheist parents do not celebrate Christmas (or similar festivals and holidays). This is often beaten up by media commentators into a "war on Christmas" (Smith, 2011).

In fact, most atheists in Western, historically Christian, countries do tend to celebrate Christmas (e.g., White, 2011). It turns out that even non-Christian followers of different religions seem to enjoy celebrating Christmas as a public holiday of a kind (e.g., Berkeley Parents Network, 2009). Atheists, along with followers of non-Christian religions, do not treat Christmas as a time of worship – as atheists, we do not believe that Jesus was the son of God or that he was born of a virgin somewhat over two thousand years ago. That does not, however, mean that we cannot enjoy the tradition. For atheists who participate in celebrating Christmas, the festival has long lost its religious significance. All the same, it provides an opportunity in the year to relax, spend time with family and loved ones, and take part in local cultural events. Quite likely atheists in Muslim countries where Eid al-Aadha (no kidding, a celebration of a father's willingness to sacrifice his son to show obedience to Allah) is a public holiday will enjoy *that* holiday, and possibly even some of its rituals, for much the same reasons.

In fact, there is nothing terribly unusual about such an attitude. In Mexico, for instance, the Dia de Muertos, the Day of the Dead, is celebrated by many atheists, Christians, and Muslims, among others, even though it dates back to the indigenous Aztecs' belief that during the Day of the Dead the souls of our deceased family members return to celebrate with us (Brandes, 2006). Many tourists visit Mexico during the Day of the Dead celebrations and join in the party. This does not mean, of course, that they actually subscribe to ancient Aztec beliefs.

Atheists do tend to be conscious that the origins of Christmas are largely pre-Christian, dating back to pagan celebrations of the northern hemisphere winter solstice. Customs such as giving presents, as well as the actual date of December 25, can be traced from pagan tradition, while many of the modern commercial trappings also have little to do with Christianity (like many Christians, many atheists find some of the excessive commercial emphasis distasteful, though not sacrilegious or blasphemous).

Richard Dawkins, perhaps the world's most famous advocate for atheism in the early twenty-first century, has often stated that he enjoys Christmas time, including traditional Christmas carols. For example, he spoke about the issue in an interview on BBC Radio Four's Today program in late 2008, saying: "I really like the kind of peripheral things about Christmas. I like the smell of tangerines and the smell of the tree and to pull crackers." He described his Christmas routine as, "We go to my sister's house for Christmas lunch which is a lovely big family occasion. Everybody thoroughly enjoys it. No church of course" (Todd, 2008).

Credited to Jesus and Mo, www.jesusandmo.net

Myth 16 Atheists Don't Appreciate the Beauty and Perfection of God's Creation

You likely will have heard this claim from Muslim or Christian friends praising the beauty and perfection of the natural world. Atheists, so the myth goes, are unable to appreciate these.

Indeed, many theists have argued for God's existence from the beauty of nature – Richard Swinburne being perhaps the most important living philosopher to take this tack (2004, pp. 121–122, 190–191). Swinburne claims that God has reason to create a basically beautiful world, especially if he creates a world with embodied intelligent beings such as us. Conversely, so the argument goes, there is no particular reason to think that the world would be beautiful in God's absence. Swinburne does not place great weight on this in itself, since he thinks the argument's force depends partly on whether beauty is an objective property of nature or something we project onto the world, and in any event his general approach is to develop a cumulative case for the probability of God's existence, rather than rely on particular phenomena whose existence settles the issue once and for all. Still, he is a modern representative of a much longer tradition of connecting the beauty of nature with the existence of a deity.

Many thinkers from earlier eras have made much of the supposed beauty and perfection of God's creation. Writing in the eighteenth century, the German philosopher Gottfried Leibniz declared, with some pride, that the whole purpose of his philosophy was to demonstrate the perfection and greatness of God and his creation. Leibniz discussed the matter in his *Theodicy*:

> M. Bayle raises the further objection, that it is true that our legislators can never invent regulations such as are convenient for all individuals, "Nulla lex satis commoda omnibus est; id modo quaeritur, si majori parti et in summam prodest. (Cato apud Livium, L. 34, circa init.)" But the reason is that the limited condition of their knowledge compels them to cling to laws which, when all is taken into account, are more advantageous than harmful. Nothing of all that can apply to God, who is as infinite in power and understanding as in goodness and true greatness. *I answer that since God chooses the best possible, one cannot tax him with any limitation of his perfections; and in the universe not only does the good exceed the evil, but also the evil serves to augment the good.* (Leibniz, 1951[1710], p. 263)

It is tempting, to answer all this with a glib, "What perfection?" We can easily point to examples of how suboptimal the natural world around us actually is. In his novel *Candide* (2005 [1759]), Voltaire rightly made a mockery of Leibniz's complacent philosophy. It is undercut throughout by the numerous horrors and disasters that strike one of the main characters, the Leibniz-inspired philosopher Pangloss.

John Stuart Mill is also well known, alongside Voltaire, to have been skeptical of any rose-tinted view of the world, though in his essay *On Nature* he excuses Leibniz on the basis that the latter did not genuinely believe in a literally omnipotent God (Mill, 1996 [1904], p. 20). *On Nature* is largely devoted to examining nature's horrors and its endless capacity for destruction. At one point, Mill reminds us that a large proportion of the world's animals are predators, "lavishly fitted out with the instruments necessary" for "tormenting and devouring other animals"; he adds that the lower animals (those other than our own species) are, almost without exception, "divided . . . into devourers and devoured, and a prey to a thousand ills from which they are denied the faculties necessary for protecting themselves" (Mill, 1996 [1904], p. 30). This is not quite the romantic, perfect blue planet that Leibniz had in mind!

Just think of the following well-known example of nature in action that William L. Rowe mentions: "In some distant forest lightning strikes a dead tree, resulting in a forest fire. In the fire a fawn is trapped, horribly burned, and lies in terrible agony for several days before death relieves its suffering" (Rowe, 1979, p. 337). Consider, too, the various forms of life that we see, including ourselves. The intricate functioning of plants, animals, and other living things is impressive, and inspires wonder in atheists and theists alike. However, we need to be clear that none of these, again including ourselves, is perfect. John C. Avise has described in extensive detail how and why the evolutionary process produces painful or debilitating outcomes (Avise, 2010). Jocelyn Selim has even created a lengthy list of bodily organs that today, on closer inspection, turn out to be utterly useless (Selim, 2004). Surely this is not an indication of perfect, harmonious beauty created by an omniscient, all-powerful, supremely good God.

As Allen Buchanan puts it, "evolution does not produce harmonious, flawless objects: it cobbles together unstable products, the majority of which are destroyed rather quickly and all of which eventually break down" (Buchanan, 2011, p. 156). Buchanan offers a litany of what, from an engineering viewpoint, would be regarded as design flaws, and describes how the Darwinian process, with its incremental selection of naturally arising traits, produces these ubiquitously. "In brief," he says, "evolution *inevitably* produces sub-optimal designs" (Buchanan, 2011, p. 157).

True enough – and any god who created the universe did not actually do a great job. Nonetheless, there is an agnostic and atheist equivalent to the reverence felt for the natural world by many religious people. Reverence does not actually require religious belief, as Paul Woodruff notes in his groundbreaking study of reverence (Woodruff, 2001). There can be no doubt that most, if not all of us, are overcome at one point or another by the awe-inspiring greatness of the nature around us. If it has not yet happened to you, try Australia's red outback, Arizona's Grand Canyon, or any number of other spectacularly beautiful nature spots. Their awe-inspiring beauty is there for anyone to experience, despite the all too obvious flaws in the system. One does not have to be religious to be overwhelmed, and to experience feelings of reverence and awe (Keltner and Haidt, 2003).

In fact, these sorts of experiences have been investigated in various contexts. Wilderness settings, for example, offer a mix of aesthetic pleasure and renewal that can lead to a triggering of peak personal experiences that provides the basis for individual spiritual expression (Williams and Harvey, 2001; McDonald *et al.*, 2009). Clearly, though, these feelings are not evidence for God's existence.

The bottom line seems to be that atheists can appreciate and respond to beauty just like everyone else without, however, thinking either that the universe is God's creation or that it is "perfect."

Myth 17 Atheists Fear Death (More than Others)

Do atheists fear death more than our religious fellow humans? Let us begin by reviewing the empirical evidence. In fact, only a few studies investigating this question have been published, most of which do not carry a sample size sufficient to be statistically predictive one way or another. The reported research results are nowhere near conclusive either. What is noteworthy is a consensus on one fact: both religious believers and atheists who are strong in their respective views of the world, and not prone to doubts about their convictions, are best able to cope with their impending death, just as they are generally happier with their lives than those plagued by self-doubts (Mochon *et al.*, 2011). In the words of Samuel R. Weber and colleagues, the reported research "demonstrate[s] a clear correlation between strength of conviction in one's religious (or nonreligious) worldview and psychological well-being, with both the most and least religious individuals experiencing the best health." Basically "strong atheists appear to enjoy the same psychological benefits as strongly religious individuals" (Weber *et al.*, 2012, p. 83).

Peter Wilkinson and Peter Coleman of the University of Southampton's Geriatric Medicine Department undertook qualitative research with two matched groups of people aged over 60, roughly half of whom held either strong atheistic views or strong religious views. They concluded that "a strong atheistic belief system can fulfil the same role as a strong religious belief system in providing support, explanation, consolation and inspiration" (Wilkinson and Coleman, 2010, p. 337). Leaving aside quibbles about whether atheism *itself* is a belief system, this suggests that atheists are not lacking in resources to make sense of the world, and to respond to its opportunities, challenges, and tragedies.

Monika Ardelt and Cynthia Koenig note that undoubtedly many people "turn to religion because religion provides order to the world even in the presence of physical decline, social losses, suffering, and impending death and offers an existential meaning that provides a sense of peace and a recognition of one's place in the broader cosmic context" (Ardelt and Koenig, 2006, p. 189). Strong religious beliefs have the potential, much like strong atheistic views, to provide us with solace in times of need. That said, religious convictions can also become a significant cause of stress for the believer toward the end of life, especially in circumstances where religious patients feel punished by God, or abandoned in their struggles (Edmondson *et al.*, 2008).

Whether or not that is so will depend on a given individual's psychological make-up as much as on his or her view of the world. Philosophical naturalists among atheists will take as a given that once we are dead our existence, with all of its good and bad experiences, ceases to be. Some will see this as a kind of "neutral" state that it is neither good nor bad to be in, simply because everything that is *us* is no longer. Others will think that nonexistence should not be feared (due to the neutrality of death for our experiences), but still regretted. They will subscribe to the view that death should be regretted by all those whose lives were, on balance, still worth living to them at the time.

Up to a point, the fear of death is a natural and healthy instinct, though it is unhealthy if it is "tuned up" too high and spoils our enjoyment of life. As we have seen, however, the empirical evidence available does not support the view that atheists are morbid or obsessive about the prospect of death.

Of course, some religious people will have more reason than atheists to look forward to death. Surely that is so if you genuinely believe that not only is there an afterlife, but also that this afterlife – whatever form or shape it might take – will permit you to continue your existence in a God-organized paradise. On that conceptualization of your demise, you would be better off dead, since you would move from an imperfect existence, with its inevitable painful experiences, to eternal bliss.

In our view, it is not healthy, much as we empathize, to concoct or accept stories about how death is not real. The inevitability of our eventual deaths is something we should aim to face head-on. We suspect that many religious people who profess the idea of a forever-blissful afterlife do not really quite buy it. How else could we explain the insistence of, for instance, the Roman Catholic Church that we ought to live as long as is humanely feasible (Mercier, 2009)? How else do we explain the measures that religious people, as much as atheists, usually take for their own safety? We note, too, that the most fanatical campaigners against voluntary euthanasia are invariably to be found among the ranks of religious organizations, as opposed to those of humanist groupings. No doubt they have theological reasons, but they often emphasize the fear of being pressured into death. By contrast atheistic humanists are the ones who seek legislation to assist people to end their lives once they become intolerable. Unsurprisingly a European survey of trends in euthanasia acceptance concluded,

> Religiosity in western European countries has decreased rapidly since 1981 and continued decreasing between 1999 and 2008 in all countries except Italy and the Netherlands. Secularization of society tends to lead to increased value being placed on autonomy in important life choices and is associated with increasing euthanasia acceptance. (Cohen *et al.*, 2012, p. e2)

Of course, such claims are all-other-things-being-equal claims. The same authors note that, in addition to increasing religiosity in eastern European countries after the fall of communism, concerns about poor health care delivery and suspicion of government intentions with regard to reducing health care costs and other such factors could have contributed to lower than average support for assisted dying in those societies.

It is perhaps worth noting the importance of not conflating fear of death with fear of dying. As things stand, most of us will die deaths that are, mildly put, unpleasant (e.g., Schüklenk *et al.*, 2011, pp. 9–12). We have good reason to be fearful of the process of *dying*, as distinct from death itself, and here atheists might find common ground with religious believers. As Julian Baggini and the British Humanist Association's Madeleine Pym note in the medical journal *The Lancet*, "dying can be as fearful for humanists as for anyone else, and although they accept the inevitability of death, that does not mean they are going to be happy when it comes, especially if it comes prematurely" (Baggini and Pym, 2005, p. 1236).

We should aim for the longest, healthiest lives we can, and we should support medical research that has the prospect of helping us do so. However, we must also accept that the race against death is one that none of us will ultimately win, not even if we greatly increase the current span of healthy human life.

Myth 18 Atheists Turn to God When Death is Near

So-called deathbed conversions do occur. There have been a number of famous deathbed (or old-age) conversions where people, religious or atheist, have taken a last stab at a true religion. Famously, Charles II of England duly reigned as an Anglican, but on his deathbed he converted to Roman Catholicism (Hutton, 1989).

Perhaps it is not surprising that some people reflect on their fundamental beliefs and values when reaching a strategic inflection point as significant as their own death. Nor is it so surprising if reflections sometimes lead to changed beliefs. Philosopher Antony Flew, who described himself as "the world's most notorious atheist," really did convert in his old age to theistic belief of a kind – though this was more a form of deism than anything like orthodox Christianity. In his book *There is a God* (Flew and Varghese, 2007), Flew explains his reasons, stressing that he still does not believe that he personally will survive his own death (which actually took place in 2010). Accordingly, we can note that this was not a deathbed conversion as that is usually understood, and it did not involve a Pascal-type wager about the afterlife (see Myth 48). Flew denies in his book that his old age and impending death had much to do with his change of heart, but it is undeniable that the philosopher's beliefs changed in his old age.

On the other hand, stories told about deathbed conversions are often false. For example, there are stories about Charles Darwin, a self-described agnostic, having had a deathbed conversion to Christianity. These go back to the British evangelist Lady Hope, who falsely claimed in 1915 to have been at the scientist's deathbed many years earlier (Darwin died in 1882), and to have heard his recantation. Her account was subsequently disputed by both of Darwin's children, who insisted that he never had a deathbed conversion and that Lady Hope was not even in attendance when their father died (Clark, 1985, p. 199; Moore, 1994, p. 21).

In 1776, David Hume bravely faced a lingering death from what seems to have been a form of abdominal cancer. Throughout the process, he took no comfort in religion or any prospect of immortality. Much to the consternation of his friend James Boswell, the great biographer of Samuel Johnson, Hume maintained that there was no afterlife and that "the morality of every religion was bad" (Boswell, 1971, p. 11). Boswell's account of his final interview with Hume makes fascinating reading, most notably for the philosopher's cheerful denial that we survive death. The experience evidently left Boswell rather shaken:

> I was like a man in sudden danger eagerly seeking his defensive arms; and I could not but be assailed by momentary doubts while I had actually before me a man of such strong abilities and extensive inquiry dying in the persuasion of being annihilated. But I maintained my faith. (Boswell, 1971, 12–13)

As he concludes his account, Boswell adds, "I left him with impressions which disturbed me for some time" (Boswell, 1971, p. 14). In an added note written considerably later, however, the biographer takes comfort that perhaps Hume had "some hope of a future state," since the latter had remarked that if such a state did exist he believed he could give as good an account of his life as most (Boswell, 1971, p. 15). Frankly, this sounds like wishful thinking on Boswell's part.

Boswell also records Samuel Johnson's denial that Hume could have died without any fear of annihilation or worse (Boswell, 1980, pp. 838–839). But this also seems like wishful thinking – on Johnson's part, this time. In fact, Johnson, the Christian believer, apparently looked on the prospect of death with horror (Boswell, 1980, pp. 426–428).

Despite every opportunity, Hume never did turn to God as his death approached. One of his last important acts was to ensure that his *Dialogues Concerning Natural Religion* would be published after his death and in his own name. This work subsequently appeared in 1779, though initially without Hume's name on it. Whether or not Hume was strictly an atheist (he may have held some kind of deistic belief), he left behind much of the intellectual foundation for modern atheist thought.

Much more recently, high-profile atheist Christopher Hitchens died in 2011 of complications related to esophageal cancer. He not only did not convert, but had this to say in his last years – commenting on Christians who prayed for his health or for a deathbed conversion (what a marketing coup that would have been for Christianity!):

> And it's also rather presumptuous, as well as illogical, to suggest that, now that I know of a nasty change in my physical condition, it's surely time for me to be thinking of an alteration in my mental and intellectual state as well. Leaving aside those who have thanked god for giving me cancer and a future in the eternal inferno, the offer of prayer can only have two implications: either a wish for my recovery or a wish for a reconsideration of my atheism (or both). In the first instance, a get-well card – accompanied by a good book or a fine bottle – would be just as bracing if not indeed more so.... In the second one, a clear suggestion is present: surely now, at last,

> Hitchens, your fears will begin to vanquish your reason. What a thing to hope for! Yet without this parody of concern, religion would instantly lose a vast portion of its power. If I was to be wrong about this, then the faithful would have been praying for me to see the light when I was not dying. But this they mostly did not choose to do. (Hitchens, 2010)

We could go on for a very long time looking at famous people who allegedly converted to this or that religious view on their deathbeds. Some of these alleged conversions may in fact have occurred, but most are dubious. In any event, let us be clear about the significance of conversions of religious people belonging to one faith opting to throw the dice one last time and choosing a competing religion. Likewise, let's be clear about the significance of any atheists placing a deathbed bet on one god or another. The philosophical significance of all such conversions is, of course zero. The truth about the existence of God (whatever god you care to name) cannot be settled by dying people choosing to place bets. That is true when religious people change horses in the face of death, as much as it is true if an atheist does decide, very late in the game, to place bets on the truth of some religion or other.

Myth 19 There are no Atheists in Foxholes

Foxholes are defensive earthworks dug by military personnel in wartime – the term is typically applied to a defensive military position for one person, though some are larger and are used by two or more soldiers. The modern style foxhole is a vertical hole, narrower at the top, where a soldier can stand to fight or crouch to take cover from artillery bombardment or other high-intensity attacks. The myth is that atheists won't be found in the military, or at least that their atheism will not last long once they come under enemy fire.

John Micklethwait and Adrian Wooldridge suggest that World War II intensified religious belief in the United States, with religious faith being used in many ways to boost wartime morale. During this period, the myth became popular: "One of the most quoted remarks of the era was, 'There are no atheists in foxholes'" (Micklethwait and Wooldridge, 2009, p. 92). In any event, this saying continues to be used.

Many countries routinely spend tax monies on military chaplains. Reportedly, in the US military there are about 3000 such chaplains, 90% of whom are Christians even though only seven out of ten soldiers are Christians. Thus, Jason Torpy, of the Military Association of Atheists and Freethinkers, and an Iraq war veteran, "wants to know why the much larger group of atheists or humanists [than Jewish, Muslim, and Hindu soldiers who have their dedicated chaplains], estimated to be about 40,000 soldiers, don't have their own chaplain" (Severson, 2012).

Here are two examples of what some of the overwhelmingly evangelical chaplains in the US army have had to say on the question of whether there are atheists in foxholes. First, CNN anchor Soledad O'Brien interviewed a US marine chaplain, Commander Kal McAlexander (O'Brien, 2004):

> O'BRIEN: It's long been said there are no atheists in a foxhole. Have you found that to be true? You do battlefield baptisms, I understand. What exactly are those?
>
> MCALEXANDER: That's true. There is no such thing as an atheist in a foxhole.

Or try Texas's Fort Bragg's 4th Infantry Division senior chaplain James Carter, who went on record as follows: "You've heard the saying that there are no atheists in foxholes. I don't believe there are any atheists in a war, period" (Vincent, 2007).

Strangely, Christians have also argued the opposite, namely that foxholes breed atheists:

> "There are no atheists in foxholes," goes the saying, but foxholes can breed atheists, when those who see war's nightmares lose all faith in dreams – and fight fire with fire and dog eat dog are the only values that survive. (Resnicoff, 2004)

The interested reader might wish to note that, however this is being twisted, the atheist remains squarely at the disapproving end of the claim made. If you are an atheist in a foxhole, it is likely because the terrible war theater has made you such an immoral person that only dog-eat-dog values remain. If you are a Christian soldier in a foxhole you are there because of your superior moral Christian values, values an atheist doesn't have, hence no atheists can be found in foxholes. Or so the suggestion goes. Against this background, we see some further irony when a staunch and high-profile Christian, such as born-again Christian and former US President George W. Bush, did not actually serve in the US military – he was like many draft dodgers of his generation, Christian or otherwise religious (Romano, 2004). The no-atheist-in-a-foxhole myth is silent on this.

The American atheist writer and war veteran Joe Haldeman is skeptical about the myth as he recalls his experiences during the Vietnam war:

> We talked a lot about religion, as I think soldiers must, and I don't recall any serious challenges to my unbelief. None of the other soldiers in my platoon

had any education beyond high school, whereas I'd stuck around college for six years, but I don't think that was a big factor. On the battlefield you have constant reminders that if there is a God, he doesn't have anyone's comfort or survival in mind. (Haldeman, 2009, p. 188)

To be fair, the corner might be turning on this particular myth. A Catholic military chaplain is notably disappointed about a lower than expected turn-out to his sermons:

> ABERNETHY: Much as he admires his troops, Chaplain Angotti also notes that soldiers in Iraq do not go to chapel as much as he has been told they did in other wars. This despite the danger.
>
> Chaplain ANGOTTI: I thought it would change them because there is the saying that there are no atheists in a foxhole. And I find that that is not true, that even in a battle zone there is still a fairly large number that is not practicing a faith, at least by chapel attendance. (Abernethy, 2004)

Today, many atheists serve as soldiers in theaters of war all over the world. The US Military Association of Atheists and Freethinkers maintains a list of active service members willing to put their names on the record, partly to confront the myth that there are no atheists in foxholes (MAAF, 2012). Let some of their members have the final word:

> SERGEANT RACHEL MEDLEY: I am an atheist and I'm a good person – have, you know, a great life and have great friends, and my service to my country is based on my personal morals which are help other people, be kind to others, treat others as you would like to be treated.
>
> SERGEANT JUSTIN GRIFFITH: This is us coming out of the closet, you know, shattering that stained glass ceiling. We want to remove the stigma about atheists and whatever they think the word "atheist" means. (Severson, 2012)

3

Atheism, Ethics, and the Soul

Myth 20 Without God There is No Morality

The basic claims propagated in this myth are that there can be no secular basis of morality, on the one hand, and that there is a sound theistic basis of morality. In its most simple form, it will be familiar to many along the lines of the following quote from the Reverend Earlmont Williams, a prominent cleric from Jamaica:

> Morality is essentially about right and wrong and surpasses human happiness, which many think is our *summum bonum* (ultimate good). The highest good of our existence lies beyond ourselves in something higher and greater than us. Atheists wouldn't embrace this because they seek answers from below where the human race faces self-destruction. (Williams, 2012)

This view is shared by Williams's countrywoman Kay Bailey:

> Secularism, the exclusion of God and, specifically, the Christian world view from decision making at all levels of society, has no real basis for teaching love of fellow man.... Can a people who believe that they were made by mindless, purposeless forces, for no purpose at all, love their children enough not to abuse them or to prevent them from being abused? (Bailey, 2012)

The latter part of this statement is quite remarkable in light of a worldwide pandemic of sexual abuse of children at the hand of Catholic

50 Great Myths About Atheism, First Edition. Russell Blackford and Udo Schüklenk.

clergymen, but we'll let that pass. Williams writes dismissively in response to one secular approach to ethics, namely that advocated by Sam Harris:

> Who says Sam Harris was right about happiness and suffering being the essence of morality? This is a ridiculously reductionist view of morality, which is more transcendental and overarching than mere happiness. If this were so, morality would have a secular humanistic foundation, which is absolutely incredible. (Williams, 2012)

To be fair to Williams, many nonutilitarian secular ethicists would likely beg to differ from Harris. However, the impartial reader will notice that the essence of Reverend Williams's argument consists of the pejorative terms "ridiculously reductionist" and "absolutely incredible," both of which are question-begging. His suggestion that our highest good lies beyond ourselves in something higher and greater is also baseless – it requires evidence.

Of course, the history of philosophy is full of nontheistic systems of morality. We can name just a few of the more influential ones: Aristotle's *Nicomachean Ethics* (1999), Immanuel Kant's *Groundwork for the Metaphysics of Morals* (1993 [1785]), Arthur Schopenhauer's *On the Basis of Morality* (1995 [1860]), John Stuart Mill's *Utilitarianism* (1979 [1863]), Jean-Jacques Rousseau's *Social Contract* (1987 [1762]), Henry Sidgwick's *The Methods of Ethics* (1981 [1874]) – and there are so many others that it is impossible to list them here. For example, some contemporary atheists argue for a form of Ideal Observer theory, in which the moral rightness of conduct is determined by the attitude that would be taken by a hypothetical observer with certain idealized properties (Martin, 2002, pp. 49–71).

Kant is included in our list, though it is true that he developed a moral argument for belief in the existence of God. This appears in his *Critique of Practical Reason*, first published in 1788 (Kant 1997 [1788], pp. 103–110). However, he was quite explicit in his published works that his actual moral system does not depend on theistic belief at all, but on quite different considerations relating to what maxims of conduct can be rationally willed. In Kant's system, God does *not* provide the ground of moral obligation (1997 [1788], p. 105). Rather, Kant argues that we must believe in God so as to trust that the highest good is achievable and that moral goodness is eventually rewarded with happiness. This is a deeply flawed argument – for a start, it is not at all obvious that moral goodness will be rewarded with happiness in all cases, even if the possession of moral virtues such as courage and kindness tends to be beneficial to the individual concerned (for a critique of Kant's argument see Oppy,

2006, pp. 372–375). Not surprisingly, Gavin Hyman observes that Kant's defense of God's existence "was an uneasy and precarious truce that was inherently unstable" (Hyman, 2010, p. 38; see also pp. 64–65).

As it turns out, secular systems of ethics or morality share a number of common features. They typically ask us to respect or otherwise value persons, and they give universal and impartial reasons to adhere to the guidance offered by moral reasoning. Doubtless these are interpreted in different ways by the different theories, but we can find a common core to the many moral systems from different societies and historical periods. So the strong claim, that atheists have *no* basis to be moral, cannot be true, as all these examples show. As long as any of the nontheistic possibilities are intellectually promising, morality can plausibly be separated from theistic religion (Brink, 2007, pp. 157–158).

Instead of arguing that particular varieties of secular ethics are bound to fail, theists more frequently choose a different line of attack. We might link this to the practical difficulty of demonstrating fatal flaws in every secular ethical approach to ethics. Instead of attacking the secular theories one by one, theists may argue that morality depends on God and cannot be grounded in anything else. John F. Haught is one of many who make this claim. More specifically, he claims of Dawkins, Dennett, and Harris, and others who think along the same secular lines: "But, again, in your condemnation of the evils of religion, you must be assuming a standard of goodness so timeless and absolute as to be God-given" (Haught, 2008, p. 26). This, of course, is not actually the case, as no such assumption needs to be made by secular ethicists. Haught complains that Richard Dawkins is unable to present an indictment of religious morality:

> As one who professes to be guided by lofty moral ideals, loftier even than any he can find in religion, Dawkins finds himself in a situation where his own moral indictment of religious faith has no firm justification if the values or standards by which he renders his judgments can themselves be fully explained in evolutionary terms. After all, a blind, indifferent, and amoral natural process, which is how Dawkins has always characterized evolution, can hardly explain why justice, love, and the pursuit of truth are now unconditionally binding values. (Haught 2008, p. 71)

Haught makes clear that he is not so much skeptical about the possibility that there could be some kind of descriptive account of how we came to have the values that we do, though he considers current accounts to be incomplete. His deeper problem is how such an account could ever provide a naturalistic justification for morality and avoid an appearance of arbitrariness (Haught, 2008, pp. 71–75). But we need to take issue with many of the assumptions being made here. For example, why should it be thought that our moral values must be "timeless and absolute," or that they must be "unconditionally binding" on us in the sense that Haught seems to mean? It seems a common assumption of religious believers that in the absence of the absolute rights and wrongs handed down from above there would just have to be moral chaos and anarchy, given that there would be no authority underwriting whatever moral guidance is proffered.

It is true that without God there would be no divine lawgiver, which many Christians and others evidently take to be of paramount importance. Authority figures matter to believers! Consider this claim by Dinesh D'Souza:

> If there are moral laws that operate beyond the realm of natural laws, where do these laws come from? Moral laws presume a moral lawgiver. In other words, God is the ultimate standard of good. He is responsible for the distinction between good and evil. (D'Souza, 2007, p. 233)

No. For a start, this betrays a crude understanding of the mechanisms of the law and what it is to be a lawgiver. The authority of a law depends on whether it is recognized as valid within a system of political institutions. In ethics it is not clear that there could or should be such a thing as moral laws – *pace* Immanuel Kant. However, even if one were to accept the possibility and necessity of a moral law, note that the immediate source of our actual laws need not be anything (such as a legislature, for example) that could be described as a "lawgiver." A particular law may, for example, be part of a body of useful customs that have come to be recognized and enforced by the courts. In common law systems we can locate several sources of law, and the trend for formal legislatures to become the dominant source of law is a relatively recent historical development. In short, the authority of law comes from the legal system's rules and institutions for recognizing laws, which may include, but certainly need not be limited to, the role of a formal lawgiver such as a king or a parliament.

In turn, the authority of political institutions, including the acceptability of various sources of law, will depend on whether or not they are accepted as legitimate by the population of the relevant territory. In human societies, no lawgiver is ever the *ultimate* standard of what is or is not lawful.

If we were to apply the analogy literally, we would have to conclude that the acceptability of God as a lawgiver depends on whether he continues to be accepted by us as a legitimate source of law, which will reflect such considerations as whether he continues to make laws that actually serve our needs. Perhaps he will if he is as wise and benevolent as theists claim he is, but what *ultimately* matters is the wisdom of his laws for serving human needs, not where these laws come from. In the absence of a divine lawgiver, we can judge the authority of various moral principles, standards of conduct, and so on, directly by how well they serve human needs. What best serves them under one set of circumstances (economic, technological, and environmental) may not do so in another.

More specifically, it does not follow from the lack of a supernatural lawgiver that there are no good reasons for us to treat each other well, oppose cruelty, and cultivate dispositions of character such as honesty and kindness. If this is what morality is really about, as a reading of the works of nontheistic moral philosophers tends to suggest, then there is no reason to posit a god in order to have morality.

Albert Einstein made the point well:

> A man's ethical behavior should be based effectually on sympathy, education, and social ties and needs; no religious basis is necessary. Man would indeed be in a poor way if he had to be restrained by fear of punishment and hope of reward after death. (Einstein, 1954, p. 39)

If we thought that some things are good because God approves of them, we would then be inclined to ask what they have in common apart from the fact that God approves. We tend to look for something that "good" things and something that "bad" things have in common, or at least for sets of properties that enable us to group them. Surely we should not accept the idea that God would approve of some things and disapproves of others *arbitrarily*?

The ultimate point of morality cannot, therefore, be obedience to the will of a god or a group of gods. This would raise the notorious problem discussed in Plato's famous *Euthyphro* dialogue (399 BCE): does conduct become morally correct because it is in accordance with a god's (or the gods') commands, or should we obey those commands because they track the independent requirements of morality? If the former, we seem to be stuck with the idea that murder and rape are wrong only because of the arbitrary commands of a powerful being (this being could have made murder morally right simply by commanding it). If the latter, then why not find out what the independent requirements of morality *actually are*, that is, the requirements that are independent of the god's will? Far from it being the case that morality needs a cosmic or divine lawgiver, it makes no sense to see morality as grounded in anything other than what humans actually desire, value, or need. If a lawgiver gave us commands that we cause each other suffering, we would have every reason to rebel against them.

All this aside, there is a practical problem with basing our moral ideas on an idea of God. God's supposed commands – for example, in holy books – must still be interpreted, implemented, and understood, but it is often surprisingly difficult to ascertain what moral lesson God is trying to get across, as Aikin and Talisse point out (2011, pp. 111–117).

Paul Henri Thiry, Baron D'Holbach, dealt effectively enough with these issues at the dawn of atheism as we now know it, pointing out the range of secular reasons that human beings can have for treating others well, abiding by mutually beneficial social norms, and generally acting in ways that fall within our ordinary ideas of moral decency. In one passage, he compares this to what he sees as the weak and unreliable guidance available from religious doctrine:

> It is asked, *what motives an Atheist can have to do good?* The motive to please himself and his fellow-creatures; to live happily and peaceably; to gain the affection and esteem of men. "Can he, who fears not the gods, fear any thing?" He can fear men; he can fear contempt, dishonour, the punishment of the laws; in short, he can fear himself, and the remorse felt by all those who are conscious of having incurred or merited the hatred of their fellow-creatures.
>
> Conscience is the internal testimony, which we bear to ourselves, of having acted so as to merit the esteem or blame of the beings, with whom we live; and it is founded upon the clear knowledge we have of men, and of the sentiments which our actions must produce in them. The Conscience of the religious man consists in imagining that he has pleased or displeased his God, of whom he has no idea, and whose obscure and doubtful intentions are explained to him only by men of doubtful veracity, who, like him, are utterly unacquainted with the essence of the Deity, and are little agreed upon what can please or displease him. In a word, the conscience of the credulous is directed by men, who have themselves an erroneous conscience, or whose interest stifles knowledge.
>
> "Can an atheist have a Conscience? What are his motives to abstain from hidden vices and secret crimes of which other men are ignorant, and which are beyond the reach of laws?" He may be assured by constant experience, that there is no vice, which, by the nature of things, does not punish itself. Would he preserve this life? he will avoid every excess, that may impair his health; he will not wish to lead a languishing life, which would render him a burden to himself and others. As for secret crimes, he will abstain from them, for fear he shall be forced to blush at himself, from whom he cannot flee. If he has any reason, he will know the value of the esteem which an honest man ought to have for himself. He will see, that unforeseen circumstances may unveil the conduct, which he feels interested in concealing from others. The other world furnishes no motives for doing good, to him, who finds none on earth. (Thiry, 2006 [1770], pp. 104–105, italics in original)

Credited to Jesus and Mo, www.jesusandmo.net

This does not, of course, amount to a "timeless and absolute" reason to behave decently and develop a moral conscience. What it shows is that morality serves needs and desires that human beings actually have. That is why moral standards will remain even if belief in God no longer prevails.

The upshot of our analysis of this myth is that it would be true if morality were understood as a system of do's and don'ts handed down by an absolute god-like authority. But if morality is understood as it is today by the vast majority of moral philosophers, namely as a system of reason-based normative guidance and normative justification, it is, of course, very much possible. On that understanding the myth is false.

Myth 21 Atheists are Moral Relativists

As with some of the other myths, it is hard to be sure what people are really getting at when they say things like this. Sometimes they just seem to mean that atheists do not believe that morality takes the form of inflexible and specific moral rules such as "Don't lie." But why should morality take this form, rather than the form of more flexible principles such as, "Do what you reasonably think will produce the best consequences in the circumstances"? At other times, the moral relativism charge seems to mean little other than what we have addressed in Myth 20, namely the odd idea that there can be no true moral rights and wrongs unless they are backed up by God's absolute authority.

Dinesh D'Souza's *What's So Great About Christianity* contains a chapter in which he criticizes secular accounts of morality, thinking, so it seems, that many atheists profess a form of moral relativism. One notable aspect of his discussion, however, is that he shows an extremely crude idea of what moral relativism might actually be. This enables him to make the startling claim that, "Relativism in its pure sense simply does not exist" (D'Souza, 2007, p. 231). How does he demonstrate this? His advice is that next time somebody professes to be a moral relativist – "a relativist who insists that all morality is relative" – we should punch him in the face, then listen to his protests that it was morally wrong to do so. This will, D'Souza seems to think, make the point that the relativist subscribes to absolute moral standards after all. Furthermore, we can provoke this person by attacking moral causes that he holds dear, such as, perhaps, the abolition of racial discrimination and slavery. This can be expected to produce a morally outraged response.

This analysis is hopelessly confused, like so many claims about how atheists think and act. It may be news to D'Souza, but moral relativism comes in many forms, some more sophisticated than others. Even the least sophisticated moral relativists are unlikely to deny that we make moral judgments. They are also unlikely to claim that we should stop doing so. Though the details of relativist theories vary considerably, they will claim that moral judgments are made relative to some sort of standard, which might, for example, be personal or cultural. They need not think that the standard is merely arbitrary or that no standards are better than others (even if they are relativist about first-order moral judgments, such as "punching people in the face is morally wrong," they need not be relativist about all values). Nor need they deny that we rely on each other to conform to much the same standards, especially when it comes to important matters about how we treat each other, such as matters to do with nonviolence and honesty.

If you do punch a moral relativist in the face, as D'Souza's edifying thought experiment proposes, you can expect that person to respond angrily, and it will be perfectly rational for him or her to do so. That is partly because the somatic response of anger is useful to us in situations of danger, but also because you will be violating a rule against gratuitous violence that we all rely on for living reasonably peacefully together. It is understandable that people respond with anger when someone violates this rule, as with any other rule where mutual reliance and reciprocity are involved.

So far, we have mentioned only some very basic considerations that even the most unsophisticated moral relativist could adduce to show the naïveté of D'Souza's thought experiment. Actual relativist theories have much more to say than this. Perhaps D'Souza is correct that there are no "pure" relativists if he means people with relativist theories so crude that they are unable to handle his thought experiment. If so, no atheists are relativists in D'Souza's "pure" sense, and this version of the myth is busted. Nonetheless, there *are* plenty of people who are relativists in less "pure" and more sophisticated senses. There are also people in between, people who do not take such a "pure," that is, naïve, view as D'Souza supposes, but who have not developed their views in the rigorous way aspired to by professional philosophers working in the field of meta-ethics.

Much the same applies to most Christians and other religious people who are not professional philosophers, and to most people who hold on to some form of absolute morality whether it is based in religion or not. Few of these people are likely to have developed their ideas about morality to the point where they are theoretically rigorous and would withstand much philosophical scrutiny.

D'Souza is right that there is considerable commonality in the behavioral standards of human societies, but that is what many moral relativists would expect. While they may think that moral judgments are made according to cultural standards, and that the latter vary to some extent, a moral relativist might expect some basics to be cross-culturally similar or even universal. A moral relativist is likely to think that at least part of the point of having moral rules is to enable human beings to get along reasonably harmoniously in societies and gain the benefits of mutual assistance and social living.

For instance, D'Souza notes that there is some commonality among marital and child-rearing practices: "One group may permit one wife and another group four or more wives, but all groups agree on the indispensability of the family and its moral obligation to provide for the young" (D'Souza, 2007, p. 230). But how are claims such as this – even if they are true – supposed to undermine any moral relativist position beyond the most simplistic and vulgar? The relativist claims (correctly) that judgments about marital arrangements are made according to one set of standards in one society and a different set in the other. Empirically we cannot reasonably quibble about this. The standards of moral judgment in Afghanistan or North Korea differ from those in Britain. The relativist is bound to concur that there are constraints on what standards can be adopted by different societies: one such constraint might be that any successful society will need to have *some* set of standards requiring family participation in caring for children. True, this could be a more limited involvement (as was the case in Stalin's Soviet Union) or a more significant involvement (as is the case in most Western liberal democracies). However, moral judgments are nonetheless made against standards. These standards themselves develop to provide for human and social needs that are, to a large extent, common across all societies. Some standards are more important than others, some change over time as needs change along with economic and other circumstances, but at any given time some will be very important and people will rely on each other's conformity to them.

In short, some people, including some atheists, really are moral relativists. Some, indeed, are moral skeptics. That does not mean that they are more likely to engage in conduct that would normally be regarded as unethical by, for lack of a better term, moral absolutists – such as murder, rape, and robbery. Moral relativists commonly claim that moral judgments are made against standards that are themselves judged against their success in ensuring social survival. Moral skeptics typically add that we go wrong when we think that we have access to absolute, inescapably binding moral standards – *this* is what they are usually skeptical about – but they do not necessarily deny (any more than relativists necessarily do) that there is a meaningful sense in which some moral standards are better than others.

Critics of atheism who claim that atheists are moral relativists, or even moral skeptics, would do well to read some of the more sophisticated accounts of moral relativism and moral skepticism. In the case of moral skepticism, the state of the art is most readily found in the work of Gilbert Harman (1977) and Jesse Prinz (2007). Moral skepticism is developed as a philosophical system by the Australian philosopher John Leslie Mackie (1977) in his *Ethics: Inventing Right and Wrong*, and more recently by

Richard Garner (1994) and Richard Joyce (2001). None of these authors advocates the sort of simplistic theory that Dinesh D'Souza appears to be imagining. All of them provide reasons to support behavioral standards not greatly different from those of commonsense morality, though their theories do leave room for moral codes to be inspected and possibly revised. Richard Garner is arguably the most radical in claiming that we should decide how to act based directly on such values as compassion and curiosity, rather than on codes of moral norms, but even he does not suggest that we should prefer harshness to compassion, cowardice to courage, miserliness to generosity, and so on. No serious theory of moral relativism or skepticism in the philosophical literature proposes any such thing.

The bottom line here is that atheists are unlikely to adopt inflexible moral rules. For some of us, this is because we think that moral rules can only be justified if they operate to achieve naturalistic goals such as reducing and avoiding suffering or contributing to the stability of human societies. Unlike Christianity, atheist views of the world do not see that there is much redemptive value in human suffering. While atheists may not encourage breaking good moral rules lightly – presumably the rule is serving some purpose by being treated as a rule – we are not inflexible. What really matter are the goals that lie behind the rule, not slavish adherence to the rules themselves for their own sake. If this is "relativism" then that kind of relativism is justified and the charge of "relativism" should not be considered a criticism.

At any rate, there is no in-principle reason related to atheism or naturalism that would force atheists to take a moral relativist or skeptical stance. Atheists can well subscribe to the view, and indeed many of us do, that morality is objective – but if so, objectivity lies in the need for consistent standards of conduct, in objective facts about such things as pleasure and suffering, in thoughtful accounts of what is needed for a good human life, or perhaps some combination of these things. Atheist writers Scott Aikin and Robert Talisse provide a lucid summary of some of the main moral theories that are available to atheists as well as to others (2011, pp. 118–125) and we refer you again to our discussion of Myth 20.

Truth be told, though, you do not have to resort to atheist literature to learn about secular ethics. Virtually all of the predominant ethical theories, whether they are consequentialist, deontological, virtue ethical, feminist, or of any other variety, quite explicitly do not rely on the invention of godly entities to provide their necessary argumentative and critical firepower.

Credited to Jesus and Mo, www.jesusandmo.net

Myth 22 Atheists Don't Give to Charity

As Walter Sinnott-Armstrong acknowledges, we would see it as "a serious defect" if secular people showed a lower than usual rate of helping out the needy, even if their lives were not otherwise degraded or depraved (Sinnott-Armstrong, 2009, p. 44). This precise accusation, however, is commonly leveled at atheists and other nonreligious people. Sinnott-Armstrong particularly discusses a recent study by Arthur Brooks that purports to show that religious people are the ones who really care about others (Sinnott-Armstrong, 2009, pp. 44–45).

Such claims are reinforced by reported findings such as this by Statistics Canada, a government agency:

> while less than one in five attend church regularly, those who do are far more likely to give to charities, and are substantially more liberal in the size of their gifts to both religious and non-religious organizations. The average annual donation from a churchgoer is $1,038. For the rest of the population, $295. (McLean's, 2010)

Atheists do give to charity, but do we do so less than others? Is it somewhat more than a myth when we are accused of giving less, or of showing less compassion, than religious people? It is a concern, but the facts here are complex. For starters, one particularly rich atheist could easily compensate for lesser giving by very many fellow atheists, so that in balance there would be no difference, once giving on all sides is averaged. Just think of atheists Bill Gates and Warren Buffett and their charitable giving. Their combined efforts amount to many billions and billions of dollars (Lowenstein, 1995, p. 13; Singer, 2006). Of course, the fact that some very rich high-profile atheists give billions to their preferred charitable causes (incidentally, reproductive health and poverty reduction are high on Buffett's and Gates's agendas) does not prove that most atheists follow suit. One thing does seem clear, however: atheists and other nonreligious people are more likely than religious people to give to charity, or to behave charitably, simply because they feel compassion or believe in the charitable cause. Religious people, by contrast, are more likely than atheists to support charitable causes for other reasons – not from a sense of compassion or a wish to help for its own sake, but because of religious doctrine and/or peer pressure.

Sinnott-Armstrong (2009, pp. 45–46) points out some of the less edifying religious motivations for giving to charity, such as Bible verses promising eternal life to the charitable and damnation to those who refuse to help the needy (he cites Matthew 25: 46 and Luke 6: 38). Another reason is the practice of tithing to the believer's church, which may itself be seen as a requirement imposed by God. It may have a heavenly reward attached to it, even apart from the issues of organizational and peer-group pressure.

Most published research on the matter indicates that there is a strong correlation between peer pressure and charitable giving. For example, a study in the Netherlands found that higher levels of giving to religious charities among Protestants (when compared to Catholics and secular Dutch people) were largely due to significant peer pressure applied to church members. According to this study, Protestant churchgoers in the Netherlands are constantly bombarded with requests to donate money – usually to religious charities. This also makes giving easier for them, as they cannot escape what are frequently public demands on their purses. In fairness, however, the same study notes higher levels of giving to secular charities among Protestants than among Catholics and the secular, and ascribes this to prosocial values instilled by the religion (Bekkers and Schuyt, 2008).

Religious donors' motives don't appear to be necessarily or even primarily compassionate ones. In a separate review of the literature on the factors influencing charitable giving, René Bekkers and Pamala Wiepking note: "the religious are not necessarily more willing to donate than the non-religious when asked to donate to pre-selected secular organizations" (Bekkers and Wiepking, 2011). Other research findings include a strong correlation between higher educational attainment and charitable giving (Wiepking and Bekkers, 2009).

A series of empirical studies undertaken by a team at the University of California at Berkeley sheds some more light on the issue. These studies found "that for less religious people, the strength of their emotional connection to another person is critical to whether they will help that person or not." Berkeley-based social psychologist Robb Willer, a coauthor of the study notes, "the more religious, on the other hand, may ground their generosity less in emotion, and more in other factors such as doctrine, a communal identity, or reputational concerns" (Anwar, 2012).

A recent US study suggests that religious belief is likely coincidental when it comes to charitable giving, because it "is less the effect of ideology than of active participation in religious, political, and community organizations that explains Americans' financial giving to religious and nonreligious organizations" (Vaidyanathan *et al.*, 2011, p. 450). If so, it is not surprising that religious people are more strongly motivated to donate to religious charities than secular ones.

Nonetheless, all of this suggests that there is an element of truth in the suggestion that more religious people give more to the needy than do less religious people, including atheists. Perhaps their motivations are less than pure, at least across the entire group of the religious, but how much does that matter if religious people actually do give more?

Even here, we are not fully convinced, and we rely on a number of strong points made by Sinnott-Armstrong (2009, pp. 47–49). First, many studies rely on self-reports, and these are known to be unreliable. In particular, churchgoers may be more motivated than atheists to exaggerate or embellish the truth about their charitable giving. After all, they are under pressure to maintain their self-images as charitable people. Second, the relevant studies tend to divide people between regular churchgoers, by whatever definition, and those who are *not* regular churchgoers. But this need not line up with the difference between theists and atheists. Indeed, the relatively small numbers of philosophically convinced atheists may be more generous toward the needy than the much larger group of relatively apathetic theists.

Third, atheists may be more prepared than others to give to political causes, some of which are aimed at helping the needy, but this sort of giving is not usually classified as charitable (we add here that much money given to the churches may be classified as charitable even if it does *not* help the needy). Atheists may also tend more than the religious to be willing to vote for public actions to help the needy, whereas the religious may tend more to disdain such public actions and to prefer private giving. Certainly, there is much evidence in the United States of a correlation between religious conservatism and resistance to government spending on social programs. Conversely, some atheists put considerable time, effort, and even money into campaigns to support government action, yet none of this self-sacrifice is counted as charitable giving.

Fourth, any study that separates people into regular churchgoers and others may be picking up a causal effect that runs in the opposite direction to that assumed. Some people who are actually theists may be motivated not to go to church regularly precisely because it imposes certain disciplines and peer pressures. If the "nonreligious" group in a study includes such people, this will bring down the average degree of charity shown in that group. Conversely, the "religious" group may actually be weighted toward those theists (and perhaps even some people who attend church but have no supernatural beliefs) who are temperamentally willing to accept such pressures and to give to charity in an organized way.

All of this leaves it unclear whether atheists, as opposed to apathetic or unmotivated people among the theistic majority, actually do give less than others to help the needy. The case has not been made out. Nonetheless, the point about peer pressure is a strong one: this is undoubtedly a powerful motivator for many people. In turn, that might explain why atheist groups have started their own charitable giving campaigns aimed at raising funds for secular charitable work, for instance for medical charities, schooling in developing countries, and other such worthy causes (Smith, 2011b). These can also apply peer pressure in support of their respective good causes. For instance, the secular initiative The Life You Can Save, aimed at alleviating world poverty, publicly lists the names of those who have pledged to donate a certain percentage of their income to fight world poverty (www.thelifeyoucansave.com/list).

Myth 23 Atheists Deny the Sanctity of Human Life

The view that atheism denies the "sanctity of human life" is expressed by theists in various shapes and forms. For instance, in his book *The Atheist Delusion* Phil Fernandes argues that, "atheism, by denying belief in God's existence, is a world view that has no basis for the sanctity of human life" (Fernandes, 2009, p. 77).

It is certainly true that there is no uncontroversial secular basis for such concepts as equal human dignity from the moment of conception, and that a society that rejects Christianity will very likely end up rejecting concepts such as these. For example, Dinesh D'Souza argues to that effect (D'Souza, 2007, pp. 77–78), and we do not disagree with this point as far it goes. It is possible, in a sense, that at some point in the future a secular ethicist will come up with a persuasive account for why human life ought to be considered inviolable, possibly even from the moment of conception. At this point in time such an account does not exist; hence atheists who reflect on the matter tend to reject the sanctity of human life doctrine (Kuhse, 1987). So is this "myth" actually quite plausible, or even confirmed?

Not so fast. A problem with the myth is that it assumes that human life possesses "sanctity" in the first place. Most atheists deny that human life possesses any supernatural property of being sacred, and this may lead them to make, or advocate, different decisions from, say, traditional Christians when it comes to issues involving the beginning and end of life. Atheists, informed by secular approaches to ethics, are more likely to be focused on what will cause, or prolong, or conversely, ameliorate, suffering, rather than taking the view that human life possesses some kind of transcendent or supernatural value (e.g., Glover, 1977; Singer, 2011). In that sense, the myth might be considered confirmed. But we classify it as a myth because it is highly misleading: it falsely implies that atheists have no respect for the life and well-being of their fellow humans.

Atheists do not think that human lives are valueless, and we are no more likely than anyone else to murder or otherwise harm other human beings. Although we understand our fellow human beings as biological creatures – closely related to chimpanzees and bonobos – we do not see other humans as insignificant or expendable. Theists and atheists alike, we are all physical and biological entities on one planet among many, but we are special in at least one way: we are extraordinarily complex beings. Our brains and nervous systems contain billions of neurons, with a seemingly unmappable intricacy of interconnections. They are the most complex entities that we know on this planet. They are also intimately connected with the other parts of our bodies, and all aspects of their functioning. Nothing else that humans have encountered to date matches our extreme organizational and functional complexity, not even the most closely related apes.

Furthermore, we are social and moral beings. Our current knowledge of human evolution suggests that our immediate precursors were already social animals. Peter Singer, an outspoken atheist ethicist, argues that our evolutionary ancestors must have restrained their behavior toward each other to the extent required for their societies to function: they showed the beginnings of morality, which involves showing concern and respect for the interests of our fellows (Singer, 1981).

It is not only our fellow humans who deserve respect or at least concern. We share with our simian relatives, and with many other animals, a vulnerability to physical suffering – and this gives us all a certain moral status (Singer, 1976). Others have suggested that some animals must not be used as mere means to our ends due to their capacity to be subjects of their own lives, just as we are, albeit to a different extent (Regan, 2004). Even if it is justifiable to kill nonhuman animals, it is not so justifiable to treat them cruelly. Of course, it is frequently claimed that human beings have a special moral worth beyond that of all other animals. But what makes us so special? According to most atheists, it cannot be anything supernatural. If we are to make comparisons between human beings and other animals, we need to look at the actual (and entirely natural) dispositional capacities of the things that are being compared.

While many other animals possess a capacity for conscious experience, fewer of them (perhaps just a small number of mammalian species) are conscious of themselves as individuals in anything like the way human beings are. None possesses our deep, sometimes troubled, sometimes joyous, inner lives. In addition, most of us possess dispositional capacities for reason and reflection (Sinnott-Armstrong, 2009, pp. 69–70), life planning, caring, emotions, language, and the many practices of cooperation, technology, tradition, and art that comprise our cultures – all to an extent that makes the equivalent capacities of other animals, even chimpanzees and bonobos, seem rudimentary. That being said, and without wanting to dwell too much here on the ethical animal rights debate, animal rights activists rightly caution that many of us do not possess dispositional capacities different from some higher mammals, either at certain points during our lives, or indeed throughout our lives. Hence, they argue, respect for equal interests demands that we treat such higher mammals no differently from how we treat humans with similar capacities.

Atheists, like many Christians and other religious people, are often impressed by the individual autonomy of human beings, in an important sense of "autonomy," where it refers to the ability to make our own decisions, particularly about important matters to do with how we live in the world. A moral or political principle of respect for others' autonomy, in this sense of the word, requires a degree of deference to the self-regarding choices of other competent people, even when we believe their choices are imprudent. This is the kind of autonomy that Jonathan Glover discusses extensively in *Causing Death and Saving Lives*, where he suggests that respect for autonomy supports an objection to killing other persons, over and above any utilitarian, or similar, consequences. On an account such as this, when we respect other individuals' autonomy we give priority to their decisions about their own future, accepting their present outlook on such matters, even if we can reliably predict it will change (Glover, 1977, pp. 78–80).

Importantly, however, Glover identifies three necessary conditions before we can meaningfully respect an individual's autonomy. First, the individual concerned must actually exist. Second, the individual must have developed to a point of being able to have relevant desires about his or her own future life. Third, the individual must *actually* have such desires – that is, we can violate a person's autonomy only if our action conflicts with desires that she or he really has (Glover, 1977, p. 77). Thus respect for autonomy cannot provide support for obligations toward embryos, babies, or even young children. When considering possible obligations to them, most atheists look elsewhere (including at general utilitarian considerations).

In addition, most humans' superior capacities for thought and feeling enable us to understand and agree that moral constraints apply to *us*. Our nature gives us both our special entitlement to moral respect from each other and our capacity to understand and assume moral burdens. We human beings are arguably an exceptional species, among those on this planet, but this need not be analyzed in quasi-religious terms such as a "sanctity" possessed by human life.

Myth 24 If There is No God We are Soulless Creatures

Can the human soul exist if God does not? Gary Demar protests that it cannot:

> an atheist creates a closed system of his own making. Only those things within his worldview are real. Of course, he defines the nature of reality.

> Those things that do not fit his rationalistic worldview do not exist. As a result, the consistent rationalist will reject the reality of God, the soul, special revelation, miracles, providence, immortality, sin, and the need of salvation. (Demar, 2006)

If the soul is understood in the popular religious sense, then the authors of this book must plead guilty as charged by Gary Demar and others like him. Neither of us thinks that there is such a thing as a soul – certainly not in that sense. However, this is not entailed by atheism alone. Someone who denies the existence of any god or gods might nonetheless believe in the existence of immortal souls.

Consider, for example, the philosophical system developed by Descartes (1996 [1641]). Descartes was not an atheist, but his belief in something like the soul, as it is commonly understood in theistic religion, comes at an earlier point in his system of thought than do his attempts at demonstrating the existence of God. That is, he argued for the existence of a mind or self that is radically different from the material body, and thought he had established this prior to going on to establish the existence of God. It would be possible to accept his arguments for the former while rejecting his supposed proofs of God's existence. Although Descartes's analysis of these issues receives little support from contemporary philosophers, it is possible to be a dualist about the mind (seen as equivalent to the soul) and the body, without believing in God or other divinities.

Many thinkers in the Eastern philosophical tradition have also put forward arguments for the existence of something much like the concept of the soul, without depending on theistic arguments. One important example is Sankara, a leading Hindu philosopher whose work was crucial in developing the doctrines of Advaita Vedanta. Sankara argued that no one can doubt his or her own existence: "For every one is conscious of the existence of (his) Self, and never thinks 'I am not.' If the existence of the Self were not known, every one would think 'I am not' " (Thibaut, 1962 [1904], p. 14). For Sankara, the existence of the spiritual self is not a mere "adventitious thing," but something no one can doubt without contradiction: "Just because it is the Self, it is impossible for us to entertain the idea of its being capable of refutation" (Thibaut, 1962, p. 14).

Rather than beginning with God, and then arguing for the existence of a soul or Self, Sankara pursued the argument in the other direction – he claimed to be able to demonstrate the existence of *Brahman* (God, the Absolute, or the Universal Spirit) by first demonstrating that we cannot deny the existence of *Atman* (the Self). Having shown to his satisfaction that the self irrefutably exists, he went on to argue that it is something unified, nonmaterial, eternal, and separate from the body (Thibaut, 1962, pp. 14–15, 268–72). While we don't endorse any of these arguments, or others proposed by classical philosophers in the Indian tradition, it is notable that the arguments do not depend on the existence of *Brahman* or any of the Hindu gods. We could accept these arguments from the Brahminical schools of Hindu philosophy without, for example, going on to embrace the mystical doctrine that *Atman* and *Brahman* are one.

To cut a long story short: philosophers from both the Eastern and Western philosophical traditions have proposed ingenious arguments for a nonmaterial mind or spiritual self, without first depending on claims about the existence of any gods. It is at least conceivable that some atheists would be convinced by similar arguments for the existence of the soul or a similar immaterial entity. We would not be surprised to find philosophical dualists who believe in the existence of something like the human soul, without believing that any gods exist – though this would be an unusual position for either Eastern or Western philosophers.

All this illustrates that there is no tight logical link between the existence of God and the existence of souls, even though they are often closely associated in the minds of the religious. Accordingly, the influential philosopher A.J. Ayer points out that even if souls existed this would not prove God's existence (Ayer, 1988). Conversely, even if a god existed, that would not necessarily give rise to the existence of souls.

Regardless of these considerations, it is probably fair to say that most religious people believe in the existence of souls, while most atheists do not believe in immortal souls for reasons related to some of their reasons for not believing in God. That is, most atheists take a naturalistic view of the world, which leaves no room for such a thing as an immortal soul that could survive the death of the body.

There remains a question as to whether we are "soulless creatures" in some other sense, perhaps a more metaphorical one, whether or not any gods exist and whether or not we literally have immortal souls. Perhaps the fear is that we might, in the absence of God, be "soulless" in lacking integrity, deep feeling, or an emotional nature. However, nothing like this follows from atheism. *This* claim, at least, is undoubtedly a myth.

4
Name Calling

Myth 25 Atheists are all Communists, Left-Wing, Liberal . . .

Clearly not *all* atheists are left-wingers or liberals. How else could the icon of modern-day libertarians, Ayn Rand, have been an atheist (Sciabarra, 1995; Benfer, 2009)? More generally, this myth is based in part on the mistaken assumption that atheists must all agree with each other across a range of issues, including political ones. Communists who closely follow Marx's views are, of course, atheists, so it might be assumed (somewhat lazily) that all atheists agree with them on political matters. Or perhaps the thought is, as George H. Smith puts it, that communism is "a logical outgrowth of atheism," making all atheists at least latent communists (Smith, 1979, p. 22). That, however, is a mistaken view: communism of any sort, including the sort associated with the ideas of Marx and Lenin, makes many assumptions that go far beyond atheism.

During the Cold War period, and especially the 1950s, the US public largely accepted a simplistic equation of atheism with Soviet-style communism. Religious differences provided a point of contrast between the USA and USSR, as church leaders and politicians alike stirred up fervor against their country's new geopolitical rival. During this period, atheism and communism were closely associated in political discussion and the public mind, with the result that many people still conflate atheism and communism, hearing an echo of the word "communist" in the word "atheist"

50 Great Myths About Atheism, First Edition. Russell Blackford and Udo Schüklenk.

(for a concise and insightful discussion of this period in American history, see Jacoby, 2004, pp. 308–316).

Associations with Soviet-style communism are still used as a rhetorical stick to beat atheists, as in John C. Lennox's book-length critique of the "New Atheism," *Gunning for God* (2011, pp. 94–95). However, we must acknowledge some people were attracted to atheism in the past as part of a total package that included communist politics.

Christian theologian Alister McGrath, for example, writes of his youthful attraction to communism as a totalizing political program that would include the eradication of religion and the transformation of society. In explaining his youthful atheistic period, he describes an intellectual direction from political commitment to rejection of God: "The principal cause of my atheism was Marxism, a movement that I believed held the key to the future" (McGrath, 2004, p. 176). Perhaps for this reason, much of McGrath's discussion of atheism links it to Marxism and to the twentieth-century communist regimes in Eastern Europe. Indeed, it becomes clear throughout *The Twilight of Atheism* that McGrath associates the supposed "twilight" with the twilight of Marxist-Leninist communism and specifically the collapse of the Soviet Union. The equation is clear in this comment on twentieth-century geopolitical developments:

> It was no longer necessary to imagine a world without God. The Soviet Union represented precisely such an atheocracy. What humanity had previously been asked to imagine as presently unfulfilled had now come to pass. And the more people learned about the Soviet Union and its European dependencies, the less they liked what they saw. It was a world evacuated of God, to be sure – but the process of extraction seemed to have sucked that world dry of many of the vital stimuli for creativity and exhilaration. There were limits to the human imaginative capacity to laud the joys of Stalinism. (McGrath, 2004, p. 187)

It should not, however, be assumed that this is, or ever was, typical of the relationship between atheism, religion, and political ideology. McGrath depicts himself as rather naïve about religion during this period, but many people become atheists from a background where they are well-informed about, perhaps even immersed in, religious practice.

Many, though obviously not all, atheists are quite hostile to communist ideas. This may be because they reject communism's political assumptions or because they see it as a totalizing worldview with many of the same faults that they find in religions. Marxist-Leninist communism is not technically a religion, as we understand the term: for example, it does not posit a supernatural or otherworldly order. Nonetheless, it offers a comprehensive view of reality, revered books (such as *The Communist Manifesto* and *Das Kapital*), prophetic leaders, canons of conduct (often including acceptable forms of art and science, and even personal behavior), and an apocalyptic vision of history. Passionate Marxists may undergo psychological transformations much like those of religious converts. None of this proves that communist ideas are false, but it helps explain why some atheists find such a belief system unattractive and even dangerous.

Communism is most certainly not the main motivator in current expressions of atheism in Western culture. Although there is a political element to forthright, public atheism, it has more to do with impatience over the influence of religion in such areas of public policy as abortion rights, same-sex marriage, and stem cell research. These are not the kinds of issues that are likely to inspire anyone to become an atheist, but they encourage atheists who might otherwise be quiet to speak out and question the credentials of religious organizations and leaders when they try to influence social and political opinion. It is not a coincidence that several of the people who were keen to contribute to our earlier book, *50 Voices of Disbelief: Why We Are Atheists* (Blackford and Schüklenk, 2009), were bioethicists interested in moral issues surrounding the beginning and end of life.

Writing in 1979, Smith took comfort that what he called "this irrational and grossly unfair practice of linking atheism with communism" was losing popularity, and was "rarely encountered any longer except among political conservatives" (Smith, 1979, p. 22). However, writings such as those of McGrath and Lennox show that the practice remains alive and well in the twenty-first century. This is still a myth that cries out to be busted.

But if atheists are not necessarily communists, might they be more left-wing or liberal in their political orientations? Again, not necessarily so. Atheism is not a political doctrine. As we have already stressed, atheism as such is not a worldview and thus does not bear directly on any political issue or position. In *Atheism: The Case Against God*, Smith presents a section entitled "What Atheism is Not" where he disassociates atheism from the many myths about it. He highlights the mistaken belief that atheism implies a world outlook, "a way of life," and suggests that atheism does not entail any substantive views about the meaning of life or human existence. While it might be, he notes, that one can infer from some substantive philosophical positions to atheism, one cannot perform an inference in the opposite direction (Smith, 1979, pp. 21–22).

Not so surprisingly, then, atheists are a politically diverse demographic. For example, Ariela Keysar presents evidence that American atheists are more often independents and are only as likely to be Democrats as the rest of the general American population (Keysar, 2007). Keysar shows that, while there are trends (atheists are more male than female, are younger, are more highly educated, concentrate in certain geographical areas, and are less likely to be Republicans), atheists can be found within every demographic.

A 2011 *New York Times* article notes that several prominent conservative pundits are atheists (Oppenheimer, 2011). This article draws attention to a community of conservative atheists who make the case that there is no necessary connection between atheism and left-wing political views. It also points out that in the United States the association between religious belief and the Republican Party is a recent phenomenon, historically speaking, emerging only in the 1970s.

Swiss evidence suggests that atheists are more likely than theists to be left-wing, but theists are more strongly right-wing than atheists are left-wing. Moreover, atheists appear to hold generally independent attitudes in conjunction with a broad distrust of many social and political institutions (Geissbuehler, 2002). Only about 70% of those who responded as nonreligious in a CNN exit poll after the 2008 US presidential election voted for Barack Obama. While this is a significant majority, it provides evidence against the view that there is anything like a *necessary* correlation between atheism and left-wing politics (CNN, 2008). Indeed, it appears that a large minority of atheists are broadly right-wing. The reason for this is that philosophically atheism does not require atheists to hold left-wing or even liberal views.

Sarah Nicolet and Anke Tresch have studied the decline of religious belief in Europe, and how it relates to political behavior. They argue that along with a drop in church attendance, there has been a shift within the types of religious beliefs that many hold. Correlating with the increasing number of nonbelievers, there is a decrease in the reliability of predictions of political behavior on the basis of religious adherence. There is now a less clear connection between nonreligious belief and left-wing (on their analysis, socially libertarian and economically socialist) political views. They conclude that religious adherence is not a useful tool for tracking political leanings in Western Europe (Nicolet and Tresch, 2008).

In any case, we might well question how useful such labels as "left-wing" and "right-wing" really are, since there are many dimensions to the political choices that face politicians and voters in modern societies.

Myth 26 Atheists Can't be Trusted

John Locke wrote an important appeal for religious toleration, published in 1689, but atheists were one group whom he believed could not be tolerated. In his *Letter Concerning Toleration*, Locke claimed:

> *Lastly*, those are not at all to be tolerated who deny the Being of a God. Promises, Covenants, and Oaths, which are the Bonds of Human Society, can have no hold upon an Atheist. The taking away of God, though but even in thought, dissolves all; besides also, those that by their Atheism undermine and destroy all Religion, can have no pretence of Religion whereupon to challenge the Privilege of a Toleration. (Locke, 1983 [1689], p. 51)

He assumed that citizens could not be trusted to keep promises and tell the truth unless motivated by fear that successful deceit in this life will be punished in an afterlife. Though Locke was a strong proponent of secular government, with political leaders making decisions solely for this-worldly reasons, his discussion assumes a residual role for religion in the sense of bare belief in God or gods, an afterlife, and divine punishment.

Similar views are widely held among religious people even today. A study group led by Will Gervais of Canada's University of British Columbia found that distrust is central to antiatheist societal prejudice. Religious people seem to use their fear of their respective deities' displeasure as a heuristic tool deployed, likely unconsciously, to establish trust among each other (even across religions). Whether or not that is necessarily justified is another question. Martha Gill reports in *The New Statesman*:

> In exams, students who believe in a forgiving deity are far more likely to cheat, and in lab studies, Christian participants who spend ten minutes writing about God's merciful nature showed increased levels of petty theft when assigned a money-based task afterwards. More recently, a comprehensive study found that crime rates are significantly higher in places where people believe in divine redemption. Researchers looked at belief surveys conducted between 1981 and 2007, which covered 143,000 people from 67 countries. In places where the belief in heaven was stronger than the belief in hell, the level of crime was significantly higher. (Gill, 2012)

In any case, Gervais and colleagues write:

> Matters are different for atheists, however. If belief in moralizing gods is used as a signal of trustworthiness, it follows that those who explicitly deny the existence of gods are not merely expressing private disbelief; they are also sending the wrong signal. A key consequence of religious prosociality,

> therefore, is distrust of atheists. A widespread view in religious societies that belief in gods guarantees morality would cause equally widespread distrust of atheists. Indeed, nearly half of Americans believe that morality is impossible without belief in God....anti-atheist prejudice should be characterized by specific distrust of atheists...rather than by general dislike of atheists or other specific appraisals. (Gervais *et al.*, 2011, p. 191)

This sort of attitude demonstrably leads to discriminatory decision making by religious believers (Gervais *et al.*, 2011, p. 1200), and has led to many laws that have disadvantaged atheists. As George H. Smith points out, many of the US states enacted laws preventing atheists from testifying in court, thus preventing them from asserting their rights in civil and criminal proceedings (Smith, 1979, p. 4).

Of course, Locke had no experience of a society where atheism is widespread. Indeed, explicit and committed atheism – atheism as thoughtful disbelief in the existence of any god or gods – was virtually unknown in Europe in 1689. During the seventeenth century, the condemnatory epithet "atheist" was commonly applied to individuals, such as Thomas Hobbes. Hobbes had unorthodox worldviews by Christian standards, but he never defended outright atheism and may have believed in a deity of some kind. There may have been genuine philosophical atheists among the intellectual elite of Paris, but if so they were a tiny proportion of the population of Europe.

Assuming there were philosophical atheists in Europe in Locke's day, they certainly were not in such numbers as to allow him to draw reliable conclusions about their behavior. In later centuries, however, atheism became a live option, culminating in the current situation where many Europeans disclaim any belief in gods or an afterlife. This has not caused social collapse in European countries or a breakdown in their legal systems. Even in a more religious country such as the United States, atheists now make up a large proportion of the population, with no ill effects. In fact, data from the US federal prison system indicate that only about 1% of prisoners are atheists, far less than their numbers in the general population would predict (Angier, 2001). While quite possibly this figure tells us more about the demographics of the USA, at a minimum there is no uncontroversial evidence that atheists are more likely than anyone else to renege on promises, covenants, and oaths (or at least solemn affirmations).

To be fair, atheists also seem to consider religious people to be less trustworthy than fellow atheists (Johansson-Stenman, 2008, p. 458). Perhaps both atheists and religious believers would do well to respect and trust each other a little bit more, despite our ideological differences. We are fellow humans first.

Credited to Jesus and Mo, www.jesusandmo.net

Myth 27 Many Atrocities Have Been Committed in the Name of Atheism

This sort of claim is often made by theists. For example, Dvir Abramovich, director of the Centre for Jewish History and Culture at the University of Melbourne, wrote as follows in an opinion piece in *The Sydney Morning Herald*:

> For Hitchens and co, religion does little good and secularism hardly any evil. Never mind that tyrants devoid of religion such as Hitler, Stalin, Lenin, Mao and Pol Pot perpetrated the worst atrocities in history. As H. Allen Orr, professor of biology at the University of Rochester, observed,

the 20th century was an experiment in secularism that produced secular evil, responsible for the unprecedented murder of more than 100 million. (Abramovich, 2009)

A story from 2010, by Miles Godfrey, reports a number of attacks on atheism by church leaders in Australia.

> The new Catholic Bishop of Parramatta, in Sydney's west, Anthony Fisher, continued the attack in his Easter message. "Last century we tried godlessness on a grand scale and the effects were devastating: Nazism, Stalinism, Pol Pot-ery, mass murder, abortion and broken relationships – all promoted by state-imposed atheism," he said. (Godfrey, 2010)

Isn't it interesting that the list of evil-doers always seems to begin with Hitler followed by Stalin and Pol Pot – sometimes with Mao Zedong added for good measure? For example, this gang of four receives plenty of attention in John C. Lennox's denunciation of all the twentieth-century atrocities that he attributes to atheism (Lennox, 2011, pp. 83–96). It's standard operating procedure for Christian apologists.

Dinesh D'Souza is another who claims that atheism was responsible for atrocities on an immense scale, concentrating on the crimes of Nazi Germany, communist China under Mao, and the USSR under Stalin. He insists that if we take into account such Christian atrocities as the Inquisition when assessing Christianity's record, we must take into account acts by atheistic regimes when assessing the record of atheism. To do otherwise, he argues, would be to employ a double standard. When the calculations are done this way, Christianity emerges as relatively innocent, whereas atheism is responsible for an incomprehensible bloodbath involving the deaths of over a hundred million people (D'Souza, 2007, pp. 214–221). Alister McGrath tries a similar tack. Throughout his book *The Twilight of Atheism*, he associates atheism closely with Stalin and the Soviet Union. He claims that "the elimination of God led to new heights of moral brutality and political violence in Stalinism and Nazism" (McGrath, 2004, p. 235). However, he offers no evidence to connect atheism with the Nazis.

To their credit, at least Patrick Madrid and Kenneth Hensley do not claim that Hitler was an atheist (a dubious proposition at best, and one that we will deal with in Myth 28 below), though they do try to taint atheism with his atrocities when they refer to "notable modern mass-murdering atheists such as Stalin, Mao, Planned Parenthood, and Pol Pot (and some heavily influenced by atheism, such as Hitler)" (Madrid and Hensley, 2010, p. 14). Note that a major reproductive health agency, Planned Parenthood, is included in this list for good measure. We assume that the odd reference to Planned Parenthood refers to its involvement in providing abortions, which we discuss elsewhere in this book (Myth 6). Never mind that most abortions conducted by Planned Parenthood are probably provided by and to theists, rather than atheists. In any event, Madrid and Hensley provide another attempt to implicate atheism in large-scale atrocities such as those committed by twentieth-century dictators. They choose to characterize Hitler as a disciple of Friedrich Nietzsche (2010, pp. 80–82), though they neglect to mention Nietzsche's well-known opposition to anti-Semitism. In fact, Nietzsche broke in 1885 with his long-time editor Ernst Schmeitzner, describing his own writings as being "completely buried and unexhumable in this [Schmeitzner's] anti-semitic hole" (Nietzsche Chronicle, 1885).

Let us review some facts. It is true that Hitler and Nazism were responsible for terrible atrocities. So were Stalin, Mao, and Pol Pot. Moreover, Stalin, Mao, and Pol Pot were actually atheists, but they acted in the name of their positive belief systems, not in the name of a liberal critique of religion. Hitler, by contrast, cannot easily be seen as an atheist. Other dictatorships that committed their share of atrocities were certainly not driven by atheism. For example, Franco's Spain was controlled by an expressly Catholic ideology (Baggini, 2003, p. 82). Under Benito Mussolini, Italy recognized the Vatican State, and Roman Catholicism became Italy's official religion. At no time did a majority of Catholics oppose Mussolini's regime, even after anti-Jewish laws were passed in 1938. Again, Mussolini's atrocities were not committed in the name of atheism (Baggini 2003, pp. 82–83). Similar comments could be made about other fascist movements and dictatorships, most notably the Ustashi in Croatia.

Nazi Germany was never an atheist state, regardless of what Hitler's personal views might have been, and none of its atrocities were committed in the name of atheism – quite the opposite. The Nazi regime reached a concordat, ironically still binding on the modern German state, with the Catholic Church in 1933 and was largely accepted by the Protestant churches, with resistance coming only from a minority group. It departed from traditional atheist values by raising such concepts as blood, soil, and nation to a quasi-religious status, treating them as sacred (Baggini, 2003, pp. 84–85).

Moreover, while the roots of the Holocaust are complex, traditional Christian anti-Semitism undoubtedly played a part, creating the mindset in which the persecution of the Jews and the Holocaust were conceivable (Baggini, 2003, pp. 85–86; Sinnott-Armstrong, 2009, p. 26). In particular, the Nazis' demonization of Jews and homosexuals owes more to long-standing Christian attitudes than to anything in the atheist or rationalist tradition. Martin Luther epitomizes a dismal record of anti-Semitism throughout European Christendom over hundreds of years, consistently rising far beyond a mere theological opposition to Judaism. Although he showed sympathy for the Jews in the first years of the Protestant Reformation, he later developed an extreme hostility to them, displayed in his own participation in anti-Semitic persecutions and in his hateful 1543 tract, *Von den Jüden und iren Lügen* (*On the Jews and Their Lies*) (see Luther, 2004 [1543]).

By contrast to all this, the Soviet Union was undeniably an atheist state, and the same applies to Maoist China and to Pol Pot's fanatical Khmer Rouge regime in Cambodia in the 1970s. That does not, however, show that the atrocities committed by these totalitarian dictatorships were the result of atheist beliefs, carried out in the name of atheism, or caused primarily by the atheistic aspects of the relevant forms of communism. In all of these cases, the situation was more complex – as, to be fair, also applies to some of the persecutions and atrocities in which religious movements, organizations, and leaders have been deeply implicated over the centuries.

Sorting out the roles played by religious or antireligious beliefs, as opposed to such things as worldly ambition and lust for glory, is often a nontrivial task, and we should be careful before adopting simplistic narratives. In the case of twentieth-century communist regimes, much of the death toll – perhaps most of it – arose from utterly ruthless attempts to effect economic transformations on a near-apocalyptic scale.

Successive rulers of the Soviet Union, particularly Joseph Stalin, were responsible for countless millions of deaths. There is no scholarly consensus on the actual number killed by the regime's actions, though Matthew White (2012, pp. 382–392) attributes 20 million just to Stalin. This may be conservative, and others have argued for far larger figures (Rummel, 1994, pp. 79–89).

While all this is a horrible indictment of the Soviet leadership and perhaps the ideology that the leaders embraced, little of it relates to atheism as such. Indeed, the Soviet Union did not have a uniformly antagonistic relationship to religion, and the Moscow Patriarchate of the Russian Orthodox Church supported the regime's military initiatives, such as suppression of the uprising in Hungary, the building of the Berlin Wall, and the invasions of Czechoslovakia and Afghanistan (Baggini, 2003, p. 88).

Can we find any grain of truth in this myth? Yes. There were persecutions of churches. They took place in the USSR's Russian heartland, in the largely Catholic countries that the Soviets occupied after World War II (some of which they annexed, as with Latvia, Lithuania, and Estonia, while others were placed under the control of their own communist governments), and notably in East Germany (the German Democratic Republic). Generally, however, Stalin and other communist leaders were more concerned with the political influence that organized churches could exercise than with the substance of any particular beliefs, or with an insistence that their populations renounce belief in God. The Soviet regime viewed the churches and their leaders as political rivals that had to be neutralized for it to succeed in its goals. Other centers of power and possible resistance, such as trade unions, the press, and even the army, were also attacked.

Similar comments can be made about the regime of Mao Zedong. Before Mao ascended to power in 1949, the brutality of his communist forces was more than matched by the Guomindang (the Chinese Nationalists) under Chiang Kai-shek. Both committed acts of terror and destruction on scales that have seldom been witnessed elsewhere, made possible by China's vast size and high population density. Mao's regime caused death in enormous numbers through the use of purges and labor camps, as part of an unrelenting campaign to repress all opposition, whether real or imagined; programs of forced collectivization and urbanization; and atrocious mismanagement of China's largely agricultural economy that led to tens of millions of deaths by famine in the late 1950s and early 1960s – the time of the disastrously planned "Great Leap Forward" (Tao Yang, 2008).

A similar pattern of utter ruthlessness, combined with attempted economic transformation on an apocalyptic scale can be seen in the conduct of the Khmer Rouge regime (Short, 2005). Pol Pot's efforts to bring about swift, total change were even more intense than those of Mao Zedong, leading to over a million deaths – likely nearer to two million – in a relatively small country over just a few years. The Khmer Rouge created a hell on earth in their desperate attempt to bring about a collectivist utopia based on "agrarian socialism."

While we do not doubt that religious people were often targeted as enemies of all these regimes' grandiose plans, this was usually because churches and other religious authorities (such as those related to Confucian tradition in China) were seen as actual or potential sources of resistance. Once again, the Soviet authorities were not always on bad terms with the Orthodox Church, and the aim of these communist regimes was to suppress any opposition, from whatever source, while carrying out massive transformations of their countries' economic bases. There was plenty of fanaticism involved, but mainly about holding onto power and engaging in mass-scale forms of social engineering – whether agricultural collectivization, forced urbanization, or, as in the case of Pol Pot's

"Democratic Kampuchea," forced deurbanization and abandonment of learning and technology.

None of this follows from mere atheism, and instead far more comprehensive political and economic ideologies were relied upon. These bear little resemblance to the views of most thinkers in the rationalist tradition that dates back to ancient Greece, and they are remote from anything found in the thinking of high-profile atheists involved in current debates – "celebrity atheists," to use Abramovich's trivializing expression – who tend to be political liberals and pluralists. Indeed, contemporary atheists tend to oppose comprehensive, apocalyptic ideologies such as Nazism, Stalinism, and Pol Pot's agrarian socialism, partly because these imitate so many of the features of monotheistic religion – aspects of religion that contributed historically to pogroms, witch hunts, and inquisitions.

One lesson to be learned from all this is that apocalyptic thinking and comprehensive worldviews can override ordinary human sympathies, not to mention ordinary caution and common sense. This seems to hold true for both religious and nonreligious adherents of particular totalitarian ideologies.

Myth 28 Adolf Hitler was an Atheist

Why would anyone care whether or not Hitler was an atheist? The function of this myth is to insinuate that atheism as such leads people to commit terrible deeds. We have seen already that Hitler's demons play an important rhetorical role in religious apologists' attacks against atheists (Myth 27). What might be described, tongue in cheek, as *argumentum ad Hitlerium* is designed to smear atheists (or others one doesn't like) with the fascist tar, hoping that some of it will stick. This is done to serve, in part, as a counterweight to criticism of Christian ideology's role in the atrocities committed during the Crusades and other historical episodes such as the sixteenth and seventeenth-century wars of religion in Europe. We have just dealt with the general strategy of saddling atheism with the blame for historical atrocities. As promised, we now turn more specifically to the case of Hitler. Let us have a closer look at this popular myth of Hitler the atheist.

It is often claimed that Hitler was an atheist and that Nazism was an atheistic ideology. A typical example is Freeman Dyson's allegation, in a speech delivered in May 2000, that Hitler and Stalin "were both avowed atheists" – Alister and Joanna Collicutt McGrath (2007, p. 22) cite this uncritically. John C. Lennox likewise discusses Hitler in a chapter on the supposedly poisonous nature of atheism, although his conclusion is the rather lame one that Hitler was "vehemently anti-Christian and anti-Jewish" (Lennox, 2011, p. 89).

What are the facts? Hitler was born to Catholic parents and never renounced his Catholicism (Speer, 1970, pp. 95–96), though his views were scarcely orthodox. As for other religions, National Socialism as such had no particular view, and we can see a variety of opinions among leading figures in the Nazi party.

The party's official chief ideologue, Alfred Rosenberg, in his magnum opus *Der Mythos des 20. Jahrhunderts*, proposed to replace the hegemony of Christianity in Western civilizations with what he described as a "religion of blood" (Rosenberg, 1930). About 1.4 million copies of this book were in circulation in Germany during the Third Reich. The Christian churches in Germany fought against the Nazi competition contained in this volume, in the face of significant threats and oppression from the dictatorship's police apparatus. Another party leader, Heinrich Himmler, had strong sympathies for Germanic mysticism. Jonathan Glover claims that Nazis were encouraged to be believers in God, in line with Rosenberg's rejection of characterizations of his work as pagan, as opposed to Christians, and this does indeed seem to have been one current within Nazism as a movement (Glover, 1999, p. 356). Be that as it may, Nazism was never an atheistic worldview, and its political programs were never carried out in the name of atheism. Some individual Nazis were atheists, but that is a very different matter.

What, however, about Hitler himself? If such a reviled figure could be portrayed as an atheist, especially if he were *motivated* by his atheism, this could do great harm to atheism as a credible viewpoint. The negative implications might not be entirely logical – more a matter of guilt by association – but damage could be done. In fact, the situation is somewhat murky, and we are bemused when we read confident claims that Hitler was, on one hand, a committed atheist, or, on the other, a thoroughly orthodox Christian. Neither of those claims seems sustainable.

Hitler spoke frequently of God or Providence or a divine lawmaker, but we should take note that such language cannot always be taken at face value; as we will also see in the case of Albert Einstein, it can sometimes be used metaphorically. One of Hitler's biographers, Alan Bullock, claims that Hitler believed in neither God nor conscience (1962, p. 216). However, Bullock's studies of the dictator's life and career have much to say about Hitler's sense of himself as a man raised up by Providence to do its grand work in history. In *Hitler and Stalin: Parallel Lives*, Bullock suggests that Hitler was led to speak frequently of Providence as a necessary, if unconscious, projection of his sense of destiny. This provided him, as it did Napoleon, "with both justification and absolution" (Bullock, 1991, p. 430; compare Bullock, 1962, pp. 215–216).

Indeed, Bullock goes on to quote Hitler as saying on one occasion: "The Russians were entitled to attack their priests, but they had no right to assail the idea of a supreme force. It's a fact that we're feeble creatures and that a creative force exists" (Bullock, 1991, p. 430; compare Hitler, 1953, p. 87). For Bullock, Hitler, like Stalin, was "materialistic" in his dismissal of religion and his insensitivity to humanity, though the biographer does not go so far as to ascribe to Hitler a naturalistic worldview (see Bullock, 1991, p. 430).

Hitler seems to have believed in some kind of God that intervenes in human history, though some of his statements suggest that he may have understood God in impersonal terms. He certainly expressed anti-Christian sentiments at times, though it can be difficult to sort out whether his objection was to Christianity as such, or to specific doctrines, or whether it was simply an objection to the influence of church hierarchies. His relationship to Christianity was ambivalent at best. At times he supported a strong state church of a kind (his regime attempted with some success to remodel the Protestant church along these lines). However, this seems to be have been driven mostly by instrumental considerations. He believed that a people might need a church because of its stabilizing influence on society and the state.

Passages in the compilation *Hitler's Table Talk* are frequently cited to support the claim that Hitler was actually an atheist or at least anti-Christian. *The Table Talk* is a compilation of comments made by Hitler in his bunker, as transcribed by secretaries at the behest of Martin Bormann. Glover quotes from the English version of the *Table Talk* to demonstrate that Hitler saw Christianity as a disease, a lie, and a Jewish conspiracy (Glover, 1999, p. 355). The relevant passage, dated February 27, 1942, is scathing about such leading doctrines of Christianity as that of sacrificial atonement, but Hitler also puts forward some obscure, perhaps confused, views about God and Providence. Readers might wish to consult the whole passage, but even as they have been translated into English these do not seem like the words of an atheist – and certainly not of someone motivated by atheism (Hitler, 1953, pp. 341–344).

One problem that must be dealt with at this point is that the passage – along with others from the *Table Talk* – reads differently in the French and English translations from what appears in scholarly texts of the German manuscripts. The English version appears, according to Richard Carrier, to be based on the French translation, and the provenance of some text not found in the German is unknown. Carrier's comparisons of several passages show that the French and English translations are, to say the least, rather loose. In some cases, the differences are so serious as to suggest outright fabrication. Having examined the evidence, Carrier suggests that passages were altered for whatever purpose by the French translator, François Genoud (Carrier, 2003).

In any event, some of the most virulently anti-Christian statements in the only English translation to date of the *Table Talk* cannot be verified from the German sources. These include the wording of a long passage in which Hitler is represented as saying:

> I realise that man, in his imperfection, can commit innumerable errors – but to devote myself deliberately to error, that is something I cannot do. I shall never come personally to terms with the Christian lie. In acting as I do, I'm very far from the wish to scandalize. But I rebel when I see the very idea of Providence flouted in this fashion. (Hitler, 1953, p. 343)

When consulted, the German text does not use any expression equivalent to the phrase "the Christian lie" though it does refer to the doctrines Hitler has been denouncing as a lie. Carrier translates the German version (which he provides) as follows:

> I know that humans in their defectiveness will do a thousand things wrong. But to do something wrong against one's own knowledge, that is out of the question! One should never personally accept such a lie. Not because I want to annoy others, but because I recognize therein a mockery of the Eternal Providence. I am glad if I have no internal connection with them. (Carrier, 2003, p. 570)

Likewise, Hitler does not refer to "the Christian disease" as he continues what is more a denunciation of "the beatifying [Catholic] Church" ("*die seligmachende Kirche*") and its claimed authority to offer salvation of souls (Carrier, 2003, p. 566). While the passage retains its anticlerical force in the original German, it does not show Hitler dismissing Christianity in its entirety in the same straightforward terms. At the same time, the German, French, and English versions of the passage from which all this comes contain references to God that are, to put it mildly, not obviously metaphorical. Conversely, the German contains text that has not been included in the French and English translations. For example, according to Carrier, Hitler says in the February 27, 1942 passage, "*Das, was der Mensch vor dem Tier voraus hat, der vielleicht wunderbarste Beweis für die Überlegenheit des Menschen ist, dass er begriffen hat, dass es eine Schöpferkraft geben muss!*" (Carrier, 2003, p. 568). Carrier translates this missing statement as: "What man has over the animals, possibly the most marvelous proof of his superiority, is that he has understood there must be a Creative Power!" The entire paragraph from which this comes is omitted from the French and English versions (Carrier, 2003, p. 568).

Hitler does not speak in the *Table Talk* as an atheist, though he expresses anti-Christian and anti-clerical sentiments, and sometimes sounds agnostic, as in a passage dated December 13, 1941: here, Hitler says that if there is a God he has given human beings intelligence to use – and using his own intelligence has led him to reject the concrete image of the Beyond offered by Christianity. But Hitler then speaks of the soul and mind migrating, as the body returns to nature, adding that he does not understand the "why" of it all as "The soul is unplumbable" (Hitler, 1953, p. 144).

At other times, he sounds as if his God is an impersonal force, though this impression is strengthened by what appear to be editorial decisions by Bormann, such as when Hitler says, "Fundamentally in everyone there is the feeling for this all-mighty, which we call God" – and the following words are added in parentheses, "that is to say, the dominion of natural laws throughout the whole universe" (Hitler, 1953, p. 6).

Like other totalitarian dictators, Hitler was hostile to the Christian churches insofar as they provided rival centers of power, and he cannot be regarded as a pious Christian by any stretch of the imagination. However, he never renounced Christianity, and his enemies at the time did not claim he was not a Christian. He expressly professed Christianity in *Mein Kampf* and in his speeches, and is also recorded as having spoken of God or Providence on private occasions when he had little to gain by doing so. In Chapter 2 of *Mein Kampf*, for example, he says that he sees himself as acting in accordance with the will of the Creator by defending Germany against the Jews. He wrote, "Therefore, I believe today, that I am acting in the sense of the Almighty Creator: by warding off the Jews, I am fighting for the Lord's work" (Hitler, 1941, p. 84).

It has to be conceded that much of what Hitler said in his public statements cannot be taken at face value – there is no doubt of his propensity for political opportunism. However, Dinesh D'Souza overreaches in *What's so Great About Christianity* when he accuses Sam Harris of ignoring evidence of Nazi sympathies for, among other things, atheism (D'Souza, 2007, p. 220) – this conclusion follows a discussion that provides no such evidence in relation to Hitler or for the Nazis in general.

The jury is out on just how much Hitler accepted orthodox Christianity at various phases of his life, and how far he moved over time to an unorthodox and idiosyncratic position, perhaps even to an impersonal conception of God. However, there is no solid case for the claim that he was an atheist. On the contrary, he appears, at least in some moods, to have been convinced that he was carrying out the divine will. The narrative of Hitler as a convinced atheist, acting from some sort of atheistic motivation, is yet another myth.

Myth 29 Atheists Give a Free Pass to Non-Christian Religions

Some people (mainly Christians) complain that atheists direct most of their criticism at Christianity. You can find such concerns frequently expressed on internet discussion sites and personal blogs, though not so much in the academic literature. For instance, one such writer asks, "How come they never ever attack anyone else like Muslims, Jews, Boodists, Hindoos, Rastafarians, Scientologists, or any other religion?" (Answerbag, 2010, spelling as in original). In a similar mood is "Jim the evolution cruncher," who asks, "Why do atheists hate Christ so much? Rarely here on R&S do they ever attack Buddha, Mohammad or any other god. Why the focus on the Son of God?" (Jim the evolution cruncher, 2012).

Our readers should note that these quotations are taken more or less randomly from internet sites. We have not verified the persons behind the pseudonyms responsible for them. Our primary interest is to show that people *are* concerned that atheists (supposedly) give non-Christian religious ideologies too easy a ride. The complaint is that various kinds of Christian belief get more flak than all the other religions, such as Islam, Hinduism, and Buddhism. This might, we suspect, even be confirmed by empirical evidence. Would this imply that atheists give non-Christians religions a "free pass"?

Obviously, there are other explanations. For a start, historically Christian nations show currently the highest percentages of atheists in their populations (Zuckerman, 2007). It is hardly surprising if atheists concentrate on criticizing the religion that has wielded local influence – both in past times and, in many cases, in an ongoing way. Furthermore, people are most free to criticize religion in the Western democracies of Europe, North America, and Oceania, all of which share Christian traditions and retain a Christian majority. It is hardly surprising if atheists in these countries concentrate on criticizing Christianity. That is a reasonable priority, since it is the religion that has the most local prestige. Opposing Christian ideas and their social or political influence can seem more important than criticizing, say, Islam, whose adherents may even be disadvantaged and discriminated against in Western countries. Many Muslims in the

West suffer from various forms of cultural and personal intolerance, and Western atheists may hesitate to add to this.

In other countries, such as Turkey, priorities are rather different. Atheists in predominantly Muslim countries are more likely to concentrate their criticisms on Islam. Note, however, that they are frequently impeded when they do so. For example, Abdullah Rıza Ergüven's philosophical novel *Yasak Tümceler* ("The Forbidden Phrases") promulgates a materialist philosophy and contains trenchant criticisms of Islam and the Prophet Muhammad. Its publication led to a conviction against the publisher's managing director under an antiblasphemy provision in Turkey's criminal code. This conviction was ultimately sustained by the European Court of Human Rights (*İ.A. v. Turkey*, September 13, 2005).

Turkey is, of course, one of the most liberal of the world's predominantly Muslim countries. The other that is often praised for its comparatively liberal approach is Indonesia, but it appears that this is not a safe place to express atheistic views at all, let alone engage in criticism of Islam. In January 2012, it was reported in the international media that one Indonesian citizen, Alexander Aan, had been attacked by an angry mob, threatened with loss of his job, and risked jail – merely for posting on an atheist Facebook page his belief that God does not exist (BBC News, 2012). Mr Aan was sentenced to two and a half years imprisonment and a fine of 100 million rupiah (about 10.500 US$) (Amnesty International, 2012). Even as we write, his ordeal continues, and Western atheists and human rights organizations have been lobbying the Indonesian government to secure his freedom. If Turkey and Indonesia are the "liberal" Muslim nations, it is not surprising that little criticism of Islam appears from atheists based in the others.

Nonetheless, some non-believers do subject Islam to trenchant criticism. One is Ibn Warraq (not his real name) who has written prolifically on the subject. Contributors to his anthology, *Leaving Islam: Apostates Speak Out* (Warraq, 2003), explain the dangers that atheists and critics of Islam are confronted with if they dare to express their views publicly.

Numerous Western writers have criticized Islam, and some were vocal even before the September 2001 attacks on the New York City twin towers by Islamic radicals. Among these was Antony Flew (see Flew, 1995), who was then an atheist, though he became a philosophical deist in the later years of his life. Since the events of 2001, Western atheists have been increasingly troubled by the influence of Islam, especially insofar as it seems to be lagging behind Christianity in adapting to liberal ideas of a separation between religious authority and the activities of the state. Christian organizations and leaders often pay only lip service to this, of course, but it is not clear that Islam has, to date, been able to embrace the concept at all. Islam is notorious for its historical reluctance to draw a boundary between the domains of religion and politics.

For these and other reasons, not least the extreme patriarchy and misogyny that is unfortunately often associated with Islam, some current forms of Islam appear to sit badly with liberal social and political ideas.

Accordingly, some atheists in the West are now highly critical of Islam, among them Sam Harris, who focuses much of his attention on Islam in his first book, *The End of Faith* (Harris, 2004). See also *Does God Hate Women?* by Ophelia Benson and Jeremy Stangroom (2009), which particularly deals with Islam's unhappy record of misogyny and patriarchy. In fact, one of us has been highly critical of Western liberal intellectuals' failure to confront the barbarism that pervades many Islamic societies' treatment of women, gay people, atheists, and others not conforming to the standards demanded by this ideology (Schüklenk, 2009, p. 329).

It must be acknowledged, of course, that issues of personal safety do deter criticism of Islam, and this must not be trivialized. One well-known example is the Ayatollah Khomeini's 1989 *fatwa* against the novelist Salman Rushdie. You might want to consider reading Rushdie's gripping account of living under the *fatwa* (Rushdie, 2012). The *fatwa* openly incited Rushdie's murder, and led to such atrocious events as the fatal stabbing of his Japanese translator, Hitoshi Igarashi, in 1991. Rushdie's Italian translator, Ettore Capriolo, was seriously wounded in the same year (Cliteur, 2010, pp. 134–135). Other such examples include the murder of Dutch film director Theo van Gogh in 2004. Many critics of Islam, such as van Gogh's one-time collaborator Ayaan Hirsi Ali, are forced to take onerous measures just to protect their personal safety. Against that background, it is encouraging that former Muslims sometimes speak out about their reasons for leaving behind the faith that they were born and socialized into (Crimp and Richardson, 2008; Namazie, 2009).

What about Asian religions, such as Hinduism, Buddhism, Sikhism, and Jainism? Do these get a free pass from atheists and secularists? In Western societies, these religions do not tend to be the ones that threaten political liberties, and so they attract less anger and criticism. One well-known exception relates to the play *Behzti* by Gurpeet Kaur Bhatti: this was the subject of violent protests in Birmingham, UK, by militant Sikhs, who objected to what they saw as an offensive depiction of the Sikh community (Branigan, 2004a). Bhatti herself received death threats, and the performance of her play was cancelled.

Behzti is undoubtedly sensational – it involves rape and a murder – though there are also light moments and a rather touching love story. It is in no way a racist or quasi-racist attack on Sikhs, but it is set in a Sikh temple and has been accused of being especially offensive in portraying violence and sexual crime within such a location. At the time of the controversy, several hundred well-known writers, actors, and directors defended the play (Branigan, 2004b) while the local Catholic Archbishop criticized it, reportedly because of its "offensive" nature (Britten, 2004). This reflects a common and long-standing view among many representatives of religious organizations that religious adherents must be protected from ridicule and anything that might offend their sensibilities. This is a courtesy that other groups in society are rarely offered by these very same religious figures.

If there were more cases such as this, involving the roles of Asian religions in Western countries, we would probably see more criticism leveled at Asian religions by Western atheists. As it is, these religions are seen as not having the social power and prestige to make them high-priority targets for rational critique. But atheists in Asian countries, such as G. Ramakrishna (1981) and Prabir Ghosh (2009) in India, have a very different relationship to Asian religions, which are far more powerful and prestigious in those countries. Accordingly, they are most definitely engaged in public criticism of Asian religions.

5

Horrible, Strident Atheists

Myth 30 Atheists are Arrogant

Dinesh D'Souza's writings are as good as any to serve as an example of the complaint that atheists are arrogant. He writes that we "assume that [our] rational, scientific approach gives [us] full access to external reality." This, he says, leads us to be arrogant:

> It is this presumption that gives atheism its characteristic arrogance. Daniel Dennett and Richard Dawkins call themselves "brights" because they think they and their atheist friends are simply smarter than the community of religious believers. (D'Souza, 2007, p.168)

His charge of arrogance essentially amounts to the claim that we are overweening in our reliance on reason and evidence:

> The atheist is now revealed as dogmatic and arrogant, and the religious believer emerges as modest and reasonable. While the atheist arrogantly persists in the delusion that his reason is fully capable of figuring out all that there is, the religious believer lives in the humble acknowledgment of the limits of human knowledge, knowing that there is a reality greater than, and beyond, that which our senses and minds can apprehend. (D'Souza, 2007, p. 178)

The first of these passages raises questions that we address in our discussion of other myths, such as for instance the idea that science and reason depend on faith or even on the presumption that God exists. We will not duplicate

50 Great Myths About Atheism, First Edition. Russell Blackford and Udo Schüklenk.

later discussions except to note the chutzpah of accusing atheists of arrogance! D'Souza portrays the religious believer as possessing esoteric knowledge – knowledge that there is a world "greater than . . . our senses and minds can apprehend." Who is arrogant here, those of us who are well aware of the practical limitations of human knowledge, or someone like D'Souza who claims to have esoteric knowledge of otherworldly agencies?

It is also worth noting in this context the patently false claim D'Souza makes about atheists: it is not true that any (or even many) atheists think that *all* questions can be answered through reason. It seems trivial to acknowledge that some questions cannot be answered at all today, through reason or otherwise. It is also possible, of course, that *some* questions that we are unable to solve by means of rational inquiry today can be solved tomorrow. Let us assume, however, for the sake of the argument, that there are external realities that we will always be unable to grasp by means of human reason and evidence. But if reason and evidence do not answer some questions, it is best to acknowledge that rather than insisting that we can obtain justified beliefs about these things in some other manner.

By the way, D'Souza's short passage mentioning Dawkins and Dennett is both simplistic and misleading – though by no means the only such example (for another, see Lennox, 2011, pp. 15–16). The word "bright" was employed as a noun by Paul Geisert and Mynga Futrell when they launched the "Brights movement" early in 2003. The idea was to find a positive-sounding word for people who have a naturalistic worldview, analogous to the word "gay" for homosexuals. While it may have connotations of intellectual superiority (as in "a bright student"), it has other positive connotations, as with cheerfulness and bright colors. Thus it does its job as a positive word for a class of people whom Geisert and Futrell justifiably saw as despised and marginalized (Edgell *et al.*, 2006). As they explain in their vision statement,

> Persons who have a naturalistic worldview should be accepted as fellow citizens and full participants in the cultural and political landscape, and not be culturally stifled or civically marginalized due to society's extensive supernaturalism. (Brights, 2012a)

Geisert and Futrell stress that the main basis of the word was its association of philosophical naturalism as well as the Enlightenment: "We hope that the newly coined 'bright' will serve the purpose of indicating *a person or persons whose worldview is naturalistic*, no more, no less" (Brights, 2012b).

Given that Dennett and Dawkins have been at the receiving end of D'Souza's criticism, it is worth investigating whether they are as arrogant as he implies. What is their take on the Brights movement? Dawkins gave support to the idea in an article published in the *Guardian* newspaper on June 21, 2003. The article was mainly concerned with the capacity of language to shape how we think (which justifies feminist consciousness-raising about sexist usages). He acknowledged the possibility of a perception of arrogance, and his article puns on the idea of "bright" as intelligent when he concludes with the possibility that "we may finally get a bright president." Still, his main emphasis was on the term's cheerfulness and its capacity to serve in a consciousness-raising exercise aimed at making nonreligious worldviews more socially welcome:

> Geisert and Futrell are very insistent that their word is a noun and must not be an adjective. "I am bright" sounds arrogant. "I am a bright" sounds too unfamiliar to be arrogant: it is puzzling, enigmatic, tantalising. It invites the question, "What on earth is a bright?" And then you're away: "A bright is a person whose world view is free of supernatural and mystical elements. The ethics and actions of a bright are based on a naturalistic world view." (Dawkins, 2003a)

Dawkins also published a shorter article on the topic for *Wired* magazine. Here he emphasizes that the idea is not a claim to intellectual superiority, though in fairness he hints in passing that future research may show that people with a naturalistic worldview are better educated, or in some sense smarter, on average than others who hold views such as those propagated by D'Souza:

> I am a bright. You are (quite probably) a bright. Most of the people I know are brights. The majority of scientists are brights. Presumably there are lots of closet brights in Congress, but they dare not come out. Notice from these examples that the word is a noun, not an adjective. We brights are not claiming to be bright (meaning clever, intelligent), any more than gays claim to be gay (meaning joyful, carefree). Whether there is a statistical tendency for brights (noun) to be bright (adjective) is a matter for research. I would dearly like to see such research undertaken, and I know the result I am betting on, but it is not part of the definition of the noun. (Dawkins, 2003b)

Dennett joined the debate with an article in *The New York Times* in July of the same year. Dennett's emphasis in this piece is rather different: he pays particular attention to the analogy with "gay" for "homosexual," and he offers the coinage "bright" as one component of a campaign to redress what he sees as the political disenfranchisement of atheists and others with similar views of the world. Once again, he stresses that the word "bright" is not intended to be a boast of intellectual superiority, and that it is not even an adjective. To be fair, once again, he sees it as connoting a degree of pride, but not as any sort of boast:

> The term "bright" is a recent coinage by two brights in Sacramento, Calif., who thought our social group – which has a history stretching back to the Enlightenment, if not before – could stand an image-buffing and that a fresh name might help. Don't confuse the noun with the adjective: "I'm a bright" is not a boast but a proud avowal of an inquisitive world view. (Dennett, 2003)

A fair reading shows that Dawkins and Dennett gave this idea some support not as an arrogant boast of intellectual superiority – something that they explicitly addressed with some concern – but in the hope that the word could operate much like the word "gay" if given some help. That may have been a misjudgment on their part, since it has been used as a stick to beat them, and other atheists, ever since. In any event, it is wrong to think that it was intended as an expression of superiority.

There remains the suspicion, expressed in passing by Dawkins, that philosophical naturalists are better educated, on average, than the general population, or even more "intelligent" (whatever that actually means). Is this true? If so, is it arrogant to say so? Surely this boils down to an empirical claim, a testable hypothesis that Dawkins encourages us to investigate – though he leaves us in no doubt as to what he suspects the results will show.

All that said, it is worth noting that in many social circumstances religious views of some sort are the default. It is what most people are familiar with, and what they are most likely to be socialized into by nonrational means. The minority who come to adopt a naturalistic worldview are more likely to have reached it through intellectual inquiry, which may suggest that they are at least better educated or more curious than the general population. If pointing out this possibility makes us arrogant, then so be it – but it is setting the bar for "arrogance" very low. We do not suggest that theists and others with supernatural beliefs are *ipso facto* stupid; nor do we deny that some have reached their views through intellectual inquiry. Clearly some have.

Or perhaps what is being suggested is that there is something unkind about questioning religious beliefs, especially if it is not done in an especially gentle and apologetic way. However, it is not clear why atheists should offer so much solicitude: why should religious beliefs be protected from being challenged in a straightforward way, especially given the amount of cultural and political power that they often wield, and which atheists often believe to be used badly (Dacey, 2008)?

Possibly the charge of arrogance is simply meant to suggest that atheists are personally overbearing, unjustifiably proud, or obnoxious. Will there be such atheists? Of course. Are there such people who also happen to be religious believers? Of course there are. We have no reason, and indeed no evidence, to think that we – *qua* atheists – are any more arrogant than anyone else. Arrogance is something that goes far beyond being passionate or outspoken, and it has to do with how we treat people rather than with what we believe or how we reach our conclusions.

Myth 31 Atheists are Intolerant

There certainly are some less than impartial observers complaining about atheists' alleged intolerance. An editorial in *Christianity Today* suggests that our intolerance shows how atheism itself is in trouble:

> The antitheistic rhetoric that erodes the ethos of respect is a clear and present danger.... This newly aggressive mood (Dawkins calls religious education "brainwashing" and "child abuse") is in danger of undermining civil society. (*Christianity Today*, 2007)

Right, and they call *us* strident! Question: is it intolerant to suggest that there are ethical problems in indoctrinating children in faith schools in their formative years with religious ideology, instead of providing them with unbiased information about the world's competing religions? Even if this is acceptable, how far should it go? Should children be cut off from alternative viewpoints? What if they are told that all other viewpoints are sinful, and should not even be considered?

Christina Odone, writing in the conservative British broadsheet *The Telegraph*, is another commentator who expresses deep worries about intolerant atheists: "I fear intolerant atheists will not be satisfied until they've driven faith underground: Christians, Jews and Muslims will be forced to resort to Masonic handshakes and hush-hush gatherings. Meet you in the catacombs" (Odone, 2011). So – what terrible actions by atheists have brought *this* on? The examples mentioned in her commentary pertain to staff members of a public housing association displaying religious paraphernalia in their car, fundamentalist Christians running into trouble with authorities when it was discovered that they were indoctrinating their foster children with antigay propaganda – and the list goes on. For Odone, it does not matter what we think about how the state, or the public housing association, ought to have acted. What is worth noting, however, is that none of the cases flagged in her commentary sustain her histrionic conclusion about intolerant atheists wanting to drive religious people to the catacombs.

Actually some atheists have rather more modest and reasonable goals: they are goals that Odone might disapprove of, but why not examine them on their merits? Yes, atheists, or some of us, might want to curtail religion-based refusals to provide certain professional services. Or some of us might protest when foster parents indoctrinate vulnerable foster children, while receiving public funds to bring up those children. Surely these are matters for legitimate argument.

Is it a sign of intolerance, then, when atheists no longer allow religious views to go unchallenged when expressed in everyday interaction? Is it intolerant to demand the end of a privilege that religious ideas enjoy, a special immunity from challenge that does not apply to political or economic ideas, for example? If this is intolerance, it is only in a very weak sense, perhaps best described (to borrow an expression used by Sam Harris) as conversational intolerance. This is remote from atheists murdering religious people over disagreements on the question of God's existence, or because of disagreements about the beginnings of the universe.

Well, then, is this a myth – or is there a grain of truth in the assertion that atheists are intolerant? That is, of course, subject to a consensus on what constitutes intolerance. Harris rightly notes that anyone who strongly believes that a certain way is the right way and is the only way to human fulfillment, happiness – insert whatever you think we ought to aim for – will inevitably be intolerant toward others who choose to stray from this way, at least if the stakes are very high:

> Once a person believes – really believes – that certain ideas can lead to eternal happiness, or to its antithesis, he cannot tolerate the possibility that the people he loves might be led astray by the blandishments of unbelievers. Certainty about the next life is simply incompatible with tolerance in this one. (Harris, 2004, p. 11)

That is a bit of a problem with many strongly religious people. Indeed, this attitudinal problem is at the core of much of the sectarian violence that continues to plague our modern world. Will Durant hits the nail on its head when he notes that "tolerance grows only when faith loses certainty; certainty is murderous" (Durant, 1992, p. 784).

In modern liberal democracies, our freedom of speech is rightly respected. We are all permitted to argue for the truth of whatever we believe, both in private and in public forums. We are permitted to persuade others, if we can, to live in certain ways and not to do certain things, to take a particular view of the good life for human beings, and to believe certain things rather than others. All of this involves the techniques of argument and exhortation, personal practice and example, and so on.

Unfortunately, far more than conversational intolerance is commonly attributed to atheists, particularly to those who are forthright about their views. John Haught is just one author who accuses some atheists of abandoning freedom of religion and advocating political intolerance of religious views. He says that Harris and Dawkins want us to abandon "respect for freedom of faith and religious thought" (Haught, 2008, p. 9). This claim is based on passages that say no such thing – for example, page 306 of *The God Delusion* (Dawkins, 2006) and passages in *The End of Faith* (Harris, 2004). Dawkins argues on page 306 that we ought to give up on the idea of automatic respect for religion, which is a far cry from asking us not to respect people's freedom to subscribe to particular religious beliefs, no matter how implausible they are. He suggests that religion and religious extremism are not entirely distinct, and adds, "as long as we accept the principle that religious faith must be respected simply because it is religious faith, it is hard to withhold respect from the faith of Osama bin Laden and the suicide bombers" (Dawkins, 2006, p. 306). Dawkins goes on to explain that this is why he tries to warn people against religious faith. That, however, is not the same as saying that he disrespects their freedom to adopt a religion.

In short, Harris and Dawkins may be among the most passionate opponents of religion among contemporary atheists, but they do not oppose freedom of religion. They do oppose respect for the religious beliefs themselves, but that is an entirely different matter: I may have good reasons to respect your right to make up your own mind what to believe, without having to respect your conclusions (in this case religious beliefs) themselves. It is remarkable that authors such as Haught seem incapable of grasping this fundamental distinction, and that they continue to propagate the myth of intolerant atheists.

Haught (2008, p. 10) claims that Harris and others defend themselves by saying that faith never had any moral or rational justification and so should never have been tendered the right to exist. However, he offers no citation or other evidence for his claim that any contemporary atheist of note actually makes such an illiberal claim.

He does later state that, for Dawkins, Harris, and Dennett, the best way to remove faith from the minds of others is not violence or political action but by "filling minds with science and reason" (Haught, 2008, p. 12). He does not notice, or does not admit, that this contradicts his earlier suggestions that these thinkers share a highly illiberal viewpoint – unless, of course, he views science and logic classes as illiberal activities. By this point of his book, atheists have been smeared, an impression has been created, and the damage is already done.

Let us be clear about this: what we must not do is attempt to impose our beliefs or preferred ways of life by the use of force, whether it be by acts of terrorist violence or through laws that suppress the alternatives. But these are not our practices as atheists. This is not to say that there are no atheists who are intolerant, but it is to suggest that atheists *per se* are no more intolerant than other members of society. It is also to suggest that atheism *per se* does not provide particular motives for atheists to behave in intolerant manners toward believers. In fact, in many cases, it is religious believers who are unwilling to tolerate disagreement and are keen to impose their particular canons of conduct on others who do not share them.

Credited to Jesus and Mo, www.jesusandmo.net

Myth 32 Atheists Want to Ban Teaching Religion to Children

Atheism does not commit anyone to an opinion as to whether, or how, religion should be taught to children. You won't be surprised to learn that many atheists think that children should not be indoctrinated with the teachings of a particular religious system. A good example of this is Bill Nye, the popular US science educator. He made no secret of his view that while parents are entitled to their religious beliefs, it surely would be inappropriate to teach their children creationism in school. He said in an interview,

> if parents want to deny evolution and live in your world that's completely inconsistent with everything we observe in the universe, that's fine, but don't make your kids do it because we need them. We need scientifically literate voters and taxpayers for the future. We need people that can – we need engineers that can build stuff, solve problems. It's just . . . really a hard thing. You know, in another couple of centuries that worldview, I'm sure, will be, it just won't exist. There's no evidence for it. (Nye, 2012, our transcription from the video)

Teaching children creationism or other make-belief stories about God and the universe can be contrasted with teaching children about religion as a social phenomenon: children could learn in school about the different beliefs held by followers of the major religions of the world.

Richard Dawkins, perhaps, as we write, the world's best-known outspoken atheist, is frequently accused of holding an extreme position on these issues. The position attributed to him is one in which teaching religious doctrines to children is child abuse and ought to be forbidden by law: thus, John C. Lennox writes casually that "Dawkins' argument for banning the teaching of religion would logically lead even faster to banning the teaching of atheism," since Lennox thinks that atheism has led to many atrocities (2011, p. 94). But when has Dawkins expressed, or argued for, such an unnuanced view?

Let's get this as clear as we can. In *The God Delusion*, Dawkins states that his main purpose in the relevant chapter is to "question" the practice of labeling children "as possessors of beliefs that they are too young to have thought about." On the same page, he does in fact call *this* "a form of child abuse" (Dawkins, 2006, p. 315). In his view, we should ascribe belief systems to other people only after they are old enough to have made up their own minds. He then discusses "ordinary" forms of sexual and other physical abuse, but argues that terrorizing children with stories of

Hell can sometimes be a worse form of psychological abuse than these (while observing, in fairness, that the Catholic Church does not make as much of Hell as it once did) (Dawkins, 2006, pp. 317–325).

Dawkins goes on to make many interesting observations. For example, he spends several pages attacking the teaching of creationism in schools, and government support to schools that do this – while noting that many members of the clergy agree with his position – before he returns to the issue of "labeling" children. As to that, however, he ultimately asks no more than that we wince when we see or hear it (pp. 337–340). He does give historical examples where the specific content of someone's religion made it harmful – as in one ancient cult which involved human sacrifice – but that is rather different from seeking to prohibit all efforts to teach religion to children. He concludes with a discussion of the importance of teaching the Bible as part of our inherited literary culture (pp. 340–342). In short, Dawkins has not argued that socializing a child into a religion is *ipso facto* child abuse, let alone that it should be prohibited. Thus the claim that Dawkins argues those things is a myth. He has, in fact, expressed far more nuanced, specific, and defensible views.

A. C. Grayling takes a harder line. He accepts that liberal political principles and the view that parents "have a right to determine their children's faith and education" point to an acceptance of indoctrinating small children into their parents' religious beliefs. But, he asks, might society actually have a duty to protect children from proselytization? He worries about children being taught what he regards as falsehoods, fantasies, and absurdities from an early age, and so being rendered incapable of challenging what they were taught. However, even Grayling's discussion of these issues is inconclusive: he merely proposes that we consider the problem (Grayling, 2009, pp. 19–20).

So Grayling, who appears more strict than Dawkins on this particular issue, does not simply claim that teaching religion to children should be banned. In fact, we are not aware of any high-profile atheist who takes such a strong position. It is simply not true that atheists *qua* atheists want to ban religious socialization by parents. Perhaps there are individuals who are committed to this approach, and whom we are overlooking, but to suggest that this is the usual view of high-profile atheists – let alone of atheists in general – is insupportable.

Related to this myth is what may be a separate one: that atheists wish to control the educational curriculum in order to brainwash children into their antireligious worldview: "They want to control school curricula so they can promote a secular ideology and undermine Christianity," says Dinesh D'Souza (2007, p. xv).

D'Souza argues for this at length, but he offers little evidence. He thinks there is an equivalence between people who object to creationist theory and the like, because it is used to support religion, and people who want evolution taught because they regard it as antireligious. But the equivalence is a false one. The state should not be in the business of teaching a body of scientific findings either because they tend to support *or* because they tend to undermine religion. Those are, we submit, improper motives for officials and government agencies. State education systems should simply teach what is considered by scientists in the relevant fields to be accurate, central, up-to-date science. It is really not that difficult.

Credited to Jesus and Mo, www.jesusandmo.net

Myth 33 Atheists Want to Strip People of their Beliefs

Alister McGrath makes a remarkable claim in his book *The Twilight of Atheism*:

> A desire to eliminate belief in God at the intellectual or cultural level has the most unfortunate tendency to encourage others to do this at the physical level. We simply cannot separate ends and means here. (McGrath, 2004, pp. 166–167)

The context of this baseless – and, indeed, outrageous – claim is his discussion of the Stalinist era crackdown on religion, though even McGrath acknowledges that Stalin's aim was not necessarily that of eliminating personal faith so much as breaking the power of organized religion (McGrath, 2004, pp. 166–167). Still thinking partly of the Soviet experience, he goes on to describe the following as an atheist view: "Faith will die out by natural means, or it should be eliminated through forcible suppression" (2004, p. 189). John C. Lennox (2011, pp. 92–95) takes a similar stance, closely associating contemporary expressions of atheism with Soviet communism and political suppression of religious belief.

Pointing to totalitarian societies that have meted out punishments against religious people and their leaders is offensive and intellectually weak. In Stalin's case, for instance, the persecution of religious organizations had more to do with a threat that the dictator saw to his power. Equally, Hitler first negotiated and dealt with both the Protestant and Catholic churches in Germany and turned only against whatever components of the churches he considered a threat to his regime. In a sense, these targets were no different from organized Boy Scouts, political opposition parties, trade unions, and all the other organizations banned by the Nazis. Attempts to constrain or suppress organized religions, then, were a response to a perceived threat that their organizational infrastructure posed to these totalitarian regimes.

What about contemporary atheists in such countries as the United States or the nations of Europe? It is always *possible* that some atheists would, if they had the power, take steps to persecute religion or to hinder religious teaching. Fanatics can be found in all movements, and no doubt individual atheists are sufficiently antireligious and illiberal in their attitudes to resort to force. Generally, however, this is not the attitude of contemporary atheists, most of whom are happy to live and let live. There is nothing in the mere concept of atheism that could justify the use of force or other forms of coercion as legitimate means of transforming religious people into fellow atheists. Many atheists – with some justification – believe that the appeal of religion will diminish over time, as has happened in Western Europe and some other parts of the world, perhaps as a natural result of better schooling, health care, scientific progress, security, and general well-being. But believing this is not the same as attempting to "strip" people of beliefs.

In any event, what is meant here by "stripping"? Is it something that would happen against the religious person's wishes? Or is it something that might occur because a religious person is persuaded by atheist arguments? The former is unacceptable, and it has been our focus in the discussion so far, but the latter strikes us as perfectly reasonable: like other ideas, religious ones are fair game for examination, critique and, yes, they should be discarded by followers if they themselves find them wanting in significant ways. The same holds true for any other view, be it scientific, historical, ethical, economic, or political.

Myth 34 Atheists Want to Ban Religion from the Public Square

It is often claimed that atheists, or some of us, wish to drive religion from the "public square" or "public sphere." For example, Dinesh D'Souza says: "Atheists no longer want to be tolerated. They want to monopolize the public square and to expel Christians from it." He then adds what is really a rather different point: "They want political questions like abortion to be divorced from religious or moral claims" (D'Souza, 2007, p. xv). Later in the same book, D'Souza speaks of atheists wishing "to drive religion from the public sphere so that it can no longer influence public policy" (2007, p. 28).

D'Souza is inconsistent about this – he objects to the idea that religious morality should have no role in shaping our laws (D'Souza, 2007, p. 53), but apparently *not* if the religion concerned is something other than Christianity: he notes, in sympathetic tones, the "horrified incomprehension" of Westerners "when an Islamic government proposes to execute a woman for refusing to wear religiously mandated garb" (D'Souza, 2007, p. 50). Clearly there is a problem with this line of reasoning: it is either legitimate or not for governments to impose religious canons of conduct on nonbelievers.

Criticism of religion has its place in the public square just as much as religion does, but antireligious speech is often criticized in a way that goes beyond attempts at refutation to a suggestion that it is socially unacceptable. Consider Tom Frame's recent attack on what he calls "contemporary anti-theism," within which he includes such books as *The God Delusion*, by Richard Dawkins:

> When it becomes acceptable, and even admirable, to mock and ridicule a person's religious convictions and customs – and especially when the intention is to provoke an indignant reaction – the next step is to prohibit the expression of religious sentiment in all public places and forums. (Frame, 2009, p. 267)

But this claim verges on paranoia. Frame is Australian, and should be well aware that there is no prospect in his home country of any prohibition of public expressions of religious sentiment – though he claims, vaguely, that there are "signs" to the contrary (Frame, 2009, p. 267). If he were writing in the United States, where the presidency is intimately linked with religious ritual and involved in interaction with religious leaders, his claim would appear even more bizarre.

We must distinguish between the public square and government. It is one thing to get religion out of the law or out of government, but quite another to ban it from the public square, where all issues are open for debate. D'Souza is wrong to elide wanting religion expelled from the public square and wanting it not to be imposed on nonbelievers by the government. In a liberal democracy, the government has no business promoting or imposing religious doctrines such as doctrines about what gods do or do not exist, how it is possible to obtain salvation, what religious canons of conduct are obligatory, and so forth. If, for example, the government bans or restricts abortion it cannot justify this on the basis that abortion is contrary to a religion or to a religious code of morality. Theological considerations never constitute sound normative foundations on which to build public policies in modern multicultural societies. Societal consensus is typically arrived at by means of a process that is best described as "public reason." These are arguments that, while they could be in dispute among individual citizens, can at least in principle be supported by all reasonable citizens, including all religious citizens. To give an example, a report issued by the Canadian Royal Society addresses the use of "human dignity" in the context of debates on end-of-life decision-making. It notes,

> The underlying premise – namely that all humans are possessed of dignity in virtue of a special relationship to a God – is, however, incapable of being used as a basis of public policy proven in the context of a democratic, multicultural and multi-faith society that must cleave to the strictures of public reason in ethical deliberation. In the absence of a societal consensus in favour of, or incontrovertible proof of the existence of the God in question, and, therefore, the absence of overwhelming societal support for the metaphysical claims underlying this grounding of dignity, this account

of human dignity cannot be relied upon to justify normative guidance on assisted dying on a societal level. Religious people might choose to avail themselves of the guidance provided by their respective religions, but it is unreasonable to enforce normative views, derived from claims about a God, uniformly on a societal level given the multicultural and multi-faith nature of Canada in the 21st century. (Schüklenk *et al.*, 2011, p. e42).

This line of reasoning has been supported by leading Catholic thinkers such as Lisa Sowle Cahill, a professor of Christian Ethics at the Jesuit Boston College. Sowle Cahill writes:

> public policy discourse is actually a meeting ground of the diverse moral traditions that make up our society. Some of these moral traditions have religious inspiration, but that does not necessarily disqualify them as contributors to the broader discussion. Their contribution will be appropriate and effective to the extent that they can be articulated in terms with a broad if not universal appeal. In other words, faith language that offers a particular tradition's beliefs about God as the sole warrant for moral conclusions will convince only members of that tradition. (Sowle Cahill, 1990, p. 11)

In a similar spirit the Dalai Lama has gone on record saying,

> Any religion-based answer to the problem of our neglect of inner values can never be universal, and so will be inadequate. What we need today is an approach to ethics which makes no recourse to religion and can be equally acceptable to those with faith and those without: a secular ethics. (Mosbergen, 2012)

Freedom of religion requires that governments restrict themselves to protecting and promoting worldly interests. The state should avoid endorsing any religion, even if the endorsement is one-off and falls well short of full-scale establishment.

On this view, impermissible state endorsements of religion need not involve something as specific as the advocacy of a particular Christian denomination. Rather, the state has no business giving its endorsement to any otherworldly doctrine, however generic. It should not, for example, endorse the doctrine that a particular god exists, that there is an afterlife for human beings, or that we undergo a process of death and rebirth. The starting point is that the state knows nothing about such things.

That is not a specifically atheist viewpoint – many Christians, such as, for instance, the above quoted Christian ethics professor Lisa Sowle Cahill, and other religious intellectuals, also embrace the view that governments should base their decisions on secular considerations. Indeed, this view was developed in the seventeenth century by Christian thinkers such as John Locke, who were painfully aware of the horrors that resulted when rival religious views competed for control of secular power (see, e.g., Blackford, 2012, pp. 39–55). In advocating the removal of religion from government and politics, atheists and religious people do *not* advocate removing it from the "square" of public discussion. It is pernicious to characterize a claim that religion should not be imposed by the government as a claim that religion should be driven from the public square.

Credited to Jesus and Mo, www.jesusandmo.net

Myth 35 Atheists Don't Understand Moderate Religion

Though we often hear this claim, it is not easy to get a handle on it: what, exactly, is it that makes a particular religion "moderate"? Is it a "liberal" one (by some definition)? Is it simply a religion that is not (by some definition) fundamentalist? Is it any religion that accepts the basic picture of the natural world given by modern science? Is it any religion that does not participate in, or advocate, acts of violence?

John Haught is one theologian who makes the sort of claim covered by this myth. He alleges that the "New Atheists" engage with creationists, fundamentalists, and the like because they unconsciously privilege literalist and conservative positions over what he calls "more traditionally mainstream types," ignoring the latter and implicitly seeing them as unorthodox (Haught, 2008, p. xv). He suggests that these much-denigrated New Atheists pick on fundamentalist forms of religion not only because it makes their demolition job easier, but also because they have a "barely disguised admiration" for the simplicity of these views. After all, "The best evidence of their own attraction to an uncomplicated worldview can be found in their allegiance to the even simpler assumptions of scientific naturalism" (Haught, 2008, p. xvi).

Warming to this theme, Haught delivers a long denunciation of high-profile contemporary atheists for allegedly failing to appreciate modern-day Christian theology that does not interpret the Bible literally (Haught, 2008, pp. 28–39). He is highly critical, for example, of what he calls the "farcical complaint" by Sam Harris (in his *Letter to a Christian Nation*, 2006a) that the Bible fails to provide information about such things as DNA, electricity, and the universe's actual size and age. Haught mentions that during his 35 years of undergraduate teaching none of his students has ever asked him such a question (Haught, 2008, p. 33).

This point is worth dwelling on for a moment. Haught's answer to the question seems to be that if the holy books contained scientific information then any factual slip-ups would cast doubt on their messages in their entirety (Haught, 2008, pp. 33–34). Accordingly, he thinks, it is good that these books are essentially science-free zones. But that is hardly persuasive. Evangelists regularly employ what they see as accurate prophecies and archeological information to argue for the divine origin of the Bible. If the holy books had conveyed accurate information about such things as DNA, how much more impressive their arguments might be (compare Stenger, 2008, p. 176). Any small errors might suggest that the words were only *inspired*, rather than literally *dictated*, by God, but if such extraordinary knowledge – far in advance of what was otherwise available at the time – had been delivered to the authors of ancient holy books, it would be powerful evidence that the authors really were in contact with a transcendent, or at least vastly better informed, intelligence.

The absence of this information does not, of course, *prove* that the holy books lack divine inspiration. However, it would have been very easy for a being such as God to provide the human authors with words or information that would amount to very powerful evidence of divine involvement. It is not "farcical" to ask why this did not happen, and if it is true that none of Haught's students has ever raised such a point in 35 years, then we might wonder about the perspicacity of those students.

Haught goes on to describe "the business of theology" as being "to make sure that our questions to the Scriptures of any religious tradition will be directed in such a way as to allow ourselves to be challenged and even shaken at the deepest levels by what the text has to say" (Haught, 2008, p. 35). His idea of good theology seems to be the work of Paul Tillich, Karl Barth, Rudolf Bultmann, Jürgen Moltmann, and Gustavo Gutiérrez, whom he refers to in a sympathetic discussion of theologians who are said to have engaged fruitfully with nineteenth-century atheistic thinkers (Haught, 2008, p. 93). But do all supposedly "moderate" thinkers consider these to be theologians in the historical mainstream of Christian doctrine? Even if that were a widespread view among professional theologians, is it taught to Christian congregations in the United States? What about in, say, the expanding Christian communities of Africa? To what extent is Haught's preferred form of Christianity one that is endorsed by most of today's practicing Christians – even those who consider themselves moderate? And is this the theological viewpoint that exercises most political influence? As to the latter, it seems reasonable to be skeptics.

In the case of Christianity, it may be possible to synthesize a position that seems moderate enough for many people's tastes – and can be represented as matching the original Gospels. In this version, the New Testament provides us with a religion of love, peace, and justice, all embodied and epitomized in the figure of Jesus (Kahl, 1971, p. 98). Many people may, indeed, believe in a stripped-down and rather inoffensive version of Christianity along these lines. We understand this, and it seems clear enough that most atheists get the point. Our criticisms of Christianity are not based on ignorance that such a form of it exists – doubtless with many minor variations.

However, we should be skeptical as to whether Christianity took such a benign form during the early centuries of its development. The epistles of St Paul and the sayings attributed to Jesus in the canonical Gospels have a dark side, with an emphasis on authority, sin, and terrifying eternal punishments (Kahl, 1971, pp. 99–100), and, in any event, we doubt that there is any single form of Christianity that can justify its claim to be the authentic one (Kahl, 1971, pp. 26–27).

Furthermore, whenever we hear a religious view described as "moderate" we tend to ask a simple question: moderate about what? A great deal of what passes as moderate religion involves doctrines that strike many reasonable people as not moderate at all. For example, Mooney and Kirshenbaum (2009, pp. 96–97) seem to think of the Roman Catholic Church as moderate – but is it really? Think of the Catholic doctrine that people who are sexually attracted to others of the same sex are psychologically disordered, and that if they act on their attraction it is a serious sin. These teachings are expounded succinctly in paragraph 2357 of the Catechism of the Catholic Church (available on the Vatican's official website):

> Homosexuality refers to relations between men or between women who experience an exclusive or predominant sexual attraction toward persons of the same sex. It has taken a great variety of forms through the centuries and in different cultures. Its psychological genesis remains largely unexplained. Basing itself on Sacred Scripture, which presents homosexual acts as acts of grave depravity, tradition has always declared that "homosexual acts are intrinsically disordered." They are contrary to the natural law. They close the sexual act to the gift of life. They do not proceed from a genuine affective and sexual complementarity. Under no circumstances can they be approved. (Catechism of the Catholic Church, n.d.)

In support of this, the Catechism cites various biblical texts, along with *Persona Humana*, a 1975 declaration by the Congregation for the Doctrine of the Faith (also available on the Vatican's official website). *Persona Humana* claims, among other things, that homosexual acts are morally wrong and depraved:

> according to the objective moral order, homosexual relations are acts which lack an essential and indispensable finality. In Sacred Scripture they are condemned as a serious depravity and even presented as the sad consequence of rejecting God. (*Persona Humana*, 1975)

Furthermore, documents such as *Persona Humana* correctly claim to report teachings on homosexuality, and indeed other matters of sexual conduct, that have a long pedigree in the teachings of the Roman Catholic Church, reaching back over many hundreds of years. These teachings are not a recent innovation; nor are they matters of much theological controversy at high levels within the Church's organizational structure. And yet much of the Church's teaching on such matters is extreme by contemporary standards. Times may have changed, but the Church maintains a highly prescriptive and illiberal outlook on sexual interaction and sexual pleasure. For all that, Roman Catholicism gets kudos from Mooney and Kirshenbaum, and from many others, as a moderate form of religion. But what is the standard here against which these authors decide what is and is not moderate? Is it the bomb-throwing Muslim who is militant while the US Congress member who explains that he literally believes that the earth was created a few thousand years ago who is a moderate? As far as, for instance, Roman Catholicism is concerned, it is not a form of religion that *we* regard as moderate, but this is partly because we understand its moral teachings all too well.

Haught castigates atheists for concentrating on what he sees as immoderate forms of religion that lie outside the mainstream. But, as we have shown, we have good reasons to grapple with these viewpoints. One is that these "immoderate" forms of religion are not as unusual, historically, as Haught makes out. The other is that they are currently very popular, especially in the United States of America, the strongest bastion of monotheistic religion among economically advanced countries. Popularity translates readily into political influence.

Many Christians in the USA have beliefs that are far from moderate, theologically and socially. As Micklethwait and Wooldridge report (2009, p. 131), using survey data from the Pew Forum on Religion and Public Life, most Americans (59%) believe in a Hell where the wicked are eternally punished, nearly eight out of ten (79%) believe that miracles continue to be performed today, as in ancient times, while 34% claim to have experienced or witnessed divine healing. A massive 44% of Americans (and 70% of Evangelicals) reject the theory of evolution.

A more recent poll, conducted in May 2012, found that 46% of Americans believe that God created humans in their present form within the past ten thousand years. Among those who reported attending church on a weekly basis, the figure was a startling 67%, showing a very strong correlation between Christian religious adherence and preparedness to reject some of the most basic findings of contemporary science (Gallup Politics, 2012).

It appears clear enough that many Americans are outright fundamentalists in their approach to doctrines and religious texts. Moreover, it is possible to take an immoderate stance, while falling well short of fundamentalism. For example, Dinesh D'Souza is not a fundamentalist, but he is scathing about Christians who "devote their moral energies to trying to make the church more democratic, to assure equal rights for women, to legitimize homosexual marriage, and so on" (D'Souza 2007, p. 3). We submit that there is not much that is moderate in this kind of view.

In conclusion, atheists are not, as a group, ignorant of more moderate forms of Christianity, or of other religions such as Islam. Indeed, many of us may know more than most religious people about the various kinds of religion that are on offer in current societies. Why assume otherwise?

Why assume that critics of religion understand the phenomenon that they are criticizing less accurately than others do? We are familiar with moderate forms of religion; however, we tend to be skeptical as to whether any of these can claim to be privileged over the others, or over the not-so-moderate forms that continue to wield power and influence.

Credited to Jesus and Mo, www.jesusandmo.net

Myth 36 We Should Fear a "Fundamentalist" or "Militant" Atheism

It has become fashionable among critics of outspoken atheists to level charges of militancy, fundamentalism, or fanaticism against them, but it is difficult to be sure what this criticism refers to. Militancy is not necessarily a bad thing if it merely refers to activism – for example, trade union officials are sometimes described as "militant" if they take a confrontational approach in disputes with management. However, religious struggles often involve people who are militant in a much stronger sense: prepared to take up arms and use violence. Given that context, talk of "militant atheism" is misleading and should be avoided.

The phrase plays into the sort of paranoid fear-mongering that we find in *Gunning for God*, by John C. Lennox. Lennox suggests that contemporary forthright atheists are dangerous. He deploys the rhetorical tool of guilt by association, attempting to taint his opponents, such as Richard Dawkins, Sam Harris, and Christopher Hitchens, with the worst excesses of the French Revolution and Soviet communism (Lennox, 2011, pp. 92–95). At one point, he even warns, "history teaches us that movements that begin with intellectual analysis and debate can end in intolerance and violence" (2011, p. 92). So be warned: atheists might only be analyzing and debating *now*, but apparently this can turn very sinister.

What about "fundamentalism"? Indeed, what is a "fundamentalist"? George M. Marsden claims that fundamentalism began as an affirming self-description used by late nineteenth-century and early twentieth-century American evangelical Protestants (Marsden, 1980; compare Ruthven, 2005, pp. 10–15 or Ruthven, 2007, pp. 7–10). According to Raymond Converse, fundamentalists – as far as the Christian variety is concerned – "call for Christianity's return to the simple faith of the New Testament." He continues, describing a form of textual literalism about the Bible and a strong emphasis on the doctrine of sacrificial atonement:

> They tend to interpret the Bible in a literal manner claiming that it is the word of God and that the word of God does not need to be interpreted. They call for a direct belief in the divinity of Christ, that he was sent to earth by God to redeem us from our sins by his death on the cross, and that all of the commandments of the gospels must be obeyed to the letter. (Converse, 2003, p. 158)

Whether or not Marsden and Converse are historically correct, it would be simplistic to claim fundamentalism as an exclusive evangelical Christian domain. Since the late nineteenth century, social conceptions of fundamentalism have clearly changed, and the idea goes beyond Bible literalism. For example, religious fundamentalism is often associated with an extreme opposition to modernity through acts of violence, resistance to science and scholarship, and subordination of women (see generally Ruthven, 2005, 2007). Beyond the context of religion, we also find references to market capitalist fundamentalists, communist fundamentalists, and so on and so forth. What the label "fundamentalist" has in common in these cases is that those appropriately described as fundamentalists are not prepared to question the basis of their beliefs. This holds true as much for Islamic fundamentalists as it held true for the late nineteenth-century evangelical Protestants in the USA, or market capitalist fundamentalists with their unshakeable belief that "the market" will resolve the world's economic problems.

Are atheists fundamentalists then? Eric Reitan concludes his discussion of faith with the insinuation that the so-called "New Atheists" – Richard Dawkins, Sam Harris, and others – are fundamentalists. Reitan describes dogmatic adherence to certain doctrines, whatever the evidence, as a kind of idolatry, but attempts to distinguish this from what he considers to be true faith: that is, trusting in God and being open to encountering a transcendent truth. He then suggests that this sort of idolatry is "rampant" among religious believers and that the "New Atheists" are correct to identify and describe it. But they go wrong, says Reitan, in identifying it with faith and thus thinking that faith itself is evil. His last word on the subject is as follows: "This is the sort of reasoning that I'd expect from religious fundamentalists. But then, maybe that's what the new atheists are" (Reitan, 2009, p. 186).

Even if we agreed with everything that Reitan says, the most that he establishes is that faith, at least in one sense, is something rather different from dogmatism. If that is so, then someone who equates the two is mistaken on a particular point. But even if what Reitan is describing is a mistake, it does not follow that the mistake is caused by fundamentalism. The further segue into suggesting that intellectuals such as Dawkins are "fundamentalists" is not supported and gives the strong impression of letting off emotional steam.

Similarly, the Australian Anglican bishop Tom Frame discusses examples of what he calls "contemporary anti-theism," which he likens to religious fundamentalism. He says that it has "some of the characteristics of fundamentalism and, like all fundamentalisms, needs to be opposed" (Frame, 2009, p. 268). But he does not actually specify which characteristics of fundamentalism this "contemporary anti-theism" is supposed to show. For example, Frame refers to no holy text that any atheist treats as inerrant: many scientifically informed atheists may give respect not only to each other's writings but also to such classics of science as Charles Darwin's *On the Origin of Species* (1859), but they hardly treat these as inerrant. Outspoken atheists do not show extreme resistance to modernity through acts of violence, resistance to science and scholarship, and subordination of women. They certainly do not adhere rigidly to a position in the face of scientific findings.

In short, it appears that Frame, like many others, uses the word "fundamentalism" for its hurtfulness rather than its accuracy, knowing that it represents a tendency that is anathema to the people he is criticizing.

Another example of this sort of name-calling activity can be found in Alister McGrath and Joanna Collicutt McGrath's essay *The Dawkins Delusion? Atheist Fundamentalism and the Denial of the Divine* (2007). *The Dawkins Delusion?* is essentially a lengthy, and rhetorically overheated, book review of Dawkins's *The God Delusion*. The McGraths' main complaint is that Dawkins engages in a deliberate smearing of organized religion and religious belief that is, they say, fundamentalist in nature. Alas, we have scoured *The Dawkins Delusion?* looking for a definition of the term "fundamentalism," only to discover that it is not defined once. At best, there are hints of what the McGraths have in mind, but they make no attempt to apply a conception of fundamentalism to the facts in anything like a systematic, analytical way.

This lack of intellectual rigor does not prevent the McGraths from declaring that "fundamentalism arises when a worldview feels it is in danger, lashing out at its enemies when it fears its own future is threatened" (McGrath and Collicutt McGrath, 2007, p. 96). In fact, there is little evidence offered in *The Dawkins Delusion?* that atheists lash out at anyone, but that does not stop the McGraths from declaring that atheists do just that and so "fundamentalism arises." In another passage, they write, "Dawkins seems to view things from within a highly polarized worldview that is no less apocalyptic and warped than that of the religious fundamentalisms he wishes to eradicate. Is the solution to religious fundamentalism *really* for atheists to replicate its vices?" (2007, p. 47).

Alas, whether atheists mimic religious fundamentalism, remains unclear, due to the McGraths' lack of any definition of fundamentalism. Still, the concept has a history and there are reasonably familiar ideas associated with it – resistance to modernity, clinging to certain texts or ideas as unquestionable, and so on (see, e.g., Ruthven, 2005, pp. 5–34 or Ruthven, 2007, pp. 4–23). But the McGraths fail to make any case that atheists in general, or any particular atheists such as Dawkins, are best understood in this way. Like Tom Frame, they seem to use the word mainly for its hurtfulness, and in something of a fear-mongering spirit.

Even Julian Baggini, whose *Atheism: A Very Short Introduction* defends atheism and philosophical naturalism, worries about so-called fundamentalism among atheists. He refers to an occasion when he heard someone say that religion is a kind of mental illness and that they looked forward to a time when religious believers would be treated medically (Baggini, 2003, p. 88). We accept his word that this happened, but such an anecdote surely does not constitute credible evidence for the existence of atheist "fundamentalism" as a phenomenon requiring serious consideration. Baggini does add, correctly in our observation, that atheists overwhelmingly do not seek to oppress religious people. Rather, we support political arrangements in which matters of religious belief are left to individual conscience, not regulated by governments (Baggini, 2003, p. 89). We do worry about undue influence of religious ideologies on public policies, and we do worry about the acceptance of religious views of the world at face value when it comes to public debate (an example as good as any is the idea, often expressed by Christian politicians, that from the moment of conception the developing cell mass is already a fully-fledged human person, something that clearly flies in the face of what we usually have in mind when we talk about other humans).

At the core of fundamentalism – one of the main indicators if not the actual definition – is belief in the literal, inerrant, and unquestionable truth of the Bible (or, by extension some other holy book, or some theory or idea that is treated as one). That is not straightforward, because it can be difficult to establish in a precise way what a "literal" interpretation of the Bible actually is. The Bible is a work, or rather a literary collection, that is obviously open to a wide range of interpretations, and many passages are treated by all comers as metaphors rather than literal descriptions of events.

As a first approximation, however, Christian fundamentalists treat the Bible as the inerrant record of actual events in historical time (Ruthven, 2005, p.77, 2007, pp. 47–48). They believe in a Young Earth, perhaps only about six thousand, rather than billions, of years old. This leads to some amusing problems that are a matter of historical record. Reportedly the Sumerians developed glue some seven thousand years ago, that is, they would have created the sticky stuff about a thousand years prior to when the earth was created according to many Christian fundamentalists (Harris, 2006b). Fundamentalists also typically believe in a narrative wherein the myth of Eden and the Fall describes actual historical events thousands of years ago, somewhere in the Middle East. As part of this religious narrative, Jesus really was born of a virgin, really did die as a blood sacrifice for our sins, really was resurrected bodily, and really will return to earth from Heaven in judgment of the living and the dead. In this view, the Bible is inerrant – and there is a strong tendency to read it, wherever possible, as an accurate and literal account of past (and future) events.

A recent example of an influential elected politician holding such views is US representative Paul Broun. At the time of writing he is a member of the US Congress's Science, Space and Technology Committee. According to him:

> All that stuff I was taught about evolution, embryology, Big Bang theory, all that is lies straight from the pit of hell. It's lies to try to keep me and all the folks who are taught that from understanding that they need a savior. There's a lot of scientific data that I found out as a scientist that actually show that this is really a young Earth. I believe that the Earth is about 9,000 years old. I believe that it was created in six days as we know them. That's what the Bible says. And what I've come to learn is that it's the manufacturer's handbook, is what I call it. It teaches us how to run our lives individually. How to run our families, how to run our churches. But it teaches us how to run all our public policy and everything in society. And that's the reason, as your congressman, I hold the Holy Bible as being the major directions to me of how I vote in Washington, D.C., and I'll continue to do that. (Pearce, 2012)

At least Representative Broun allows a few more thousand years than many of his coreligionists, so there is time in his version of events for glue to have been invented. But one problem with Christian fundamentalism is that it collides with the outcomes of rational inquiry into the mechanisms of the natural world whenever they fail to confirm the "literal" biblical account. Thus fundamentalism can have antirationalist and antiscience tendencies. It also tends to be apocalyptic and to resist modern ideas of morality, justice, and sexual equality, as Broun indicates in the statement just quoted, when he stresses that his votes as a legislator will be determined to an overwhelming extent by the Bible. Fundamentalism's essential weakness is its inflexibility: its adherents' inability or unwillingness to depart far from the actual words of ancient texts or to question the doctrines that they find there.

Against this background it seems inappropriate to speak of "fundamentalist atheists," since even the most forthright atheists do not match this description. It is sometimes claimed that atheists go too far in disbelief. For example, it might be said that atheists can never be sure that there is no life after death. But we do not apply a policy like this in other areas of human experience, such as by suspending belief on the question of whether the Pope is a robot or whether eating a piece of chocolate might turn someone into an elephant (Baggini, 2003, p. 22). A firmly held belief is not the same as dogmatism or fundamentalism. Dogmatists do not merely hold firmly to a certain view but hold it to be indefeasible – that is, they will not countenance the possibility that they are wrong. A dogmatic atheist would be someone who holds that there is no way he or she could be wrong about the issue. As long as people sincerely acknowledge the possibility of being wrong, even if they cannot imagine a situation that would make them change their mind, they are not being dogmatic.

This is not to deny that there are atheists who are very strongly opposed to religion, or even that some atheists may sometimes show an element of unfairness when dealing with religious opponents – in fact, it would be extraordinary if this never happened. But that is not fundamentalism. There may be some people who could, by analogy, be described as "fundamentalist" in the way they cling to a political ideology and perhaps its founding texts, but we cannot think of any significant figure who could meaningfully be described as a "fundamentalist atheist." The same holds true for the other colorful monikers proffered in this myth, namely "militant atheist" or "fanatical atheist."

Myth 37 Atheists are to Blame for Religious Fundamentalism

Although it seems strange, it is sometimes argued that atheism – or at least certain atheist approaches – pushes people in the direction of religious fundamentalism, particularly by alienating them from science. The idea seems to be that if you tell some people that there is an inconsistency or tension between religion and science they will respond by saying, "So much for science!" and will thereupon adopt a more fundamentalist version of their religion. This concern appears to be driven primarily by parochial issues confined to the USA, where religious belief is much higher than in other economically advanced countries. If it came to the crunch, so the argument goes, the majority of US Americans would rather give up science than religion and its spiritual comforts.

Something like this is argued by Chris Mooney and Sheril Kirshenbaum in *Unscientific America* (2009). As they put it, "If the goal is to create an America more friendly toward science and reason, the combativeness of the New Atheists is strongly counterproductive" (2009, p. 97). "America," they say, "is a very religious nation, and if forced to choose between faith and science, vast numbers of Americans will select the former" (2009, pp. 97–98). Alvin Plantinga has advanced much the same thesis, that many Americans are hostile toward evolutionary theory (with a hostility that carries over to science more generally) because Daniel Dennett and Richard Dawkins, among others, have claimed that religion is incompatible with it (Plantinga, 2011, pp. 53–54).

Relying on polling data (Gallup Politics, 2012), Robert Wright has even suggested, though he notes that his suggestion is "highly conjectural," that there is empirical evidence for such a thesis (Wright, 2012). His point is that the data show a strong rise in 2012 in the number of people who agree that, "God created human beings pretty much in their present form at one time within the last 10,000 years or so." In 2012, 46% of Americans polled agreed with this, whereas the figure had been only 40% a year or so before. This, thinks Wright, could be the effect of atheistic scientists arguing against religion on grounds based in evolutionary theory.

Is any of this fair analysis? First, let us step back for a moment and look more broadly at the proposition put forward in this myth. What is meant when we speak of "blame" attaching to atheists? Is it blame in the sense of mere causal efficacy, or is some kind of moral responsibility involved? In the former case, it is at least conceivable that people's visceral reaction to atheist arguments and rhetoric could lead to them hardening their religious viewpoint into a more conservative, or even fundamentalist one. That revised viewpoint might, we suppose, be very antiscientific. We shall return to this in a moment.

But if you accept the view that we are morally responsible for the choices we make, surely it is the responsibility of the religious fundamentalists just what viewpoint they adopt. Attributing the responsibility to someone else is deeply disrespectful of a religious person as a moral agent.

That said, strategies of accommodation such as those suggested by Mooney and Kirshenbaum are problematic for other reasons. For a start, they insult the intelligence of religious believers, those who hold deliberately to a fundamentalist view of the world, presumably for their own reasons that seem persuasive to them. They also insult the intelligence of scientists, if the latter are asked to provide room for religious interpretations as they examine evidence and attempt to explain the world. Science should not have to operate with such restrictions, and scientists should not have to shut up (or compartmentalize their own thinking) if some of what they discover sits poorly with religious ideas.

Surely it is not surprising that religious believers who subscribe to the view that the earth is less than ten thousand years old, or who believe that we walked our planet with dinosaurs, will feel threatened by scientists who dismantle their fantasies. Some may fight back with their own pseudoscientific rationalizations of the evidence. As Mooney and Kirshenbaum note, however, "the vast majority of their followers aren't really operating on that level," that is, on the level of scientific reasoning. Hence, perhaps, the befuddlement experienced by some well-intentioned scientists when they "keep laying out the facts but [see] no one swayed who wasn't already on the pro-evolution side" (Mooney and Kirshenbaum, 2009, pp. 99–100).

But much of this discussion ignores large elements in the motivations and understandings of fundamentalist Christians, a group who are often patronized as if they are stupid, irrational, and driven by raw emotion. What commentators such as Mooney and Kirshenbaum fail to understand is that fundamentalists have reasons of their own for advocating the doctrines that they do, and for retaining their very conservative theological orientations. Yes, some of those are emotional reasons, but contrary to what is widely assumed, fundamentalists are not always unsophisticated, and their theological positions are integrated and complex. They are well aware of "moderate," "modernist," or "liberal" varieties of Christianity, but they reject these on theological grounds, generally with loathing. It is not just that they read the Bible literally wherever this seems possible – treating it, wherever they can, as an accurate historical narrative. Beyond this, they subscribe to a thought system that would fall apart if the narrative of a literal Garden of Eden were discarded. For these Christians, the approximate age of the earth, the specific creation of each kind of living thing, and the temptation of Adam are not dispensable elaborations but core doctrines.

Thus we are dealing with a structure of ideas that includes the introduction of sin and corruption into the world at a specific point in historical time, God's covenant with the Jews, Jesus Christ's sacrificial atonement for sin, and an ultimate, world-cleansing victory of God over Satan. All of this forms a single historical narrative that the Bible is thought to convey accurately, and it must not be watered down by treating it as merely metaphorical. Here, then, we have a closely integrated set of beliefs about the world in space and time, human history, and humanity's transcendent importance in the universal scheme of things.

For strict adherents to such a system of belief, a shift to some different theological position is likely to be enormously painful; in fact, it might be a psychologically impossible task for some or even many. The same holds true for Islam. Taner Edis, for instance, in his book *An Illusion of Harmony: Science and Religion in Islam*, notes that the majority of Turks reject the theory of evolution (Edis, 2007). For a true believing Muslim following the teachings of the Qur'an, the world was created in six days, with two allocated to putting together the planet itself, while others were needed for mountains, rivers and such features, as well as the stars and the seven heavens.

All this suggests the likely ineffectiveness of marketing biological evolution in a package with liberal theology, or a variety of possible liberal theologies, as Mooney and Kirshenbaum seem to suggest. For the most vehement opponents of evolution, it is not a matter of abandoning merely peripheral aspects of their religious faith. Evolution, along with the entire structure of scientific ideas that accompanies and supports it, is directly inconsistent with doctrines that these people do not construe as optional extras.

It should also be mentioned that the doctrines taught by fundamentalists are not out of line with those taught by the Church Fathers and other great Christian theologians. Although it is often claimed that early theologians favored nonliteral interpretations of scripture, that is somewhat simplistic. The methods used varied among early theologians, but it was not typical of major theologians in the initial centuries of Christianity to depart from the truth of the literal text. It would be more true to say that they adopted complex interpretations in which the narrative of actual historical events was preserved *along with* interpretations at other levels. Moreover, the accounts to be found in early theologians are similar to expositions by modern biblical literalists, in so far as the "literal" meaning can appear rather surprising and contrived when it is explicated.

Consider St Augustine, whom Gavin Hyman sees as a prominent practitioner of allegorical exegesis (Hyman, 2010, p. 86). We do not dispute this, but Augustine also emphasized the importance of the literal biblical narrative. For example, in *The City of God* he expressly defends such doctrines as that Adam and Eve were actual persons, that Paradise was an actual place, that the first generations of men and women lived for hundreds of years, that Noah's flood actually happened, that there are good and evil angels, and that hellfire is real. These are not recent doctrines developed in response to scientifically based atheism, but were orthodox in antiquity.

Although we could go on and deal with many other theologians in the long tradition of Christianity theology, this is not the place for a detailed history of the subject (fascinating though that might be). For now, let it suffice to say that fundamentalism is a modern phenomenon, but not because the actual doctrines of fundamentalist Christians are theologically unorthodox. In reacting to modernity, fundamentalists defend positions that traditionally had widespread acceptance – an acceptance that was threatened by modern developments, such as those in science, biblical scholarship, theological reasoning, and political ideas. Emphases may change, but the central points defended by fundamentalists are not historically innovative or heretical (see, e.g., Ruthven, 2005, pp. 16–18, 2007, pp.10–12).

Fundamentalist religious believers have strong reasons to stick to their positions, whether or not atheists are also criticizing more "moderate" or "liberal" religious positions. Those reasons are partly emotional and partly to do with the nature of the theological systems that they have been taught. The latter, in turn, are not as far from traditional theological orthodoxy as is often asserted – and indeed, nothing prevents fundamentalists from finding moral, allegorical, typological, or other meanings in the narratives that they take to be historically accurate, just as was done by the theologians of earlier times. Once all that is understood, it is not so surprising that the long-term polling trend has been for creationist views of human origins to maintain steady numbers of about 45% in the USA, dating back over the last few decades, with the very recent, but unsustained, dip to 40% now looking anomalous.

Conversely, we find it unlikely that less literal-minded religious people will be driven toward fundamentalism as a result of atheistic attacks on their beliefs. Leaving aside the unconvincing data used by Wright, we know of no empirical evidence for this claim, and it is implausible when assessed against all our other knowledge. Many religious people accept that the process of evolution really happened and that we are one of its products. Even if they have difficulty reconciling aspects of their own faith with the harsh realities of evolution, they are unlikely to run from the scientific evidence and fall back into fundamentalism. Like their coreligious fundamentalist brethren, they have their own well-integrated theological understandings that they are unlikely to abandon.

All that said, there may be another group that is worth considering, and here is where some effect such as Mooney and Kirshenbaum describe is theoretically possible. There is some evidence of a component of the American population who are not, generally speaking, Bible literalists, but are, nonetheless, hostile to evolutionary theory in particular (Coyne, 2012, p. 2655). Perhaps some members of *this* group could be cajoled toward acceptance of evolution if they thought it more consistent with their overall religious views.

That, however, is speculative. First, recall that the overall level of acceptance of evolution has been fairly stable for decades – so we doubt that it is being kept high by atheists' arguments. Second, members of this last group presumably have their own reasons to be hostile to evolutionary theory, perhaps because they see it as challenging human exceptionalism. In any event we cannot assume that they are much (or any?) more ready to let go of their concerns than those who adhere to a more thoroughgoing literalist theology. Accordingly, we doubt that good evidence will ever be produced to support Mooney and Kirshenbaum's thesis. An effect such as they describe cannot be ruled out, but it would probably be marginal, and, bluntly, we don't see it at all. Accordingly we reject as a myth the idea that atheists are causally responsible for the rise of religious fundamentalism.

6

Faith and Reason

Myth 38 Atheists Don't Understand the Nature of Faith

The idea behind this myth is that atheists mistakenly think that faith is just a matter of belief without evidence. Many theologians, in particular, insist that this is a naïve understanding of faith, and they describe more sophisticated or elaborate concepts of faith that atheists supposedly do not understand. These theologians try to persuade us that something more intellectually respectable is involved when religious believers speak of "faith."

Of course, atheists do not understand the nature of faith if that means *sharing* the particular faith. However, many atheists are former religious practitioners and are well acquainted with religious ideas of faith. We are also quite capable of developing a rational understanding of what it means for someone, and for his or her community of like-minded believers, to hold a faith or to believe on the basis of faith. At least in the United States, furthermore, atheists apparently know more about religious matters than their religious counterparts. That is the finding of a survey reported by *The New York Times* (Goodstein, 2010).

All that said, the real issue may be how far religious faith can be relied upon in understanding our world. Perhaps, then, we should delve a bit deeper into the question of what it is to have faith. Is faith merely belief without evidence, or is there something more to it? As we will see, theologians offer varied answers. Some offer definitions that would be familiar to any thoughtful atheist, as when Alister McGrath writes of

50 Great Myths About Atheism, First Edition. Russell Blackford and Udo Schüklenk.

"judgments made in the absence of sufficient evidence" (McGrath, 2004, p. 179) and "belief lying beyond proof" (p. 180). To be fair, though, McGrath thinks that *everyone* takes some matters on faith.

In any event, different definitions or explanations of faith are available. If atheists are not familiar with all of these, that is hardly surprising. They may still be on the right track in their understanding of how faith works in the minds of most believers. To get some perspective on this, we turn to some popular works by philosophers, theologians, and Christian apologists, in which they defend varying concepts of faith.

Importantly, Alvin Plantinga, perhaps our century's leading philosopher of religion who defends traditional Christian theism, distinguishes between faith and reason. He understands reason as an "ensemble of such faculties or processes as perception, memory, rational intuition (the source of beliefs about, for example, elementary logic and arithmetic), induction, and the like" (Plantinga, 2011, p. 44) or

> the cognitive faculties that are employed in everyday life and ordinary history and science: perception, testimony, reason taken in the sense of a priori intuition together with deductive and probabilistic reasoning, Thomas Reid's sympathy, by which we discern the thoughts and feelings of another, and so on. (Plantinga, 2011, p. 156)

Although this is a bit vague, it is perhaps sufficiently recognizable and clear for Plantinga's purpose. The question is then whether there are truths that cannot be known by reason, as thus defined or evoked, but which are known through an additional source or faculty: that of faith (Plantinga, 2011, pp. 46–47).

Surely, however, this is just what most atheists who have thought about the issue take faith to be: an additional source of knowledge that would, if reliable, deliver truths that are not available to reason (and are thus not based on evidence in the ordinary sense). Atheists might *deny* that it is possible to obtain such (alleged) truths as "God created the world" through faith. But why think we *don't understand* what is involved when a religious person claims to know such (alleged) truths through faith?

Things get more complicated when we read more widely in the theological and apologetical literature and encounter various explanations of faith that cannot be easily reconciled. For example, John C. Lennox is scathing about the idea that "faith" is primarily a matter of belief in the absence of evidence. He claims that faith is a matter of belief or trust, and that this can be either blind or based on evidence – he then attempts to argue that religious faith is based on evidence (Lennox, 2011, pp. 37–57).

Alternatively, consider the views of John F. Haught, a theologian who takes Sam Harris and other atheists to task for understanding faith as simply "belief without evidence," where evidence is understood as "whatever is scientifically testable, empirically available, or publicly observable" (Haught, 2008, pp. 4–5). He adds that contemporary theologians understand faith as "commitment of one's whole being to God," so Harris and others are using "a now-obsolete theology" (Haught, 2008, p. 5).

Haught elaborates by discussing faith as "a state of self-surrender," in which your whole being, intellectual and otherwise, "is experienced as being carried into another dimension of reality that is much deeper and more real than anything that could be grasped by science and reason." So asking people to give up faith in this sense is asking them to give up what they understand as "their lifeline to the infinite greatness of a divine mystery" and be content with the finite, if vast, universe described by science – which may be like being content with one less dimension (pp. 12–14). Later in the same book, he presents an even more elaborate explanation:

> Faith, as theology uses the term, is neither an irrational leap nor "belief without evidence." It is an adventurous movement of trust that opens reason up to its appropriate living space, namely, the inexhaustibly deep dimension of Being, Meaning, Truth, and Goodness. Faith is not the enemy of reason but its cutting edge. Faith is what keeps reason from turning in on itself and suffocating in its own self-enclosure. Faith is what opens our minds to the infinite horizon in which alone reason can breathe freely and in which action can gain direction. Reason requires a world much larger than the one that mere rationalism or scientific naturalism is able to provide. Without the clearing made by faith, reason withers, and conduct has no calling. Faith is what gives reason a future, and morality a meaning. (Haught, 2008, p. 75)

This is all very well, but how different is it really from the idea of believing in the "divine mystery" without what would ordinarily be regarded as evidence? However much he might protest, Haught is still describing a situation where the believer does, in fact, believe certain claims that are not based on what we would normally consider reliable *evidence*. To someone who hears this language from outside the circle of believers, and without the experience of being carried into "another dimension of reality," it all sounds somewhat delusory. Importantly, Haught fails to show how the total commitment of one's being to God that he describes and extols could enable us to know that God exists in the first place.

There are, however, still other explanations that we might consider. Much like Haught, Eric Reitan sees his task as defending the idea of faith against the charge that it "is just another name for intellectual and moral irresponsibility," that it is belief without justification, or that it means you believe something dogmatically, inflexibly, and "for no reason at all" – even if the logic of your belief leads you to commit atrocious acts (Reitan, 2009, pp. 165–167). Reitan does not dispute that this phenomenon exists, but he wants to convince us that it is not typical of how religious believers hold their beliefs. For example, he says, only a minority of his Christian students at a Bible Belt university have faith in such a sense: "For most, faith appears to be a decision made when reason and evidence can take them no further, a decision to live in hope, a hope that calls them to trust in a God of love" (Reitan, 2009, p. 167).

Reitan actually distinguishes two theological senses of faith, one of which he associates more with the Roman Catholic tradition and the other more with Protestantism. The first of these is the concept of *fides*, or "belief-faith," which is a matter of assent to religious teachings whose truth cannot be demonstrated by reason. The second is *fiducia*, or "trust-faith," which means placing your trust in someone, in this case God or Christ (Reitan, 2009, pp. 167–168). Might atheists go wrong if they imagine that faith always takes the form of *fides*, whereas *fiducia* is the more important concept?

But how far can belief-faith and trust-faith actually be separated? Reitan's own discussion acknowledges that they are related. The relationship should have arrows both ways: we may trust someone on the basis of beliefs we have about them, and we may obtain belief-faith as a result of the testimony of someone we trust.

However, there is an obvious evidentiary problem if the "someone" concerned is an invisible being such as the Christian God. You cannot know this being through ordinary this-worldly interactions in the same way that you can know, say, a friend – someone whom you have actually touched, spoken to, and shared everyday experiences with. Once you are asked to trust a being such as God, an inevitable circularity enters the picture. You cannot simultaneously believe certain things, such as religious doctrines, because you trust an invisible, supernatural source such as God, who has supposedly revealed these things to you, while *also* trusting the supernatural source on the basis of your acceptance of religious doctrines. At some point, you need to have a basis for belief that comes from outside of this circle. But what could it be?

To place your trust in an invisible, supernatural being, you must first believe that it actually exists. If that belief is not based on anything that we would ordinarily consider evidence, it seems that trust-faith presupposes belief-faith. In that case, atheists such as Harris do not, after all, seem so wrong.

All this brings out the fact that we often believe the testimony of other human beings because we have ordinary evidence that they can be trusted in the particular context. Think of a friend whom you trust not to lie to you about important matters that concern you, or a competent scientist who can be trusted about what well-established findings have been made in his or her particular field. By contrast, once we start to talk about trust in God, we are relying on a source whose very existence is open to doubt. Those outside the circle of faith cannot legitimately be asked to trust God on the same basis that, say, they trust a friend – based on ordinary dealings in the social world. Likewise, you cannot trust the authority of a holy book on such topics as the existence of God in the same way that you can trust the authority of a reputable science textbook on the current state of science in a particular area.

Indeed, Reitan acknowledges that we are not in a position to put our trust in the authority of either an institution such as the Catholic Church or a holy book. He responds to this problem by invoking what he sees as an alternative: faith is about trusting in God, not as a credible authority or reliable source of knowledge but as a savior, especially a savior from our sins. But this still does not escape the circle: any such trust, in turn, needs to be based on a whole raft of grounding beliefs, such as the belief that God exists, the belief that God loves us, and so on, and there remains a question as to where *these* beliefs come from. For Reitan, their grounding is ultimately in a decision to live in hope. This is essentially an inner conviction that such beliefs are consonant with our deepest yearnings that a hopeful picture of the world is true and that the beliefs could be true (Reitan, 2009, pp. 173–182).

If we follow Reitan's analysis, then, faith is something more akin to hope. However, this approach is unconvincing. Theologians cannot expect us to trust a being – God – whom we *hope* exists, but whose existence has not been established by what usually counts as evidence. Really, it is one thing to hope, despite the lack of evidence, that the world is under the control of a benevolent power. It is another thing to have experienced the actions of this power in such a way that it is rational to place your trust in it.

One very popular figure among contemporary Christians is the British author and Christian apologist C.S. Lewis, whose discussion of faith in his book *Mere Christianity* will be familiar to many of our readers. Lewis also describes two kinds of faith. In one sense, he thinks, it is about having the courage of your convictions, holding to beliefs that you initially formed through rational thought, even when they run counter to your fears, your current mood, and so on (Lewis, 1952, pp. 109–113). In the other sense, it is, once more, about trust, in the sense of putting all your trust in Jesus Christ, rather than in your own capacities (Lewis, 1952, pp. 114–118).

We think that one point should be conceded to Lewis. Many theologians and religious philosophers claim that there really is evidence for the existence of God, or that it can somehow be proved by an exercise of reason. This is, in fact, the official position of the Roman Catholic Church (e.g., John Paul II, 1998), and there is a large body of literature produced by theistic philosophers who argue that the existence of God can be demonstrated or shown to be probable.

We submit, however, that this is not what is normally meant by believing on faith – and it evades a problem that atheists correctly point out. The problem is that, at least for most people, beliefs about gods and the supernatural are not formed through rational thought but through such things as socialization, familiarity, and emotion. We submit that atheists are correct to see this as a problem that underlies talk of "faith."

At any rate, even theologians and religious apologists offer varying definitions and conceptions of faith. As a result, there is no single agreed-on understanding of faith about which atheists could be ignorant. What, then, can we say with any confidence? Well, the most common ideas that we find in the religious literature relate to believing certain claims about an invisible, supernatural reality on the basis of faith – something that is often urged on nonbelievers – or to trusting God, or Jesus, or some other supernatural source, throughout life's vicissitudes. We doubt that any thoughtful atheists are unaware that these usages can be found in the language of theologians, apologists, priests, and so on.

Let us concede, then, that a distinction can be made between (on the one hand) believing in God on faith and (on the other hand) trusting the God whom you believe in. The fact remains that religious believers typically believe what they are socialized into believing, or what they came to believe through some emotionally powerful event in their lives. In either case, the belief is not based on reason and evidence, but is rationalized as believed on the basis of "faith."

This is consistent with the depiction of faith in both the Hebrew Bible (the Old Testament) and the New Testament. Abraham was asked to sacrifice his son as a test of his faith, and Thomas was shown as believing only after he felt Jesus's wounds. He did not need faith that Jesus had died, which he could have observed, but until he actually felt the wounds he needed it to believe that Jesus has risen from the dead, something contrary to experience and evidence. Jesus says in John 20:29 that we are blessed if, unlike Thomas, we believe without seeing. Likewise, the Epistle to the Hebrews (traditionally, though no longer, attributed to St Paul) describes faith as "the substance of things hoped for and the evidence of things not seen" (Heb. 11:1).

Accordingly, even Dinesh D'Souza, whose *What's So Great About Christianity* stands as an ambitious contemporary work of Christian apologetics, acknowledges that there is something special about religious faith. D'Souza presses the point that we all need to show an element of trust in everyday life when we assume without direct evidence that, for example, our votes will be counted in an election, that the cereal we eat is not poisonous, or that our spouses can be counted on. In some cases, as he acknowledges, we obtain this sort of trust from experience of how somebody has acted in the past. In other cases, it is because such things as banks, maps, and electoral systems tend to be reliable. D'Souza might

Credited to Jesus and Mo, www.jesusandmo.net

well add that even when these fail we can explain the failures on the basis of wider systems of reliable and evidence-based knowledge.

But religious faith goes beyond any of this in making claims that are radically different. Claims about whether our souls will survive death, for example, go beyond our experience of the world – not just our experience as individuals, but our collective experience as we build an overall web of reliable knowledge (D'Souza, 2007, pp. 192–193). D'Souza nonetheless believes that faith-based claims can be reasonable, even vindicated. He is entitled to that view, but atheists are not wrong when we distinguish faith-based claims, for which ordinary evidence does not exist, from ordinary human knowledge, based on reason and evidence.

Throughout this book, we have much to say that is critical of D'Souza, but he is correct about one thing: religious believers should not claim to know about gods, immortality, Heaven and Hell, or an afterlife (D'Souza, 2007, pp. 194–197). He suggests that we should take an attitude to these things that combines doubt with trusting in what cannot be known. Well, that's one approach. We atheists take what we submit is a more reasonable one: we distrust beliefs that are not held on the basis of rational consideration, and on ordinary evidence such as used by scientists and historians – and by all of us in our everyday lives. If extraordinary claims cannot be supported through reason and evidence, it is wisest not to give them credence.

Myth 39 Atheism Depends on Faith, Just the Same as Religion

One approach to defending religion claims that atheism itself depends on faith. If that can be demonstrated, then atheists are no better off than the religious, and it becomes just as arbitrary to deny the existence of the gods as to believe in them.

That, of course, is not how atheists see it. Consider the distinction between reason and faith drawn by leading theistic philosopher Alvin Plantinga, and discussed in the previous myth. Plantinga understands reason as an "ensemble of such faculties or processes as perception, memory, rational intuition (the source of beliefs about, for example, elementary logic and arithmetic), induction, and the like" (Plantinga, 2011, p. 44) or "the cognitive faculties that are employed in everyday life" (2011, p. 156). Do atheists rely on reason in this sense, or do we also rely on some additional source or faculty that could be called faith?

If we use this understanding of reason and faith, atheists stick with reason and do not rely on faith at all. In applying reason, we have regard for *evidence*. For us, a crucial question is simply this: does the evidence point to the existence of gods, or does it not? Is there positive evidence against the existence of certain gods or conceptions of God? Questions such as this require standards as to what counts as good evidence and what does not, but those standards are not especially mysterious. For example, evidence is stronger if it is available to be tested by more people on repeated occasions, rather than relying on the testimony of a small number of people on limited occasions, or at the extreme a single person relating an incident.

As Julian Baggini states, ordinarily we reach conclusions on the basis of what we experience. For example, we conclude that the tea we are drinking will not poison us, that the chairs we sit on won't suddenly turn to liquid, and so on. These beliefs are not one hundred percent certain, but it would be wrong to call any belief that is not one hundred percent certain an act of faith. Atheists argue in a similar way when we expect events to be explained by naturalistic phenomena and naturalistic laws (Baggini, 2003, pp. 25–27). We draw conclusions from ordinary evidence and experience all the time, whether we believe in God or not. At the least, we need to be able to say that some propositions place a greater burden on faith than others: for example, it requires less faith to think that water is good for us than to think that Jesus is the Son of God (Baggini, 2003, pp. 30–32).

But might atheists have faith in some *other* sense? Let us consider what else "faith" might refer to in a debate like this, where we are looking beyond religious conceptions. For example, Alister McGrath argues that the practice of science relies on faith, in the sense that scientific theories cannot be proved to a standard of certainty. As an example, he notes that Einstein's theory of relativity was believed by most scientists even before the "gravitational redshift" that it predicted was observed in 1960. Thus, he suggests, Einstein had faith, in about 1930, that his theory would be proved. More generally, so McGrath's argument goes, scientific theories are believed to be true even in the absence of final confirmation that they are so, so long as they are sufficiently plausible to gain our trust (McGrath, 2004, pp. 95–98).

Relativity theory was attractive to scientists early in the twentieth century because it provided a unified and mathematically elegant contribution to fundamental physics, one that avoided anomalies that bedeviled the Newtonian system. In particular, relativity theory provided an accurate explanation of the precession of Mercury, which had been observed in the 1860s and stood as an embarrassment to Newtonian physics. It also made novel predictions, one of which was the deflection of light by the gravitational field of the sun, observed in the 1920s. McGrath's point is that the theory was believed before the gravitational redshift was observed – but why shouldn't it have been? Even before this point, there was good reason to hold the theory to be well supported by evidence, including by its demonstrated power to make novel predictions, one of which had already been shown to be true.

This was not a reason to think the theory had been *proved* in an absolute sense. Science does not purport to find that kind of proof. Rather, it seeks to discover explanations that are supported by evidence. These explanations are given provisional belief, though, as more and more evidence accumulates, a position may come to seem robust and very unlikely to be overturned. Conversely, a position may not be given up as soon as one of its predictions fails, since there may be some unknown explanation for that failure. Nonetheless, science does in fact abandon theories if they accumulate too many problems. Thus McGrath's argument fails. In the case of relativity theory, there was supporting evidence in its favor even in the 1920s. Physicists had good reasons to adopt the theory, and were not taking it on faith. Philosophers of science are very much aware of this. They have come to realize that with every new experiment that we make, the results of which support a particular hypothesis or body of theory, we strengthen the hypothesis or theory, even though we are unable to prove its truth in some absolute or definitive way. This is so, because the next experiment might prove that there is a fatal flaw in what was hypothesized (perhaps one that could be demonstrated for the first time only when a very large sample size was used). There is a well-known sense in which hypotheses and theories can be proven wrong, but they cannot be proven right (this is a leading theme of Karl Popper's work – e.g., Popper, 1963).

Religious apologists sometimes offer more fundamental arguments as to why atheists depend on faith. Dinesh D'Souza provides us with a good example. According to D'Souza, Kantian reasoning shows that there are limits to how far ordinary evidence available to the senses and ordinary human reason can take us in understanding reality. It shows that we must know in some other way than via reason and evidence that there is a greater reality beyond the empirical (D'Souza, 2004, pp. 167–178). This is a common theme of modern religious apologists. For example, John Haught argues that we have to start somewhere and that wherever we start is rightly called faith: for example, we have to trust that the universe has some kind of intelligibility (Haught, 2008). Similarly, Eric Reitan claims that scientists have faith – not in the sense of belief without evidence, but in having a kind of hope that naturalistic explanations will be available for the phenomena they study (Reitan, 2009, p. 11).

Reitan offers us a further clue to his own thinking when he disparages one kind of faith:

> I share with the new atheists their disdain for those who stubbornly cling to religious beliefs for no reason at all, without regard for arguments or evidence, with no thought to the implications of their beliefs or the objections that might be leveled against them. This kind of stubborn attachment to religious beliefs is what Dawkins and Harris call "faith." And while Alister McGrath, in *Dawkins' God* (2005), rightly criticizes the adequacy of this understanding of faith, it would be a mistake to think that no religious believers conceive of faith in precisely these terms. Many, in fact, live out their religious lives in the grip of a "faith" that is just as Dawkins and Harris describe it: they cleave to their beliefs out of mere willful stubbornness, without regard for truth, and they proudly call it a virtue. While there are (as I will argue) understandings of faith according to which it may be the virtue that religious believers claim it to be, this understanding is not one of them. (Reitan, 2009, p. 8)

Reitan's own understanding of faith is "a species of hope and a decision to live as if a hoped for reality is true," and he adds that this attitude "precludes intolerance, fear-driven violence, and persecution" (Reitan, 2009, p. 15). Is there an element of truth in any of this? Well, we all make some tacit assumptions. Consider the assumption that it is wrong to believe claims that lack some kind of observational or scientific evidence. If applied strictly, such a claim could not itself be established by observational or scientific evidence. The point is that our ultimate standards for believing some claims and not others, whatever exactly these standards may be, cannot themselves be supported by evidence or anything like it – the whole idea does not make sense. If we tried to support these standards, we could no longer say that they were our ultimate ones. We must also acknowledge that some scientists speak of faith in a sense that involves nothing supernatural – for example Einstein spoke of having "faith" that we will find the empirical world comprehensible (Einstein, 1954, p. 46).

But an obvious question then arises: if science is a matter of faith, perhaps along with all of our everyday judgments, how is religious faith distinctive? Given the emphasis that religion typically gives to faith, it would be surprising if religious claims were simply like all other claims. If everything we believe is a matter of faith, this suggests that nothing we believe is better evidenced than anything else. In that case, you might just as well believe that you are a poached egg and that this book was written by purple centipedes from Mars.

Thus there are limits. If we are going to say that ordinary beliefs – such as the belief that drinking clean, fresh water is good for you, or that jumping from tall buildings is a bad idea – are based on faith, then we have robbed the idea of "faith" of any distinctive character. And the same applies if we claim that science operates much like religious faith, despite understandings held by mainstream philosophers of science with regard to the state of scientific method. In particular, religious thinkers are usually not prepared to make novel predictions about what we will observe or to abandon positions that begin to generate an embarrassing number of anomalies. On the contrary, some will hang on to beliefs that were initially formed in nonrational ways (such as through socialization) no matter how embarrassing the facts may become.

A true faith position is very different from ordinary beliefs about the world, and it is likewise different from the established findings of science. It involves believing something for which there is no strong evidence – by our ordinary evidentiary standards – or which is actually contrary to the available evidence. At least for most people, belief in such supernatural claims as the existence of God and an afterlife can rightly be called a matter of faith: it is not supported by evidence, experience, or logic, and requires something additional.

Atheism is not a faith position because atheists do not require something extra that can be called "faith" to bridge the gap between experience of the world and extraordinary beliefs about a transcendent realm.

Meanwhile, Reitan's interpretation of what faith means to him is pleasantly peaceful. Unfortunately, most religious leaders and believers conceive of their faith in less modest terms. The history of Christianity, before its political power was largely broken, was one of a nakedly persecutory religion. Even now, many religious leaders and organizations display theocratic vestiges when they lobby for their specifically religious standards of conduct to be imposed on nonbelievers by means of political power. The claim that "faith" is something personal and modest is unconvincing when viewed in the light of history and contemporary political reality in many countries.

Myth 40 Atheism is Self-refuting, as Rational Argument Presumes the Existence of God

This myth appears in many forms – it is now a commonplace among theologians and religious philosophers, and we will say bit more about it in Chapter 9, where we will scrutinize a version of the argument especially favored by Alvin Plantinga: that biological evolution could not have been expected to give us reliable cognitive faculties. If atheism were true, so this version of the argument goes, and if our cognition had merely been honed by the evolutionary process, then we could not confidently draw any conclusions about the world (including the conclusion that atheism is true or that our cognition was honed by biological evolution).

While that particular argument deserves its own discussion, the idea often seems simpler. Whenever we draw conclusions about *anything*, we eventually need to make some assumptions for which no further argument can be given. We seem to have some basic standards for obtaining knowledge that cannot themselves be argued for, since any argument would appeal to those very standards. This raises the specter of extreme skepticism – a radical skepticism about everything we know, all at once.

How, on this approach, can we know that our senses and cognition are reliable *at all*? How can we draw any conclusions at all that we can place our trust in? An extreme skeptic might note, for example, that the world has seemed to show causal order in the past, but question whether it will in future (this is a version of David Hume's problem of induction). Such a skeptic might even describe fantastic scenarios in which we could be constantly deceived, for example, by a powerful and malevolent demon, and might ask how we could ever know this from within the deception. Descartes (1996 [1641]) notoriously tried to escape from skepticism of this kind by first proving the existence of himself and, from there, the existence of a God who is not a deceiver.

As this plays out in the work of contemporary religious apologists, we are told that we cannot trust our senses, the intelligibility of the universe, or our own capacity for reason, unless we first presume the existence of an omnipotent being who acts as a guarantor of these things.

Let us have a closer look at just one example of this line of reasoning. John F. Haught claims that we all start with a basic trust that the universe will prove to be intelligible and that truth about it is worth seeking. He claims that theology is about whether this can be justified, and (like Plantinga and others) adds that it won't inspire confidence if our ability to understand the world comes about through a process such as Darwinian evolution (Haught, 2008, pp. 47–50). In a rhapsodic passage, Haught claims that the reason we are able to have this kind of trust is that each of us is "encompassed by Being, Meaning, Truth, Goodness, and Beauty" to which we reach out with a trust that "arises from the deepest and most hidden recesses of our consciousness." We all participate in this when we believe that reality is intelligible and truth worth seeking. It is not unseemly to begin with this sort of trust, but only to cover it up and refuse to look for its justification (Haught, 2008, pp. 50–52).

Theists who wish to argue from a situation of extreme skepticism are in a difficult position. They want to take extreme skepticism seriously, while simultaneously making the assumption that it is not true. But once we go down the path of taking extreme skepticism seriously there is no way back: none of our attempts to reason our way out of it can be successful, because all of them are eroded by the extreme skepticism itself. If we take extreme skepticism seriously, we have no way to be confident of anything, including the existence of God. Anyone who tries to demonstrate the existence of God from within extreme skepticism will inevitably fail. Even Descartes had to make assumptions, such as the assumption that certain of his own reasoning processes (and some of his highly abstract intuitions about the world) were reliable.

What if, conversely, theists do *not* take extreme skepticism seriously? Once they take that approach, like everyone else does in practice, they begin to abandon their entire line of argument.

In fact, even the most extreme attempts at a total skepticism have limitations, as with Descartes, who held on to certain assumptions while trying to doubt everything. How, in fact, *could* we abandon the most basic elements of logical reasoning even if we agreed that God did not exist? Our commitment to these is anterior to any belief in a god or gods. Indeed, theists will often develop theological positions on the basis that even God is limited in the sense that he cannot do anything that it would be logically inconsistent to do.

The fact of the matter is that none of us *really* are extreme skeptics. Atheists and theists are at one in not taking extreme skepticism seriously and in working within a framework where our senses and cognitive faculties, including our memories, have some, admittedly limited, reliability. If we are told, as atheists, that our disinclination to take extreme skepticism seriously shows a kind of "faith" (which, of course, takes us back to Myths 38 and 39), this is an equivocation. Atheists depend on nothing more than our ordinary reasoning abilities and ordinary evidence, whereas religious adherents do depend on something more in reaching conclusions about supernatural beings and otherworldly states of being.

As Georges Rey points out, the ordinary practice of justifying beliefs does not require that we find a definitive answer to the doubts raised by extreme skeptics (Rey, 2007, pp. 251–252). Instead, we are continually involved in processes of obtaining and weighing evidence, which we do in the context of our vast, ever-adjusting, networks of beliefs about the world. For example, beliefs based on your memory can be checked against the evidence of your senses and *vice versa*. All these can be cross-checked against written records, the testimony of others, and so on – which can also be checked in various ways, including by obtaining the testimony of still others. To some extent, we can go out and test conjectures by seeing what happens in defined circumstances. Notwithstanding our cognitive and perceptual limitations, we slowly make progress in our knowledge of the world. Even if there cannot be an ultimate justification for all our beliefs at once (once more, how could there be, since this itself would not be justified if it is truly *ultimate*?), we have more reason to trust many of the things that we know than to trust any arguments that might be offered to us in support of extreme skepticism.

Rey observes that "almost everyone knows all this" – these standards are obvious, uncontroversial in everyday life, and shared by both theists and atheists (Rey, 2007, p. 252). Extreme skeptical doubts are not relied upon to settle other issues that arise in our lives. We engage in rational argument all the time without thinking we must settle these extreme doubts, which are wheeled out only in attempts to discredit atheism and to offer a contrived reason for believing in God despite the lack of anything that would normally count as evidence. You might want to ask yourself what the rhetorical purpose of this argument is in the arsenal of believers trying to discredit atheism, seeing that it would discredit their own takes on the world, too.

7

Religion and Science

Myth 41 There is No Conflict Between Religion and Science

None at all? The relationship between religion and science is complex, and we will discuss it in far more detail later in this book (see Chapter 9). For now, let's note that many contemporary atheists find support in what they take to be the methodology and findings of science. In response to this, it is often suggested that these atheists are wrong-headed, and that religion and science are completely compatible.

Consider, for example, the views expressed by Chris Mooney and Sheril Kirshenbaum: they note that religions such as Christianity have adapted themselves to modern developments, including scientific ones. Thus many Christians no longer read the Bible literally or take its every word as eternally true. They do not embrace the Ten Commandments as a complete guide to moral behavior. Many religious believers have found ways to reconcile their ancient faiths with new developments in, say, conceptions of human rights, and, indeed, with modern scientific discoveries. On that basis, Mooney and Kirshenbaum conclude by emphasizing the wide variety of religious responses to challenges from science and elsewhere, and they endorse the idea that religion and science are completely compatible with each other:

> The official position of the National Academy of Sciences and the American Association for the Advancement of Science is that faith and science are

50 Great Myths About Atheism, First Edition. Russell Blackford and Udo Schüklenk.

perfectly compatible. It is not only the most tolerant but also the most intellectually responsible position for scientists to take in the light of the complexities of history and world religion. (Mooney and Kirshenbaum, 2009, p. 103)

But this is weak. For a start, it is an *argumentum ad verecundiam*, as it appeals to the authority of the US National Academy of Sciences and the American Association for the Advancement of Science. Such arguments are more often than not deployed in lieu of sound analysis and argument, hoping that the relevant credentials will impress discussants to concede a point they were making. We do not know what motivated these two associations to make the statements they made according to Mooney and Kirshenbaum, though we might suspect some political motivation. It is, of course, true that any system of religious beliefs can adapt systematically to whatever well-established findings come out of science, so that any direct inconsistencies between the religious system and the scientific findings are removed. Over time, the religious system may come to look very different from its original form, but it can always avoid outright falsification simply by modifying its doctrines. For example, a religion that originally taught that our planet is a few thousand years old can come to teach that it is really whatever age has been discovered by science (a few billion years, in fact), while interpreting the original doctrine as a metaphor or a mistake. In fact, a religion can be interpreted *entirely* in metaphorical or symbolic terms, leaving no room for any inconsistency with scientific findings.

It appears that all Mooney and Kirshenbaum mean, when they say that "faith and science are perfectly compatible," is that it is always possible for a religion's doctrines to be modified to remove inconsistencies with scientific findings. If that is all that is meant, they are correct, but it is such a weak claim that no one is likely to dispute it. The fact remains that at any given time many religions make claims that clash with scientific findings, and many religious people resist modifying their beliefs to remove the inconsistencies. That is partly because they subscribe to integrated theological systems that cannot be tampered with easily: the beliefs that are inconsistent with science may not strike them as merely optional extras, but rather as core doctrines, logically related to other such doctrines.

Mooney and Kirshenbaum themselves acknowledge that science and religion have, historically, "posed tremendous challenges for each other" and that "science has continually usurped terrain previously occupied by Christianity" (2009, p. 101). Many assertions in holy scripture have been exposed by science as not literally correct; science has offered explanations for events that previously appeared supernatural, as with disease and impressive natural phenomena such as lightning; while the Darwinian revolution contributed to a broader desacralization, or disenchantment, of nature, when the intricacy and variety of living things came to be explained in naturalistic terms. As a result, we have reached a point where religious reasoning is no longer invoked, at least by scientists, to explain puzzling natural phenomena (Mooney and Kirshenbaum, 2009, pp. 101–103).

None of this, then, looks like a picture of perfect compatibility. That terminology can only be employed if it is intended in a very weak sense – a sense not well conveyed by such dramatic language. The most that can be said is that religions have considerable resources to adapt so as to remain formally consistent with scientific findings if they choose to do so.

Credited to Jesus and Mo, www.jesusandmo.net

At the same time, they also have constraints on their ability to adapt: for example, the new, adapted version of a theological system may be too watered down or thinned out to be psychologically acceptable to many believers, or it may involve abandoning an integrated set of doctrines that many believers have good reasons (by their own theological lights) to retain.

Furthermore, even if a particular religious system is modified so as to conform to all the well-established findings of *current* science, there is no guarantee that it will conform to whatever new findings constitute *future* science. In that sense, the religion would still be incompatible with science: its adherents would still be stuck with unchanging, faith-based dogma, while scientists remained "open to change tomorrow, next week, or whenever new evidence is found" (Stenger, 2012, p. 29).

In principle, of course, the religion might make further theological modifications: its body of dogma might not *necessarily* be unchanging. But, as indicated earlier, there is no guarantee that the required changes would happen, at least not without internal resistance that could lead to splintering. The problem here is that religion and science do not employ the same methods: epistemologically, they are very different. Though there may be no single "scientific method," and the actual practice of any scientific discipline may be messy and somewhat politicized, science is guided by empirical evidence in a way that religion is certainly not.

Myth 42 Atheists Confuse Two Forms of Naturalism

Most modern-day atheists are philosophical naturalists in a fairly general sense. We do not believe in supernatural agents, entities, forces, and so on, in addition to the physical world studied by science – though this does not mean that we must deny, say, the existence of the mind. We merely deny that the mind is a mental substance that exists in addition to the physical brain and its activities.

It is often claimed by critics, however, that the widespread acceptance of philosophical naturalism by scientifically informed people results from a simple mistake. We fail, so it is alleged, to understand the difference between philosophical naturalism and a merely "methodological naturalism" that science is committed to. Accordingly, we make an intellectual blunder when our regard for science leads us into philosophical naturalism – which entails atheism.

To make this a bit clearer, the critics argue that some, perhaps many, atheists confuse the two forms of naturalism. The critics thus attribute an obviously fallacious argument to the atheists concerned: science adopts an approach of methodological naturalism; therefore, philosophical naturalism is true.

See, for example, the views of Chris Mooney and Sheril Kirshenbaum, who begin their argument with a strong claim about scientific methodology: "scientific hypotheses are tested and explained solely by reference to natural causes and events" (Mooney and Kirshenbaum, 2009, p. 103). This is what they mean by the expression "methodological naturalism," and they go on to argue that adopting such an approach does not involve making any claim about fundamental reality. Rather, methodological naturalism is "simply a rule that is justified on pragmatic grounds" because of its record of "dramatic success" (2009, p. 104). Thus, they suggest, it cannot preclude the existence of God or of other supernatural entities. Mooney and Kirshenbaum appear to think that Richard Dawkins and others are confused here, deducing the nonexistence of God from science's practice of merely methodological naturalism, a move that they condemn as "an intellectual error" or even "a nasty bullying tactic" (2009, p. 104).

As usual, this myth has variants, and different critics of atheism elaborate it in different ways. John Haught claims that various high-profile atheists, including such authors as Dawkins (2006), Sam Harris (2004, 2006a), and Christopher Hitchens (2007), are purveying a philosophical position that he calls "scientific naturalism" and summarizes as follows:

1. Apart from nature, which includes human beings and our cultural creations, there is nothing. There is no God, no soul, and no life beyond death.
2. Nature is self-originating, not the creation of God.
3. The universe has no overall point or purpose, although individual human lives can be lived meaningfully.
4. Since God does not exist, all explanations and all causes are purely natural and can be understood only by science.
5. All the various features of living beings, including human intelligence and behavior, can be explained ultimately in natural terms, and today this usually means evolutionary, specifically Darwinian, terms.

Haught adds two other points that he believes are maintained by the "New Atheists" in addition to this description of "scientific naturalism." We provide these for completeness, but they are not of immediate relevance:

6. Faith in God is the cause of innumerable evils and should be rejected on moral grounds.
7. Morality does not require belief in God, and people behave better without it.

(Haught, 2008, pp. xiii–xiv)

The first five points constitute a reasonably fair description of views held by many contemporary atheists, and passes as a description of what we have referred to as "philosophical naturalism." Again, note that Haught speaks of "scientific naturalism." Other expressions that cover similar conceptual territory are "metaphysical naturalism" and "ontological naturalism" (Pennock, 2000, p. 190). The terminology involved in this debate can be confusing.

Dinesh D'Souza uses different terminology again. According to D'Souza, "The adversaries of religion, like Crick, Weinberg, Dawkins, and Dennett, frequently conflate procedural atheism with philosophical atheism." As he puts it, these atheists "pretend" (surely a better word would be "believe" or "imagine," since sincerity is not the issue here) that, since "God cannot be discovered through science, God cannot be discovered at all" (D'Souza, 2007, p. 263). Elsewhere in the same book, he makes a similar point when he says that science cannot simply rule out the existence of God a priori. He adds that, "It cannot make the case for naturalism or materialism because it operates within naturalism and materialism" (D'Souza, 2007, p. 164).

Thus a myth has grown up that atheists, or at least some of us, are confusing a naturalistic view of the world with the methodological naturalism frequently attributed to science. Sometimes the myth is embraced by science advocates who fear that science will suffer politically if it is seen as in any way undermining religion. These people may fear a decline in public funding for science, political opposition to teaching evolution in schools, or general distrust of science from the public.

Whatever the motivation for this myth, is it at all plausible? Well, there could, of course, be some atheists who make such a blunder – or use such a "nasty" and dishonest debating tactic. However, we doubt that the individuals named by Haught, D'Souza, and others make such a straightforward mistake. Nor does anything like this seem involved for most scientifically informed people who have been led to a perspective of philosophical naturalism.

Before we take this further, we need to be clear about what is involved in methodological naturalism (which is what D'Souza seems to mean by "procedural atheism"). In essence, the idea is that scientists avoid positing supernatural *causes* or *explanations* for the phenomena they study. Why might they do this? One reason would be if they began with reasons to believe that supernatural causes do not exist, or in other words that philosophical naturalism is true. If we knew that, we would infer that positing supernatural causes is futile. The direction would go from accepting philosophical naturalism to adopting an approach of methodological naturalism, and the argument for this would be a strong one if philosophical naturalism really were true. Alvin Plantinga makes the point succinctly: "Of course if philosophical naturalism were known to be true, then MN [methodological naturalism] would presumably be the sensible way to proceed in science" (Plantinga, 2011, p. 169).

Doubtless, however, many scientists support methodological naturalism without first being committed to philosophical naturalism. Indeed, some scientists do believe in the existence of supernatural entities such as gods, but they still refrain from introducing hypotheses about supernatural causes of phenomena in the natural world. Why would they do this? It might just be how they were trained, but their rationale might go deeper. They are probably aware that science has, historically, learned a lesson about the greater fruitfulness of using naturalistic explanations. Since the sixteenth and seventeenth centuries, science has established a good track record of explaining phenomena in this way. Conversely, positing supernatural causes has not proved to be fruitful for the purpose of explaining – and predicting – natural phenomena. A naturalistic approach to predicting earthquakes and tsunamis has proven to be more fruitful than engaging in a God-calming auto-da-fé such as described in Voltaire's satire *Candide* (2005 [1759]) to prevent earthquakes from happening.

This gives scientists good reason to develop a working protocol or policy of positing only naturalistic causes and explanations – this was, it appears, first adopted by physicists, but eventually it appealed to scientists more generally. It does not, however, give them a reason to refuse, dogmatically, to consider supernatural causes and explanations – even when these are proposed by others who are not scientists – or to claim that these are necessarily beyond the capacity of science to investigate. Indeed, the fact that such causes and explanations have been investigated in the past, and disconfirmed, shows that they *could have been* corroborated by scientific investigation if they had actually been true.

Science would not prove those claims to the point of certainty, of course, but it never does any such thing: it considers hypotheses and organized sets of hypotheses, and examines what evidence is available to support them. Often, though not always, that evidence will take the form of success in making novel predictions. There is no reason in principle why hypotheses relating to the existence, powers, motivations, and actions of supernatural agents could not be used to make novel predictions about what traces we will discover in the natural world. We could, for example, work out the likely order of fossils in rock strata if the story of Noah's flood were true, then check to see whether that is the pattern we actually find. Indeed, nineteenth-century scientists attempted this without finding the evidence they wanted (Kitcher, 2007, pp. 25–36).

To summarize to this point, it is true that modern science, as a social institution, employs a procedure of methodological naturalism. Furthermore, this may be justified. As Maarten Boudry and his colleagues have argued, we have good reasons to adopt a "provisional methodological naturalism" – committing ourselves to positing naturalistic causes and explanations, based on the historical success of this approach, without claiming dogmatically that supernatural ones lie beyond all scientific investigation (Boudry *et al.*, 2010).

If we accept this, we are certainly not required to take the illogical step of arguing from science's (provisional, historically conditioned) commitment to methodological naturalism to the claim that the supernatural (including God) does not exist. However, the same track record that supports provisional methodological naturalism also gives some support to philosophical naturalism: that is, the fruitfulness of a naturalistic approach to science, together with the fruitlessness of supernatural hypotheses when they were sometimes used by earlier generations of scientists, suggests that we live in a world without miraculous agents and powers. This is all part of the story of science's historical tendency to undermine religious views of the world.

The case for methodological naturalism is made by the past success of science in considering naturalistic causes for observed phenomena, and by the fruitlessness of past attempts to posit supernatural causes. If at some future time that situation changes then we may need to start invoking causes that are ordinarily thought of as otherworldly, miraculous, or supernatural – such as demons, spirits, magical objects, or even an intelligent Creator. If that happened, the practice of science would change dramatically, and would become more like what it was in the seventeenth and eighteenth centuries.

However, we have moved very far indeed from that point. At the moment, there is no realistic prospect of ever returning to it.

Myth 43 Atheism Implies Scientism

Atheists are frequently accused of something called "scientism." To take just one example, John F. Haught repeatedly accuses Sam Harris, Richard Dawkins, and Christopher Hitchens of "scientism" without defining what it is (Haught, 2008, pp. 18–19, 63). When we see such accusations, we need to ask first: what is scientism? Once we understand exactly what it is, we need to ask secondly: why is it supposed to be a bad thing? If scientism is simply signifying an uncalled for confidence that science by itself can determine public policy, or answer all questions, or displace the humanities, then atheism does not imply any of these things. There might be atheists who commit naturalistic fallacies – arguing naïvely from how the world is to how it should be – or other logical errors, but atheism as such is not committed to such views and does not depend on them to survive (Ridge, 2010).

In Haught's reading, scientism amounts to the idea that scientific methodology can answer all questions, including those relating to meaning, values, and the existence of God. Elaine Howard Ecklund offers a definition along these lines, which she attributes to campus talks given by Ian Hutchison: "the philosophical belief... that the only meaningful knowledge is scientific and that scientific knowledge has the authority to interpret all other forms" (Ecklund, 2010, pp. 108–109; see also p. 137). These understandings of scientism are broadly consistent with current-day dictionary definitions. They are also consistent with a long history of pejorative use of the word "scientism" by philosophers and sociologists who are hostile to certain philosophical trends that became prominent in the late nineteenth and early twentieth centuries – particularly logical positivism. In some cases, as Pennock mentions, the talk of "scientism" is favored and promoted by "antiscientific cultural relativists" who deny the ability of science to obtain knowledge about the world (Pennock, 2000, p. 211).

But is the scientism charge a straw man? Does anyone seriously involved in modern debates about the existence of God literally believe in scientism, as defined above? Perhaps Alex Rosenberg gets close (2011, pp. 6–8): he attempts to reclaim the term, and indeed flaunts it as a badge of honor. But Rosenberg's position is a truly extreme one within current philosophy (for example he denies that our thoughts ever actually manage to be about things in the real world). Rosenberg notwithstanding, is scientism, as we have defined it, a position that typifies, or is entailed by, atheism?

Scientism, defined strictly and formally, would appear to be self-contradictory, since it makes a philosophical claim that does not itself seem to be arrived at by applying a scientific methodology. Or if it is, the concept of scientific methodology is being stretched so far as to render any statement in support of scientism almost trivial. At the same time, Haught and others are unnecessarily limiting the contribution that science can make to knowledge. Haught gives such examples of science's limits as: how do I know someone loves me? How do I understand a work of literature? How do I, or should I, respond to nature? In all these cases, he thinks, a leap of trust is necessary. We should open ourselves and make ourselves vulnerable in such cases, and so it is with the experience of God (Haught, 2008, pp. 44–47).

However, these examples are poor analogies with claims about an unseen, supernatural being such as God. For a start, atheists do not have to deny that we are responsive to each other and that most of us have considerable innate or learned ability to know when someone loves us. That is true, but there is also objective evidence that can be pointed to in arguing whether someone actually does love someone else. Prabir Ghosh discusses this well. He points out that somebody else's love manifests itself in quite tangible ways:

> It comes in the form of a cool touch on your fevered forehead when you are sick or in the form of a plate of hot rice carefully served with your favorite curries. A friend's love is explicit when he spends sleepless nights in the hospital corridor during your father's illness or when he goes home with a bruised arm trying to save you from the local goons. (Ghosh, 2009, p. 265)

It is not simply a matter that belief in someone's love *works*, in the sense that it might provide comfort or inspiration. There are manifestations that can provide justification for our beliefs that we are loved by various people in our lives, even if we process the information somewhat intuitively rather than trying to weigh it up consciously. It is worth noting that there is no in-principle reason why we should not be able, at some point in the future, to know whether someone loves us, provided we can get a definitional handle on the complex human phenomenon of love. Once that is achieved, conceptually nothing would stop neurobiologists from investigating this phenomenon. Haught has no reason to assume that love is beyond the realm of scientific investigation and understanding. In fact, scientific work on the neural correlates of both romantic and altruistic love continues apace (e.g., Bartels and Zeki, 2004).

When we respond instinctively or intuitively to nature, it is unclear precisely what knowledge we are gaining. We may experience natural phenomena as beautiful, sublime, astonishing, and so on, but that is not primarily a cognitive experience. Perhaps our emotional responses do short-circuit some of our reasoning and give us factual knowledge in advance, but that can only be because this knowledge (perhaps of the immensity of a canyon or the intricacy of a spider's web) is available through our senses – and of course these sorts of things are objectively measurable.

The process of interpreting and evaluating works of literature is rather different, but even this is not a process that transcends all evidence. Imagine, for example, that a novel leaves some events implicit and does not state that they happened in so many words. Here we can argue about whether or not they took place by proposing hypotheses that are then testable at least to the extent that they make such things as character motivations more coherent. There is nothing about this that transcends ordinary rationality. That is not to claim that the processes followed by literary critics (or ordinary readers) are exactly the same as those of scientists – certainly they are rather remote from those used by physicists or chemists. We agree that it is possible to engage in rational inquiry in fields such as literary scholarship and criticism without using the methods of, say, physicists, or even those of cognitive psychologists – and no atheist need dispute this. Nor, however, need an atheist conclude that something supernatural is involved. Again, reasoning in secular ethics does not ape the methods of the natural sciences but nor does it require the belief in a god.

Just as literary critics and other scholars working in the humanities make use of the processes of reason, the methods of science involve conjectures, or imaginative leaps. Scientists do, in fact, make themselves vulnerable when they propose hypotheses. But what gives science a degree of reliability – and this also applies to the work of historians and even that of literary critics – is that conjectures are subjected to various kinds of cognitive scrutiny. That is what atheists typically see as lacking in claims about the existence of God. It is one thing to conjecture that God exists, but quite another to provide the conjecture with intellectual support.

Finally, we acknowledge that some atheists – us included – are, indeed, very impressed by science and its achievements. So we should be. Over the past four or five hundred years, science has achieved great successes in investigating phenomena that had previously eluded all human efforts. As it has progressed, science has developed a new, and increasingly complete and compelling, description of the cosmos. Although that description is, and may always be, incomplete, scientists continue to discover more, and science is the only reliable guide that we have to the overall reality in which we find ourselves. Without science, we are greatly confined in how much of the world we can even begin to understand. If merely acknowledging this is "scientism," then it's not clear why scientism is a bad thing.

However, we can appreciate the power and success of science without denigrating the work of scholars in disciplines that are not usually regarded, at least in the English-speaking world, as part of science. There is much of importance to be discovered and assessed using techniques that we don't usually label "scientific," especially about human history and culture. Some of the contemporary criticism of so-called "scientism" comes from humanities scholars who fear that the humanities will be dishonored, and perhaps deprived of future political – and, as importantly, financial – support. This might happen if the power of scientific investigation is exaggerated or the ability of the humanities to shed light on important questions is doubted.

Though this fear is understandable, it does not follow that we have reliable ways of investigating and justifying claims about the existence of gods and other invisible, supernatural entities or forces. In principle, the hypothesis that God exists might be testable by some scientific means, if its proponents were prepared to make predictions about how God acts and affects the observable world (then accept falsification of the hypothesis if the predicted effects were not observed). In practice, however, it does not work like that. Any falsification will be explained away in one manner or another. Thanks more to the attitudes of theists than the limitations of science, the God hypothesis is untestable by researchers in either the natural or social sciences. As formulated by believers, it is not a scientific hypothesis to begin with.

Myth 44 Evolutionary Theory is a Form of Atheistic Religion

There is something strikingly unreal about creationists' attempts to discredit the theory of evolution, when they equate it with their religious view that the earth was formed by a single magical creator a few thousand years ago. It is discouraging that at this point in time in the twenty-first century we would still have to defend the view that evolution led to our being what and who we are. But that is the situation.

Earlier in this book (see Myth 1) we discussed the idea that atheism itself is a kind of religion. A variant of this idea is that evolutionary theory is best regarded as a sort of atheistic religion. This myth crops up frequently, as does the idea that evolutionary theory is inherently antireligious. To take an older example of this way of thinking, an opinion piece in *The Evening Independent*, dated December 14, 1961, is entitled "Bar Atheism From Schools." Here, Paul Harvey, an American radio broadcaster, demands that evolutionary theory should not be taught in American schoolrooms:

> If Christmas in the classroom is to be outlawed by our genuine determination to preserve, protect and defend our Constitution . . . Then let's be consistent! I'm fed up with hearing my son come home mouthing "scientific" theories in diametrical contradiction to the Word of God. If we are going to keep religion out of the school, then get the schools out of religion!

Harvey was not just any broadcaster: according to ABC News (Zecchino and Schabner, 2009) he was the "most listened to man" in broadcasting. Harvey goes on to add:

> parents are constantly bombarded by their youngsters with questions on evolution. These questions are brought home from the public schoolroom, the public schoolteacher, the school textbook. There is no foundation of fact, whatever, in the scientific supposition that men came from monkeys and they, from lower creatures. These theories may satisfy the feeble finite intellects of atheists and agnostics who have no better explanation for creation. But these teachings, opposing religious teachings, are at least as much out of bounds as they say Christ is in the classroom. (Harvey, 1961)

The writer may be confused about what the United States of America's First Amendment requires. It does not forbid the teaching of any facts or opinions that may be inconsistent with one or another of the many religious views that are on offer, though it certainly does forbid the teaching of religion as fact (if the teaching happens in public schools). Though Harvey's argument is not expressed rigorously, perhaps he thinks evolutionary theory is itself a religion, or something similar. Such views are certainly not uncommon, and they are not confined to moralistic broadcasters and journalists.

In their scholarly and well-regarded study of religious freedom, Rex Adhar and Ian Leigh complain about the attitude taken by the American courts to evolutionary theory. They suggest that the courts have embraced "a liberal form of rationality" by treating evolution as "an objective theory (lacking in religious assumptions or foundations), rather than a rival, quasi-religious worldview, as many of its critics maintain" (Adhar and Leigh, 2005, pp. 250–251). Their discussion refers to the *Tangipahoa* case (*Tangipahoa Parish Board of Education v. Freiler*, 185 F.3d 337 (1999)). This was decided by the United States Court of Appeals for the Fifth Circuit, and the US Supreme Court subsequently declined to hear an appeal (530 U.S. 1251 (2000)). In this case, the courts struck down the following disclaimer that was prescribed for reading before any presentation of evolutionary theory to students:

> It is hereby recognized by the Tangipahoa Board of Education, that the lesson to be presented, regarding the origin of life and matter, is known as the Scientific Theory of Evolution and should be presented to inform students of the scientific concept and not intended to influence or dissuade the Biblical version of Creation or any other concept.

Ahdar and Leigh claim that the courts do not provide a level playing field if a school teaching evolution cannot offer a disclaimer that involves calling it a theory and advising students to form their own opinions. They view the *Tangipahoa* disclaimer as a "mere invitation to exercise critical rationality and . . . reminder of [the students'] right to hold differing beliefs" (Adhar and Leigh, 2005, p. 252).

But contrary to the view favored by Ahdar and Leigh, modern evolutionary theory is not a quasi-religious alternative to religion, any more than any other body of well-established scientific theory. It is, in fact, a synthesis of scientific developments since the mid-nineteenth century. It draws on Charles Darwin's masterpiece, *On the Origin of Species* (1859), but also on more recent work in paleontology, genetics, and many other fields. Many lines of inquiry converge to provide empirical support, and evolution has emerged as *the* central organizing theory in the biological sciences.

We can now trace the evolution of particular forms of life, date the age of the earth and the sun, and correlate the required ages of particular fossilized organisms to the ages of independently dated rock strata. There is an enormous, and constantly growing, body of data that consistently supports the story of life's evolution, and new observations from all relevant fields of science invariably slot into the "right" places in the narrative. Indeed, the theory of evolution, the overall Darwinian model, is now so well confirmed, by so much data, that it has become almost inconceivable that its essentials could be wrong. Though all scientific findings are considered provisional, it would be very surprising indeed if it turned out, after all, that the sun revolves around the earth. Something similar can be said about the in-principle possibility that evolutionary theory's essentials are incorrect.

The essentials of contemporary evolutionary theory are robust – they have so much empirical support that they are almost certainly true. They fit, moreover, within an emerging scientific picture of the universe in space and time, one that has been developed by such fields as geology and astrophysics. Evolution is well-established science, not quasi-religion. Even the term "theory" is something of a misnomer, if the word is taken in its everyday sense of "speculation" or "conjecture" or even "guess." In science, a theory is an explanatory model that may well, as is the case with evolution, be confirmed by overwhelming evidence. Scientists usually employ the word "hypothesis" for a more conjectural idea that stands in need of testing, but the theory of evolution is not a mere hypothesis.

For better or worse, evolution does conflict with some religious claims, but that is because some religions, particularly some popular kinds of Christianity, make themselves vulnerable to refutation by making claims that are open to empirical refutation. That is their prerogative, but it has consequences. Meanwhile, evolutionary biology was not contrived for the purpose of discrediting religion, or particular theological positions. It is the result of incremental investigation of nature using the ordinary methods of rational inquiry supplemented by the more precise "scientific" methods that became increasingly available during the past four centuries – such as instruments that extend the human senses, mathematical modeling, and apparatus that enables many decisive experiments to be done. Evolutionary theory is science. It is sound, well-supported science. In no way can it be dismissed as some kind of religion or quasi-religion.

Myth 45 Albert Einstein Professed a Belief in God

Given Einstein's reputation as one of the crowning geniuses of the twentieth century, and one of the greatest contributors to our scientific knowledge of the universe, his endorsement of theistic religion would bring considerable prestige to the theist cause, and thus he is often commandeered for it. For instance, Dvir Abramovich, a Jewish Studies scholar at the University of Melbourne, says in a commentary published in *The Sydney Morning Herald*:

> Yet that iconic scientist Einstein, believed that God represented a great mind that sustained the laws of nature. We know for sure that he was not stupid or delusional. He famously remarked, "God doesn't play with the universe" and noted, when referring to the extraordinary intricacies of the universe: "The most beautiful thing we can experience is the mysterious. It is the source of all true art and science." Einstein believed that a humble, open-ended religious attitude to the cosmos was preferable to a completely non-religious approach. (Abramovich, 2009)

In context, Abramovich is defending theistic religion against the views of outspoken atheists. He appeals to the authority of Einstein as if this makes theistic religion more plausible and undermines atheism.

In fairness to Abramovich and others, Einstein did sometimes express sympathy for religious viewpoints, and he often referred to God. Indeed, he was unwilling to contest others' belief in God, and preferred that they have such a belief if it was their only way to conceptualize a "transcendental outlook" on life. Based on this point, Karen C. Fox and Aries Keck conclude: "Einstein may have had a complex understanding of the term, but he did believe in God" (Fox and Keck, 2004, p. 126). Alister and Joanna Collicutt McGrath criticize Richard Dawkins for refusing to acknowledge Einstein as a religious believer (McGrath and Collicutt McGrath, 2007, p. 22), though in an endnote to their book they are at least prepared to acknowledge pantheism as "one aspect of Einstein's religious ideas" (p. 69).

Very well, but what are the facts? Einstein was at pains to explain that he did not believe in a personal deity. He also did not believe in polytheistic gods, but it did not prevent him from composing the aphorism: "Whoever undertakes to set himself up as judge in the field of Truth and Knowledge is shipwrecked by the laughter of the gods" (Einstein, 1954, p. 28). He was, in short, willing to invoke God or the gods in figures of speech. In a famous letter written in German to the philosopher Eric Gutkind, he set the record straight: "the word God is for me nothing more than the expression and product of human weaknesses, the Bible a collection of honourable but still primitive legends which are nevertheless pretty childish" (CBC, 2008).

Though born into a Jewish family, Einstein clearly had little time for Judaism, since he writes, in that same letter, "for me, the Jewish religion like all other religions is an incarnation of the most childish superstitions" (CBC, 2008). In another letter, written in 1954, he states, "I do not believe in a personal God and I have never denied this but have expressed it clearly .... If something is in me which can be called religious then it is the unbounded admiration for the structure of the world so far as our science can reveal it" (CBC, 2008).

As Dennis Overbye states in a 2008 *New York Times* article, Einstein "lost his religion at the age of 12, concluding that it was all a lie, and he never looked back" (Overbye, 2008). Overbye sums up the issue clearly and, in our view, correctly:

> Einstein consistently characterized the idea of a personal God who answers prayers as naive, and life after death as wishful thinking. But his continual references to God – as a metaphor for physical law; in his famous rebuke to quantum mechanics, "God doesn't play dice"; and in lines like the endlessly repeated, "Science without religion is lame, religion without science is blind" – has led some wishful thinkers to try to put him in the camp of some kind of believer or even, not long ago, to paint him as an advocate of intelligent design. (Overbye, 2008)

Einstein's particular understanding of science, and especially of religion, led him to reject the existence of such a personal God. The more we become imbued with a sense of the "ordered regularity" of events, he thought, the less we would find room for other causes by its side. He agreed with Spinoza that a limited causality is, in reality, no causality at all. He added that, "the doctrine of a personal God interfering with natural events" cannot be definitively refuted, since there will always be gaps in our scientific knowledge where God's activities can be placed. In Einstein's view, however, such a strategy would be both "unworthy" and "fatal":

> For a doctrine which is able to maintain itself not in the clear light but only in the dark, will of necessity lose its effect on mankind, with incalculable harm to human progress. In their struggle for the ethical good, teachers of religion must have the stature to give up the doctrine of a personal God, that is, give up that source of fear and hope which in the past placed such power in the hands of priests. (Einstein, 1954, p. 48)

In a piece entitled "The World As I See It," first published in 1930, Einstein succinctly stated his views about God and conventional theistic religion. He claimed to be a religious man only in his powerful sense of the mysterious. In this piece, he equates the experience of mystery with, "A knowledge of the existence of something we cannot penetrate, our perceptions of the profoundest reason and the most radiant beauty, which only in their most primitive forms are accessible to our minds." He goes on to express his disbelief in any conventional God who rewards, punishes, and possesses volition:

> I cannot conceive of a God who rewards and punishes his creatures, or has a will of the kind that we experience in ourselves. Neither can I nor would I want to conceive of an individual that survives his physical death; let feeble souls, from fear or absurd egoism, cherish such thoughts. I am satisfied with the mystery of the eternity of life and with the awareness and a glimpse of the marvelous structure of the existing world, together with the devoted striving to comprehend a portion, be it ever so tiny, of the Reason that manifests itself in nature. (Einstein, 1954, p. 11)

According to John Haught, Einstein can be seen as representing "countless scientists and philosophers" who reject the idea of a personal God "by insisting firmly that the lawfulness of nature is incompatible with trust in a personal, responsive deity" (Haught, 2008, p. 78). Haught goes on to explain that although Einstein considered himself religious it was only in the sense of having "a strong sense of cosmic mystery and a passionate conviction that we need to commit ourselves to superpersonal values." For example he believed that what Haught calls "a religious devotion to truth" was required for good science, and that this was what he meant in his famous assertion that "science without religion is lame." Likewise his claim that "God does not play dice with the universe," meant in context that the universe is lawful and intelligible. For Einstein, indeed, the idea of a personal God was the main source of conflict between religion and science (Haught, 2008, p. 80). On occasion in this book we have criticized Haught, but here he appears quite accurate. Einstein's "religion," if it can be called that, was not a theistic one.

As we have seen, Einstein's assertion that "science without religion is lame" is part of his aphorism "science without religion is lame, religion without science is blind" (Einstein, 1954, p. 46). In context, this sums up his view that science can provide knowledge of the world that could guide us in actually achieving, or obtaining, the goals and values posited by religion. Without this, our attempts are "blind." Conversely, for Einstein, the practice of science requires what he saw as a kind of "religious" faith – a trust that the empirical world will yield intelligible answers when we investigate it. Elsewhere in *Ideas and Opinions*, he suggests what seems to be a stronger assumption, "that this universe of ours is something perfect and susceptible to the rational striving for knowledge" (Einstein, 1954, p. 52). In the absence of that assumption, science would be "lame."

In his book *The Unexpected Einstein*, Denis Brian devotes a chapter to Einstein's religious views. He puts the position like this:

> Throughout his adult life, in his conversations and writings, Einstein constantly used God's name to explain the universe. Yet he didn't believe in the popular concept of God as the Supreme Being. This confused people almost as much as his theories did. He didn't believe in angels, either, or devils, ghosts, hell, or heaven, nor in the theory that one's fate is written in the stars, nor that prayers can move mountains. All ancient superstitions, he would say, echoing his father. (Brian, 2005, p. 172)

Indeed, Einstein referred to God so often that one might easily think that he did hold to or advocate belief at least in some kind of distant, though personal, deity. Brian lists in detail many occasions when Einstein either referred to God or was specifically asked about his religious beliefs. His answers to questions were not entirely consistent, and some might seem evasive. On occasion he denied being either an atheist or a pantheist, but he also consistently denied believing in a personal God, an afterlife, the effectiveness of prayer, or other supernatural concepts.

On one occasion, an ensign serving in the Pacific during World War II wrote to Einstein to say that he had met a Jesuit priest who claimed to have converted Einstein from atheism. In response, Einstein categorically denied the story and expressed astonishment that such "lies" were being told about him. He stated that from the viewpoint of a Jesuit priest he had always been an atheist because he did not believe in a personal God. He added, however, that he did not consider himself an atheist because he did not share what he called "the crusading spirit of the professional atheist whose fervor is mostly due to a painful act of liberation from the fetters of religious indoctrination received in youth." In the following words, he then expressed his visionary understanding of the natural world:

> I prefer an attitude of humility corresponding to the weakness of our intellectual understanding of nature and of our being. We have to admire in humility the beautiful harmony of the structure of this world – as far as we can grasp it. And that is all. (Brian, 2005, p. 187)

By any standard definition of atheism, this is clearly an atheist position, but we freely acknowledge that Einstein did not favor the application of the word to himself.

In reporting Einstein's views, we do not necessarily express agreement with them. In particular, we do not believe that science requires faith in any meaningful way. But even if Einstein would have disagreed with us on this, it does not follow that he believed in, or sought to promote the idea of, a personal God.

Myth 46 Atheists Can't Explain Miracles

Miracles are the subject of endless popular debate between religious apologists and religious skeptics, and there is a more specialized academic debate about this in philosophical journals. Whatever the rights and wrongs of it, it seems as if all religions have in common that their respective deities impress us with miracles, *real* miracles, that is, miracles that are well and truly impossible to achieve other than by transcending the laws of nature as we know them. "The literature of religious traditions is filled with stories of strange and mysterious events," as Michael Martin puts it (1990, p. 188). The important point here is that these events, if we accept the reports as accurate, defy naturalistic explanation: they "cannot be explained in either commonsense or scientific terms" (Martin, 1990, p. 188).

Let us grant for the sake of argument that an all-powerful God, or perhaps even a less powerful supernatural being, could produce miraculous events, however defined (perhaps by overriding natural laws). Someone who *already* believes, on some other, independent, ground, in the existence of a god or gods might go on to believe that miracles take place, without committing any logical blunder or other error of reasoning (Oppy, 2006, p. 381). Nonetheless, should we believe that these events actually happen if we do not have a prior belief in supernatural beings? If only gods could produce miracles, would the (supposed) occurrence of miracles make atheism untenable? Can atheists *explain* miracles, or at least the many accounts of them?

A typical argument for the existence of God, based on reports of miracles, proceeds like this (we follow closely Martin, 1990, pp. 188–189): since certain events cannot be explained in ordinary terms, they are miracles. By definition, miracles can only be explained by the actions of a supernatural power. The most plausible such explanation is that they are the actions of God. Hence it is probable that God exists. Christian philosophers continue to use similar arguments: see, for example, Richard Swinburne in *The Existence of God* (Swinburne, 2004, pp. 273–292).

Martin defines miracles as events that are brought about by a supernatural power rather than as events that breach natural laws, since he imagines that there could be laws about what can be done by a god, and these might not be breached when a miracle occurs (Martin, 1990, pp. 189–190). This raises the question of what is a supernatural power, which Martin answers by referring to the powers possessed by beings such as angels, gods, Superman, and devils – beings that are markedly superior in their powers to beings like us (Martin, 1990, pp. 190). These beings may or may not be constrained by causal laws of some kind.

Martin goes on to argue that even if miracles took place it would not support the existence of God, since some other supernatural being might be responsible (pp. 191–192). Given the wide range of supernatural beings that might exist even in the absence of God, we cannot be confident that the existence of miracles makes the existence of God more probable. Martin thinks that some alleged miracles would more likely be the actions of other supernatural beings, rather than those of a kind and merciful deity or an all-good/all-powerful one. An orthodox version of God would be able to achieve his purposes in other ways, without acts that are scientifically inexplicable. Likewise, some alleged miracles seem capricious, while others seem trivial and do not fit with traditional images of God. Much of this analysis might strike you as a kind of skirmishing activity, however, given that as atheists we generally do not believe in any supernatural entities and powers.

So, leaving aside issues relating to the specific supernatural source of the miracle, do we need to accept that these events happen at all? It is worth noting that many of the miracles reported in the Hebrew Bible and the New Testament were standard fare in ancient times. To give just a few examples mentioned by Jean Meslier in his 1729 *Testament*: Jesus was born to a virgin (Christian miracle), while Romulus and Remus were also born to a virgin (corresponding pagan miracle); Moses struck a rock with a rod, and water sprang from it (Hebrew Bible miracle), while

Pegasus the winged horse achieved the same feat by striking a rock with his hoof (corresponding pagan miracle); Moses parted the Red Sea to permit the Israelites free passage (Hebrew Bible miracle), while Flavius Josephus reportedly claims that the very same thing happened to the Macedonians fleeing Alexander's troops at the sea of Pamphylia (corresponding pagan miracle); last but not least, the Egyptian pharaohs and their magicians were capable of delivering the same array of miracles that Moses had on offer (change rod into serpent, water into blood, bring forth vermin and insects – the list goes on) (Meslier, 2009 [1729], pp. 81–87). Meslier concludes, "But how could these so-called miracles be decisive proofs and evidence of the truth of a religion, seeing that it is not even certain that they were really done and seeing that there is no certainty in the narratives . . . ?" (2009[1729], p. 88).

For his part, Michael Martin offers a detailed discussion of David Hume's classic account in *Of Miracles* (Martin, 1990, pp. 195–199). Hume dedicated a whole section (1777, Section X) of his *Enquiry Concerning Human Understanding* to the subject. Here, he suggests that a miracle necessarily constitutes a violation of a law of nature. He defines a miracle accordingly, as "[. . .] *a transgression of a law of nature by a particular volition of the Deity, or by the interposition of some invisible agent*" (Hume, 2010 [1777], italics in original).

On Hume's approach, someone who believes in the occurrence of a miracle thinks both:

1. Event E violates a law of nature; and
2. E actually took place.

But here, Hume argues, our judgment about 1. will be based on overwhelming evidence of how nature operates – for example, dead people do not come back to life – whereas 2. will be based on human testimony, which is notoriously fallible. In support of the latter point, Stenger, in his discussion of eyewitness-based miracles, notes that many people in the USA have been freed from prison because their innocence could be proven by DNA evidence. The eyewitness accounts that were responsible for their convictions turned out to be unreliable and downright false: "In a recent decade, sixty-nine convicts were released from prison, seven on death row, based on DNA evidence. In most cases, these people were convicted primarily on the basis of eyewitness testimony" (Stenger, 2008, p. 177).

In any case, Martin thinks there are problems with Hume's argument as it stands: for example our knowledge of natural laws is based largely on the testimony of others. Also the argument is weakened if it assumes the nonrepeatability of the experience (so there can only be testimony relating to one event of this type). And conversely there may be good evidence other than just someone's testimony that E happened – for example, video recordings, EEG records, and so on (Martin, 1990, p. 196).

But there is something to be said for Hume. He is talking about events so extraordinary that they contradict thousands of years of human experience. Whether or not we rely on a concept such as a "law of nature," we have acquired evidence, cross-checked our perceptions and memories, cross-checked with each other, and built up a great deal of robust worldly knowledge. We know, for example, that – sadly – in the absence of advanced technological intervention water does *not* suddenly turn into wine. The dead do not rise from their graves. Severed limbs do not grow back. When claims are made that these things happen, we are entitled to give them virtually zero credibility, at least if we don't *already* believe (presumably on some other ground) in the existence of a miracle-working supernatural being. The probability that such an event actually happened as described on a specific occasion will always be lower than the probability that there is some other explanation – perhaps some sort of mistake, misunderstanding, or fabrication – even if we don't know which specific explanation is the correct one. The probability that the extraordinary event happened is negligible, while the probability of the disjunction of all the other possible explanations is a virtual certainty.

Believers have other problems, too. First, they must explain why E is not covered by scientific laws that we do not yet know. After all, we have made much progress to date, and many past miracles are now scientifically well explained. For example, we can confidently explain some apparent miracle cures as psychosomatic responses. So why would we not make more such discoveries in the future? The case for the existence of gods – and their interventions – does not follow merely from our current inability to explain certain events. Second, we know that appearances are often misleading: there are many ways they can deceive us, whether through deliberate trickery (it was very difficult to rule out trickery in ancient times, and even now people can be tricked in laboratory settings); self-deception resulting from gullibility, religious zeal, bias, or willingness to believe; or incomplete knowledge of the applicable natural laws. Third, some events may be governed by laws that are merely statistical.

Christopher Hitchens notes rightly that "most of the 'miracles' of the New Testament have to do with healing, which was of such great importance in a time when even minor illness was often the end" (Hitchens, 2007, p. 18). Indeed, this has not changed so greatly: even in an era of science-based medicine, most miracles (so called) probably relate to healing the sick.

In that respect, Martin offers a useful discussion of the many allegedly miraculous cures at Lourdes, in France (1990, pp. 202–207). These have all been documented and individually considered, so much so that if even these "miracles" are suspect then the claims for others, especially those recorded in earlier and more superstitious times when there was no objective documentation, are not worth taking seriously.

The story of the Lourdes miracles begins with a vision in February 1858 when a 14-year-old girl, Bernadette Soubirous, had a vision of a beautiful lady at the grotto of Massabielle in Lourdes. Various seemingly miraculous events took place. The Roman Catholic Church subsequently declared the lady in the vision to have been the Virgin Mary. Many supposedly miraculous cures have taken place ever since, and millions of pilgrims now visit Lourdes each year.

The Roman Catholic Church has a procedure for investigating and recognizing these miracle cures, which involves the work of a full-time physician at a medical bureau in Lourdes, who works with others to examine and question pilgrims. Documentation is kept, relatively strict evidence is required, and cases are submitted to an international medical committee that meets in Paris. If they decide that the cure is inexplicable, the final determination that a miracle occurred is made by the Church (a canonical commission headed by the bishop of the diocese where the pilgrim lives). Martin observes that the international committee can really only determine whether the cure is inexplicable given the current state of medical science, not that it is scientifically inexplicable in a more absolute sense. He questions whether they even do the former properly (Martin, 1990, pp. 204–207). Perhaps Michel Montaigne got things right when he wrote in his *Essays*, in 1580:

> Miracles are according to the ignorance wherein we are by nature, and not according to natures essence.... If we terme those things monsters or miracles to which our reason cannot attaine, how many such doe daily present themselves unto our sight?... Man's spirit is a wonderfull worker of miracles. (Montaigne, 1580)

Martin discusses an illuminating case, that of Serge Perrin. At the time of Martin's writing, this was the most recent case where a miracle was found. In 1970, Perrin was supposedly cured of organic hemiplegia – a paralysis of one side of the body. However, numerous problems were found with the documentation and the analysis by the international medical committee, when the case was reviewed by a group of specialists in the USA. The specialists doubted that Perrin had suffered from any organic illness at all, and concluded that if he had it was most probably multiple sclerosis – which can have severe flare-ups followed by remissions that are sometimes complete.

Likewise, the preceding case, involving Vittorio Micheli in 1963, was investigated by James Randi. In this case, a sarcoma had destroyed part of the patient's pelvis, iliac, and surrounding muscles. There was remission of the tumor, and the Lourdes team said that X-rays confirmed an unprecedented reconstruction of bone. However, such remissions are sometimes observed, and the allegedly complete regrowth of bone could not be confirmed without exploratory surgery (which was not done). Randi also found a very similar case reported in 1978 for which no miracle was alleged. When the dossier was examined by medical authorities to which Randi submitted it, they found anomalies, including conflicting information about what treatment Micheli had received prior to his visit to Lourdes.

Martin discusses the fact that all doctors have seen spontaneous remissions and the like. In addition, there has been a huge decline in accepted inexplicable cures at Lourdes, as judged by the Lourdes medical bureau, as medical knowledge has increased. This suggests that many of the earlier "cures" were accepted only because of the state of medical knowledge at the time. This, in turn, casts doubt on the accepted miracles, especially the earlier ones (Martin, 1990, p. 207).

Suspiciously, documented miracles – at least those documented in modern times, with the involvement of doctors and other health professionals – relate to diseases for which occasional remissions are observed, with no religious involvement. They include cancers and some recoveries of brain function. They do not include such things as regenerations of lost limbs, though an omnipotent deity that is capable of causing the remission of cancer, and even raising people from the dead, could doubtlessly help amputees grow back their lost limps. Skepticism with regard to religious claims about such miracles has sometimes led to state authorities forcing churches to stop making miraculous claims in their marketing materials. For instance, the New Zealand-based Equippers Church was prohibited by that country's Advertising Standards Agency from claiming – falsely – that Jesus heals cancer (Field, 2012). On the other hand, in the USA, where much is possible in terms of misinformation, partly due to a generous freedom of speech provision in the country's constitution, you do find Christian church leaders – in one particularly egregious case the director of a Christian university – claiming that prayers can regenerate lost limbs. In a YouTube video, the university director blames the lack of completion (as far as regrowth of a lost finger is concerned) on unfinished prayers. It goes without saying that other than the university director saying so, there is no documentary evidence for his claims (Joyner, 2012).

Martin also discusses indirect miracles, where there is no direct interference with natural causation, but God supposedly establishes a chain of events to produce an extraordinary and fortuitous outcome as a sign of his presence. One problem with this is that it becomes impossible to say how an indirect miracle differs from a fortunate coincidence. Another may be that it seems to deny free will for the human beings who took part in the chain of causation (Martin, 1990, pp. 207–208), though this might depend on our conception of free will.

Credited to Jesus and Mo, www.jesusandmo.net

We wonder why God does not provide more convincing, less equivocal, better-studied miracles, especially if he wants to make himself known to nonbelievers. Perhaps, it might be replied, he has reasons – maybe he does not want to make it too easy to believe in his existence. But this is not particularly convincing.

Let Christopher Hitchens have the last word on miracles:

> In much the same way as prophets and seers and great theologians seem to have died out, so the age of miracles seems to lie somewhere in our past. If the religious were wise, or had the confidence of their convictions, they ought to welcome the eclipse of this age of fraud and conjuring. But faith, yet again, discredits itself by proving to be insufficient to satisfy the faithful. (Hitchens, 2007, p. 49)

Myth 47 Atheists Can't Explain the Resurrection

The argument that atheists cannot explain Jesus of Nazareth's (supposed) resurrection is based on claims that certain events can only (reasonably) be explained if Jesus really did rise from the dead. William Lane Craig is one prominent Christian apologist who makes this sort of claim. In his own words, "the resurrection appearances, the empty tomb, and the origin of the Christian faith – all point unavoidably to one conclusion: the resurrection of Jesus" (Craig, 1985a, p. 89; see also, for example, Craig, 1985b, Craig and Sinnott-Armstrong, 2004, pp. 21–25, and Lennox, 2011, pp. 189–225).

Christian apologists tend to argue along the following lines:

1. Jesus was buried in a tomb by Joseph of Arimathea, who was supposedly a member of the Jewish Sanhedrin. It cannot be explained, so it is often said, why anyone would falsely claim that such a person was involved.
2. His tomb was found to be empty.
3. This was discovered by some of his female followers. This is where the Gospel of Mark originally ended – apologists can ask why it would be claimed that women did this if it was not so, given that women were not highly regarded in Jewish society.
4. Various individuals had experiences of seeing Jesus risen from the dead.
5. The disciples came to believe that this had happened.

In responding to Craig, Victor Stenger notes that the Gospels are inconsistent in their accounts of the Resurrection (Stenger, 2008, p. 178), and, perhaps more importantly, that no historical sources outside the Bible provide confirmation (Stenger, 2008, p. 177). The fact is that we have almost no nonbiblical sources dating from the first century CE that even mention Jesus, let alone describe his miracles and the Resurrection. There are two passages in the work of the Jewish historian Flavius Josephus, but even these are from the final decade of the first century, and one is generally believed by scholars to have been significantly redacted at a later date to suit Christian theological interests. We do not put this forward to support the relatively extreme position that Jesus is an entirely mythical or legendary character (we hold no considered view on this matter), but the fact remains that there is nothing reliable in the historical record to corroborate any biblical claims about his life, execution, and supposed resurrection from the dead.

Some atheists doubt that there was ever an actual Jesus, or at the least are highly skeptical that his existence has been demonstrated. They include Richard Carrier, an expert in ancient history who argues that Jesus of Nazareth was a literary fabrication (see Carrier, 2012a, 2012b). But disbelief in the historicity of Jesus is not necessary to be an atheist and is probably not the predominant view among atheists. In the preface to his 2012 book, *Proving History*, Carrier notes, "I have no vested interest in proving Jesus didn't exist. It makes no difference to me if he did" (Carrier, 2012c, p. 8). As he puts it in an interview with John Loftus:

> it really doesn't matter to me, in the way it does to believers. I'm not invested in any theory proclaiming otherwise, and the historical Jesus, or perhaps I should say Jesuses (as there are several) proposed by mainstream scholars today pose no challenge to my worldview. (Loftus, 2012b)

In a book arguing that Jesus was *not* an entirely mythical character, Bart D. Ehrman acknowledges that "as the mythicists have been quick to point out . . . no Greek or Roman author from the first century mentions Jesus." To be fair, he immediately adds that this does not prove Jesus's nonexistence, since the same applies to millions of other people from the time (Ehrman, 2012, p. 43). Indeed, but we are left without an evidential case for the details about him alleged in the Christian Gospels. Ehrman actually concludes, "Many Christians do not want to hear that Jesus did not make an enormous splash on the world of his day, but it appears to be true" (2012, p. 46).

Importantly, it misstates matters if we talk in terms of explaining the Resurrection. If anything has to be explained it is merely the presence of various statements in the biblical texts. These, however, are reported in contradictory terms, like much else in the Bible. Writing three hundred years ago, Jean Meslier mentions that the resurrected Jesus appeared to the apostles at the same time in Jerusalem (the Gospel of John) and Galilee (the Gospel of Matthew). Luke describes Jesus's ascension to Heaven, as does Mark (in material that was later interpolated after the original ending); alas, Matthew and John forget to mention this minor detail (Meslier, 2009 [1729], pp. 111–112). The inconsistencies in the Gospels are numerous, and their seriousness and pervasiveness have only become clearer as textual-historical scholarship has developed since Meslier's time.

One thing that we cannot do is to take the New Testament as a whole to be a single reliable source on Jesus's life and actions. There is no historical or textual basis for doing so. Unless you start out by making theological assumptions, you are stuck with the various books that make up the New Testament, each of which needs to be approached on its own merits, taking into account what historical-textual scholars believe about its provenance. In fact, it is well known to scholars that the Gospels were not actually written by their traditional authors – Saints Matthew, Mark, Luke, and John – but by unknown authors writing many years after the events that they narrate, and probably based in urban centers remote from Palestine. The first of the Gospels, traditionally attributed to Mark, was probably written about 70 CE, some 40 years after the Resurrection allegedly took place. Ehrman says:

> Our earliest Gospel account of Jesus's life is probably Mark's, usually dated – by conservative and liberal scholars of the New Testament alike – to around 70 CE (some conservatives date it earlier; very few liberals date it much later). (Ehrman, 2012, p. 75)

Thus Victor Stenger gets it right, when he expresses skepticism about biblical "eyewitness" accounts:

> that testimony is only recorded in the Bible, second hand, and years after the fact. Eyewitness testimony recorded on the spot would still be open to question two thousand years after the fact. Eyewitness testimony recorded decades later is hardly extraordinary evidence. (Stenger, 2008, p. 179)

The more general question is how we should assess what probably happened in the past, given that we are not able to observe past events directly (as we are not able to observe very small or very distant things directly). Some historical events seem probable based on the evidence that we have, but with others we cannot be confident. Ideally historians want hard physical evidence, such as photographs, and products such as houses and other buildings that can be dated confidently to the relevant time.

These can offer important information or at least clues. In addition, it is useful to have multiple, independent, and relatively extensive accounts of events from as close to the time as possible. Ideally, all of this will converge on the same set of facts, at least in the main respects (Ehrman, 2012, pp. 39–42).

At this stage, the arguments of apologists are in trouble. Unless you already believe the story on some *other* ground (perhaps what you take to be a mystical vision of Jesus), why trust narratives that were written long after the purported events and appear on their face to be heavily mythologized? It is no proof of Jesus's supposed resurrection, as Lennox wrongly assumes, that these narratives contain various correct details about the historical and geographical setting (Lennox, 2011, pp. 195–197). Why wouldn't they be correct on many matters of public knowledge, given that they were at least written in the approximate era concerned?

Was a figure like Joseph of Arimathea somehow involved? Perhaps, but we do not really know. Likewise we do not know what role was actually played by Jesus's female disciples, such as Mary Magdalene. If these people actually existed that might explain their mention in the Gospels, but we cannot draw any clear conclusions about their involvement in specific events. If claims about their involvement logically entailed that such an implausible and extraordinary event as the Resurrection took place, it would be simpler to doubt those claims than to conclude that somebody really was raised from the dead – unless of course we *already* felt inclined to accept the latter.

In passing, we doubt the common claim by Christian apologists (e.g., Lennox, 2011, pp. 218–219) that women and their testimony were so stigmatized in Jewish society that no story about women's involvement would have found its way into the Gospels unless it were essentially true. There might be all sorts of literary or other reasons for Christian documents written long after the events to mention the involvement of women, whether or not those women ever existed and whether or not, if they did, there was an empty tomb for them to discover. But in any event, it is far from clear that the stigma supposedly attaching to the testimony of women was anything like what apologists need for this to assist their arguments (Carrier, 2009, pp. 297–321).

We have noted earlier that the Gospels were written long after the time in which they are set. Perhaps, however, there is a shorter line of transmission to Paul the Apostle, who claims in his First Epistle to the Corinthians that Jesus appeared to hundreds of people after his death (and that many of these individuals were still alive). Since this epistle predates the Gospel of Mark, it does show that *some kind* of resurrection story was in place before the Gospels were written. However, even I Corinthians was probably written 20 years or so after Jesus's crucifixion allegedly took place, and we have no other records of what happened on the occasion that Paul mentions. Secular historians of the time say nothing about it, and nor do the Gospels, and it is not clear what Paul's source was. His own experience of Jesus on the way to Damascus seems to have been a visionary one, if we can rely on his account in the Epistle to the Galatians (Galatians 1: 11–16). There is another mention in Paul's letters (1 Corinthians 15: 8), but the only New Testament narrative of the actual road to Damascus conversion is in the Acts of the Apostles (chapter 9), traditionally attributed to Luke. Even this is consistent with a visionary experience rather than one of encountering a resurrected corpse on the road.

Paul makes no mention of a resurrection in that sense, and nor does he speak of an empty tomb. As Richard Carrier puts it, Paul "never mentions anyone finding an empty tomb, for example, or the testimony of a Doubting Thomas, or anything else," but claims to know of the Resurrection from scripture and revelation (Carrier, 2010a, p. 301). The absence of these doctrines in Paul's epistles suggests that they were later embellishments as Jesus's legend grew.

What are we left with? Sometimes we cannot find out the answer to a question of how an event happened, but that is not a reason to suggest an extreme explanation that contradicts everything we know about the nature of the world around us. Some claims are easy to believe given our ordinary background knowledge – for example, you would probably believe either of us if he claimed to have recovered from a cold, or even if he said that he had been resuscitated after drowning. If he claimed to have died and been entombed, then resurrected supernaturally a couple of days later, you would require far stronger evidence, even if he used the claim to explain some event that you were not in a position to account for in other ways.

Like many other authors, Kevin Smith (2012) points out that extraordinary claims require extraordinary evidence – this formulation of the idea was popularized in a 1980 episode of Carl Sagan's television program, *Cosmos*, but versions of it date back at least to the Enlightenment era. It is good advice with a long pedigree among rational thinkers, and we ought to follow it. Smith quite rightly presses the point in an article on – or actually against – homeopathy. Homeopathy has little, if anything to offer in the way of extraordinary evidence, and the same applies to claims about a Jewish wonder-worker who was raised from the dead.

8

No Future for Atheism?

Myth 48 Atheism is a Bad Bet (Pascal's Wager)

Pascal's wager originated with the seventeenth-century French philosopher, mathematician, and physicist Blaise Pascal. It has been hugely influential primarily because it marked the beginning of what is known today as decision theory. The argument that atheism is a bad bet starts off with an invitation to acknowledge an uncertainty as to whether or not God exists. We can bet either way. If we bet on belief we are vastly better off if we are right, and not much worse off if we are wrong. If we bet on nonbelief, we are not much better off if we are right and vastly worse off if we are wrong. It is best, so goes the argument, to bet on belief. Some religious apologists continue to press this argument, among them Dinesh D'Souza, who concedes that we cannot have knowledge of otherworldly matters such as life after death and the existence of Heaven or Hell. D'Souza writes that it is, nonetheless, best to take the risk of metaphysical error and ask God for faith (D'Souza, 2007, pp. 197–199).

It is worth stressing that nowhere in this wager is the claim made that the existence of God has been proven (logically or otherwise) (Pascal, 1910; Carrier, 2002). Nonetheless, the wager confronts us with a big question: how should a sensible person, possibly informed by decision-theoretical approaches, respond to Pascal's challenge? If there is genuine uncertainty regarding the question of whether God exists, should we

50 Great Myths About Atheism, First Edition. Russell Blackford and Udo Schüklenk.

believe, and follow religious dictates (also known as God's rules) just in case God does exist? There is an ongoing philosophical debate about this, and – as an entry point to it – readers might find Alan Hájek's article on Pascal's wager in *The Stanford Encyclopedia of Philosophy* illuminating (Hájek, 2011).

One immediate difficulty is that belief is not volitional in any simple way. No matter how hard you try to will it, you will not be able to get yourself to "just believe" that there is currently a live rhinoceros in your living room – not unless you live a *very* unusual life. While conceding this point in his discussion, D'Souza insists that we can, meanwhile, ask God to give us faith, live good and moral lives, and, indeed, "live as if God did indeed exist" (D'Souza, 2007, p. 199). This point should, in turn, be conceded: even though belief is not simply volitional it can be influenced indirectly to a certain extent, such as by involving yourself in religious practices (Mackie, 1982, pp. 175–176). Using such methods, you can sometimes trick yourself into believing something for which you have no evidence.

In the case of Pascal's wager, all that is required for the wager to be a coherent possibility is that we have some ability to shape our beliefs. Furthermore, someone who takes the wager seriously might already be somewhat inclined to believe in God. That could be the case with many uncommitted people in Western countries – they may never have looked deeply into the intellectual considerations favoring atheism, and they may have been familiar with religious ideas from an early age.

In those circumstances, in particular, those who wish to believe in God, but who do not currently do so, can take some practical steps even beyond those recommended by D'Souza. First, they can make a point of avoiding atheistic books, speeches, and the like, especially those that offer arguments in favor of atheism. Beyond this, the following might work as a way for them to develop belief in God: they can go to church (or mosque, or other equivalent) regularly and frequently; surround themselves with religious people; enjoy the singing and the rituals, and the general mystique of participation in an emotionally engaged group of people; establish relationships with those people; immerse themselves in religious literature; and above all stop thinking critically about religion and religious morality.

All this might incline you toward belief – and you can know that in advance. Thus it is quite possible to take steps that you know will at least make it easier for you to believe if you continue them over time. There is a very good chance, though far from a guarantee, that you will eventually feel comfortable with belief in God, and "take on" that belief. So it is, up to a point, possible to "bet" for or against atheism.

However, contrary to Pascal's claims, manipulating yourself like this is doing violence to your reason and understanding – you are suppressing your critical faculties – and thus there is a real cost that Pascal conceals (Mackie, 1982, p. 176). There is also a related question: do we really want to acquire beliefs in such an intellectually dishonest way? How desperate would you have to be to attempt something like this? Importantly, how could you justify imposing beliefs on others if they are acquired in that way, rather than through evidence? We will return to the issue of the costs of following Pascal's advice.

In any event, how, at this stage, before you set out on such a path of dishonesty with yourself, can you feel confident that any deity that actually existed would reward you? One possible answer is that any such attempt would likely be futile, even if a god existed. The reason for this is that there are so many religions and gods on offer that you would be virtually certain to miss the right god and his or her rules, so you might as well not bother at all. We are assuming, of course, that the rules of the gods competing for our compliance are contradictory – but it requires no great study of history and anthropology to show that they frequently are.

Given that the monotheistic religions' gods usually insist, in the religious scriptures associated with them, that there is one God only, and that no others are to be worshiped, it is impossible to obey all of the possible gods at the same time. There is no prospect of abiding by all their rules, as Pascal's proposition would require of us, if their rules include that we must believe in only one of them.

Furthermore, there are various possibilities that Pascal neglects. Perhaps, as individuals, we are destined to salvation or otherwise no matter what we do, so we might as well do whatever advances our worldly happiness (Mackie, 1982, p. 203). After all, believing can have its downside, such as being time-consuming and troublesome, perhaps expensive, especially if financial demands such as for tithes are made by the church or sect concerned, and perhaps oppressive, especially if the church or sect has ascetic practices, or requires extreme forms of penance, an emphasis on guilt and shame, and so on (compare Martin, 1990, pp. 235–236). These costs must be added to the cost in intellectual dishonesty and suppression of your critical faculties.

Then there is the problem that whatever god exists might be angrier if you worship the wrong deity than if you worship none at all, and the true god might be one that is unfamiliar to you (Mackie, 1982, p. 203; Baggini, 2003, p. 34). Or perhaps the true god looks with more favor on honest atheists or doubters than on "mercenary manipulators of their own understandings": people who deliberately set out to believe in a god for the sorts of reasons that Pascal offers (Mackie, 1982, p. 203). Indeed, the true god might be well aware of the epistemic uncertainty, for human beings, about its own existence and the correct rules for humans to follow. This god might not be so petty and small-minded as to punish us (or deny us eternal bliss) for getting these things wrong. To be fair, this is, of course, all idle speculation.

However, there is one thing these speculations do actually demonstrate: it's by no means obvious that atheism is a bad bet, even if a god does exist, or that betting on the existence of, say, the Christian deity will lead to salvation – even if some god exists after all.

This brings us to a related point. As we have just mentioned, believing can have its downside. One assumption in Pascal's wager is that the price one would pay for not believing (eternal damnation, or at least denial of an infinite heavenly reward) is much higher than any price one would pay for believing. But that, of course, is in the eyes of the beholder. It will depend on the nature of damnation, the nature of the heavenly reward, the worldly benefits that are lost from following the god's rules, and how much cost one assigns to each of these. Bear in mind that the lifestyle-related dictates of whichever religion one is willing to place one's wager on might be quite onerous.

Some atheists might, at least provisionally, assign a zero probability to the existence of God. While we might be open to changing our minds if we hear new arguments, we can, or perhaps must, select 0 as the probability that a particular god exists if the description of that god appears contradictory (see Oppy, 1990; compare Oppy, 2006, pp. 246–247). If we assign the probabilities in this way, we should wager against Pascal's recommendation, because the calculus changes. Hájek discusses this in his entry in *The Stanford Encyclopedia of Philosophy* mentioned above (Hájek, 2011). Expressing the point formally, he writes the respective expectations, or expected payoffs, as follows, assuming a probability of 0 for God's existence:

$$\text{E(wager for God)} = \infty * 0 + f_1 * (1 - 0) = f_1$$
$$\text{E(wager against God)} = f_2 * 0 + f_3 * (1 - 0) = f_3$$

Here, ∞, or infinity, is your payoff if you correctly bet that God exists, while f_1 is your payoff if you bet on God, but God *does not* exist (it's an entirely this-worldly payoff). On the second line, f_2 is your payoff if you bet against God, but God *does* exist, while f_3 is your payoff if you bet against God, and God does not exist (again, an entirely this-worldly payoff). If the assigned probability of God's existence is 0, then your expectation if you wager for God is a payoff of f_1. If the assigned probability of God's existence is 0, your expectation if you wager against God is a payoff of f_3.

Might it still be better to live your life as if God exists, even though there is no such being? We cannot rule that out with certainty, given the possible benefits in attending church, such as belonging to an emotionally supportive community, networking with other church members, and so forth (see, e.g., Micklethwait and Wooldridge, 2009, pp. 146–147). But as we have seen, there is a downside to leading your life as if God exists (especially if it requires you to engage in efforts of self-manipulation and intellectual dishonesty). For anyone for whom the question seriously arises, we think it is better to receive f_3 as the payoff than f_1.

What should we conclude about Pascal's wager, given these and other problems (for which, see Hájek, 2011 and Oppy, 2006, pp. 241–258)? Julian Baggini suggests that if an all-good, all-knowing, all-loving being exists we would expect it to be most concerned about whether we acted well (we take it he means this in the sense of, for example, treating others kindly). Such a being would be understanding that those who did not do so were largely damaged people who had terrible childhoods; it would not be so insecure as to want worship, and it would understand that we are faced with a multitude of choices of what and how to worship. It would also be unfair for this being to chastise us for using the intelligence that it gave us, even if this leads us to decide that it does not exist. In all, our best bet, according to Baggini, is to be good people rather than opting for a particular religious doctrine – and atheists are well poised to do that (Baggini 2003, pp. 34–35). This sort of advice sounds about right to us.

Myth 49 Atheism is Only for an Educated Elite

In his book *Is God a Delusion?*, Eric Reitan vividly describes the true horror in the lives of many people. Some endure unimaginably awful life events, while for others it is the more common kind of life story that involves extreme poverty, with its accompanying deprivation and hopelessness (as far as any worldly prospects are concerned) (Reitan, 2009, pp. 198–201). It is not too hard to make these horrors very vivid indeed, and to conjure up feelings of pity, sorrow, and outrage.

Reitan attacks Richard Dawkins for "speaking from a place of extraordinary privilege" when Dawkins describes how good life can be. This is, adds Reitan, not just naïve but plain "appalling"(Reitan, 2009, p. 201).

All this is a clever piece of rhetoric on Reitan's part: an attempt to employ the terrible suffering in the world – so hard to reconcile with the existence of a perfect God – as a stick with which to beat atheists. Karl Marx suggested ingeniously that religion is the opium of the people precisely because it gave the ruling classes a tool to delude the lower classes with false hopes, motivating them to forget the injustices committed against them while waiting – in vain –for a better afterlife. Marx put it thus:

> Religion is the sigh of the oppressed creature, the heart of a heartless world, just as it is the spirit of a spiritless situation. It is the opium of the people. The abolition of religion as the illusory happiness of the people is the demand for their real happiness. To call on them to give up their illusions about their condition is to call on them to give up a condition that requires illusions. (Marx, 1970 [1844], p. 131)

Whether or not you agree with Marx, we should not be too impressed by Reitan's line of reasoning. Surely the onus is on the religious believer to reconcile the facts of the case with orthodox claims about God, something that theologians have been struggling to do, with little success in our judgment, for hundreds of years. At the same time, Dawkins is correct that life can be very good, indeed. As far as it goes, there is nothing naïve, appallingly or otherwise, in drawing attention to this.

Perhaps there is a grain of truth in what Reitan is saying, hidden among his rhetoric: religious faith can offer comfort, and it seems harsh to take it away from people whose lives are so bad that it is all the comfort they have left. In that sense, we need to be careful before we think that atheism is an emotionally viable option for everyone, no matter what their circumstances. Even assuming atheism is true, there's a legitimate question as to whether this might not be too harsh a truth for some or many people, one not easily embraced by people who have no worldly hopes.

The writings of religious thinkers often display a yearning for values that unite all humanity, and these thinkers obviously believe that atheistic philosophies do not meet that test. For example, Swenson seeks a "fundamental source of inspiration" that is available to everyone, not just the few who may be fortunate in various ways (Swenson, 2000 [1949], p. 25). Similarly, the Protestant theologian Reinhold Niebuhr wishes to find a means of fulfillment for "humble spirits" who cannot be fitted into historical schemes of meaning (Niebuhr, 1981 [1955], p. 49). The claim here is that religious faith is deeply reassuring for such people, and that atheistic philosophy is not for them.

However, all of this runs the risk of being elitist and condescending in its own right, rather than supportive of the idea that atheism as such is an elitist enterprise. Indeed, such arguments are invariably put forward in print by highly educated leaders among the religious. So who is calling the kettle black here? Many people who are not from the highest levels of education are atheists, perhaps because they grasp the key point that there is no good evidence to support the extraordinary claims made by theistic religions, and perhaps out of a sense that many of those claims simply do not add up.

Ariela Keysar (2007) has collected information about America's atheist and agnostic population. She shows that while there are trends (atheists are more likely to be male than female, are younger, are more highly educated, concentrate in certain geographical areas, and are less likely to be Republicans), atheists can be found among every demographic.

One does not have to be a very well educated or privileged person to recognize fake reassurance for what it is. Furthermore, the prevalence of atheism in Northern and Western Europe shows that it extends far beyond a narrow demographic that could be described as an "intellectual elite." All the evidence to date suggests that atheism is likely to become widespread in any society that guarantees security for its people and allows them to prosper.

Myth 50 Atheism is Doomed in a Postsecular Age

Dinesh D'Souza argues that there is a global revival of traditional religion, including Christianity in particular, but also Islam, and Hinduism, though he sees Europe, Canada, and Australia as excluded from this. He speculates that the phenomenon of reverse missionary activity – evangelists from the developing world now preaching to populations in the developed world – could mean a reversal of secularization in its European stronghold (D'Souza, 2007, pp. 1–11). He concludes:

> Christianity may come in a different garb than it has in the past several centuries, but Christianity is winning and secularism is losing. The future is always unpredictable, but one trend seems clear. God is the future, and atheism is on its way out. (D'Souza, 2007, p. 11)

D'Souza also argues, probably quite rightly, that religious believers have much higher fertility rates than atheists; accordingly, he thinks, they inevitably outbreed atheists over time (D'Souza, 2007, pp. 15–19).

John Micklethwait and Adrian Wooldridge point to evidence that religious belief is even making a comeback in secular Europe: they refer to large numbers of people taking the faith-based Alpha course in the UK, an increase in the number of adult confirmations, immigration bringing more Christians and Muslims to the continent, and, once again, higher fertility rates among the religious (Micklethwait and Wooldridge, 2009, pp. 134–135). John C. Lennox also emphasizes a gap in fertility rates between believers (or at least regular worshipers) and the irreligious, though he acknowledges that irreligion can be spread by way of ideas or "memes" (2011, p. 25).

Alister McGrath also points to a resurgence of interest in religion in "postatheist Russia" (McGrath, 2004, p. 189). He also talks about a greater sympathy toward religion in popular culture, and the growth of bookstore sections devoted to "Body, Mind, and Spirit" (McGrath, 2004, pp. 190–192). Elsewhere, he writes of the rise of modern fantasy in the Victorian era – later developed by J.R.R. Tolkien and C.S. Lewis – as showing a loss of public confidence in "the existential adequacy of scientific rationalism" (McGrath, 2011, p. 86). He also claims that "serious political debate in Western Europe" has turned increasingly to "how best to work with faith groups and use faith to generate social cohesion and consolidate cultural capital" (McGrath, 2011, p. 96).

McGrath elaborates on the international success of Pentecostalism (and the charismatic movement within mainline Christian churches), pointing out how its success relates in large part to an emphasis on spiritual transformations and on God as something to be experienced. For McGrath, the only forms of religion that are in danger of losing adherents are those that emphasize a purely cognitive approach to the divine, primarily in the form of preaching from the Bible (McGrath, 2004, pp. 192–216).

Finally, it is often claimed that postmodernism can give comfort to religion. Indeed, it is possible that postmodern forms of religious thinking that avoid making specific claims about God can thereby avoid philosophical or scientific refutation – though only at the risk of becoming vacuous or unintelligible (see, e.g., Hyman, 2010, pp. 155–85).

Does all this mean that atheism is doomed? Not as we see it. Admittedly, religion may well survive into the future, with the proselytizing religions continuing to gain converts. Organized religious groups will continue to seek political power and influence – and will obtain some successes. For all that, religion is unlikely to regain the privileged position that it once enjoyed in the economically advanced nations of the West. There clearly is a connection between rises in better education, personal security, and individual material wealth, on one hand, and a decline in religious belief (and certainly in religious practices), on the other. This makes us wonder whether the successes that many fundamentalist churches experience, in terms of attracting new believers in many developing countries, might be relatively short-lived, given that increasing development also means better education as well as material wealth. We have seen in the developed world that this leads almost inevitably to a decline in religious belief.

Yes, as McGrath notes, some aspects of contemporary popular culture may seem to imitate religions in their depiction of wondrous events and powerful beings. But this need not indicate any yearning for religion or dissatisfaction with science and reason.

In some cases, the actual message conveyed may be far from compatible with traditional religious views – as with McGrath's example of *Star Trek*. As any fan of the series will be aware, *Star Trek* was a fundamentally secular science fiction show, frequently addressing ethical dilemmas without any references to God at all. Indeed, Gene Roddenberry, its creator, was an avowed humanist (Alexander, 1991). Perhaps McGrath is on stronger ground in his comments about fantasy literature – after all, Tolkien and Lewis were both devout Christians. Even here, however, he seems naïve about the cultural phenomenon that he invokes. Many writers in the modern tradition of fantasy literature were, or are, far from being religious (and the same applies to fantasy literature's numerous fans). You can be fascinated by mythic archetypes, wondrous places and events, and so on, without feeling any particular distrust in science and rationality, or their "existential adequacy."

So when we step back, how are atheism and religion actually faring in the twenty-first century? It is not always straightforward to interpret statistical data, but atheism does not appear doomed even in the relatively religious United States. If anything, it is slowly becoming more prevalent. A recent report on religious attitudes by the Pew Research Center (2010) shows that young American adults (aged 18 to 29) were more likely than Americans from previous generations to be in the "unaffiliated" category: that is, they responded as "atheist," "agnostic," or "nothing in particular." For this young demographic, the figure for the unaffiliated group was 26%, compared with 20% for members of Generation X (born between 1965 and 1980), 13% for baby boomers (born between 1946 and 1964), and figures below 10% for earlier generations. To be fair, the difference partly reflects an intergenerational difference in the number of people who are unaffiliated but nonetheless *do* have religious beliefs. It is worthy of note, however, that the percentages of agnostics and outright atheists are also highest in the youngest age cohort.

The Pew study acknowledges that people can become more religious as they grow older, but it reveals how little comfort the religious can take in this. Longitudinal data collected from a variety of sources show that the "unaffiliated" figures for Generation X and baby boomers are the same as when people of those cohorts were the age that the youngest group are now. The "unaffiliated" figure was 20% for Generation X when they were young and 13% for baby boomers when they were young. By contrast, the "unaffiliated" figure for the youngest cohort in the Pew study is 26%.

Even more recently, an American Values Survey conducted by the Pew Research Center (2012) shows a decline in the number of the youngest cohort who are prepared to answer: "I never doubt the existence of God." The percentage who answer this question affirmatively remains high – at 68%, but this compares to 81% in 2003, 83% in 2007, and 76% in 2009. Even if the decline is a short-term effect, there is certainly no indication in the Pew data of increased religious adherence among young Americans. Moreover, the data show the youngest cohort as more likely to doubt (at least) the existence of God than any of the older cohorts surveyed.

Just to be clear, none of this information proves that *religion* is doomed in the long term in the USA. According to the Pew (2010) study, younger Americans are about as religious as their elders by some measures, such as their propensity to believe in an afterlife. Accordingly, we are making a relatively modest set of claims: the overall picture is decidedly not one of atheism being doomed in a supposedly postsecular American culture. Instead, the gradual drift is away from organized religion and church attendance, with outright atheism more than holding its position.

We are cautious about the future. Perhaps Albert Camus was correct, even if he engaged in a degree of hyperbole, that human beings, or many of us, have an unmet expectation that the world be intelligible in a particular way. We want to understand our universe in terms of human concerns, as if it could "love and suffer" like us (Camus, 1975, p. 23). Many of us want the universe to be caring, or so it seems – why else would people engage in misleading metaphors, such as that of "Mother Nature," when they talk about our natural environment?

If some of us have the expectation that Camus speaks of, atheism will disappoint it, for the universe, taken as a whole, is impersonal and uncaring. Supernatural explanations of natural phenomena have a very poor track record. Once we move outside of a narrow range of phenomena that involve the agency of other human beings, or at least the precursors of it in other animals, explanations in terms of agency are a failure. We have seen this again and again in the history of science: we now know that emotions are not caused by gods like Ares and Aphrodite; that the lightning does not come from Thor or Zeus; and that the multiplicity of human languages has perfectly naturalistic origins, and is not explained by the wrath of Yahweh when human beings tried to build a tower to the heavens.

It seems to us that we can live lives that strike us as good, taking responsibility, perhaps succeeding in living with commitment and zest. Camus likely would have agreed, but it may not be so obvious for people whose lives are undermined by poverty, insecurity, inequality, or even by personal frustrations or heartbreaks. Many people do not have the freedom, or resources, for projects that express their personal values to more than a minimal extent. Individuals whose lives are seriously constrained by personal circumstances may continue to seek meaning in some external purpose, perhaps provided by God, rather than in their "inner freedom."

For atheism to become more widely attractive it may be that much social and economic progress will need to be made, altering the conditions in which people actually live and work. However, this has already happened to a great extent in northern and western European countries, with their high levels of economic security, education, and personal freedom. The prospect of any reversal of Europe's secularization currently appears remote.

We are not engaging in false triumphalism, and we don't know what the future will bring. Right now, however, atheism is very far from doomed.

9

The Rise of Modern Atheism

A Very Short History of Atheism

As we've noted in earlier chapters, there is a tendency for atheists to be philosophical naturalists: people who explain the world without invoking anything otherworldly, supernatural, or "spooky." Although some atheists do believe in the existence of powers or agents that transcend the world we experience with our ordinary senses, that is uncommon, at least among those of us who deny the existence of God after intellectual reflection on the issue. For us, atheism is accompanied by a more general rejection of any otherworldly reality (see Baggini, 2003, p. 3). While intellectually reflective atheists may have various reasons for denying the existence of God or the gods, the rise of modern atheism results, in large part, from the rise of modern science over much the same period of time. Science has tended in numerous ways to undermine religion – and supernaturalism more generally.

Western atheism is a relatively new historical phenomenon, but one with deep intellectual roots in the philosophical traditions of ancient Greece, which developed a number of materialist and skeptical schools of thought. Precursors can also be found in the classical civilizations of India and China, particularly the Carvaka school in India (see Law, 2011, pp. 8–9, for an introductory discussion).

The origins and antiquity of the Carvaka school are disputed, but it drew on materialist traditions that date back perhaps 2,500 years. It appears

50 Great Myths About Atheism, First Edition. Russell Blackford and Udo Schüklenk.

to have taken on a recognizable and organized form by the sixth century CE, though few relevant texts survive. We know its exponents were highly critical of the Brahminical priesthood, and opposed to asceticism. They rejected the concept of duty in the orthodox Hindu teachings, seeing this as a fabrication by the Brahmins to further their own interests, and particularly to avoid participation in what the Carvakas viewed as reputable work (that is, such worldly activities as trade, cattle grazing, and administration). In opposition to orthodox teachings, Carvaka exponents denied the existence of any spiritual self distinct from the body, and claimed that consciousness, memories, and living movement exist only where the body does. In the Carvaka view of things, the living, functioning body sustained consciousness and could be equated to the individual person.

This view of the world strikingly prefigures modern forms of philosophical naturalism. However, the more direct lines of influence on modern atheism emerge from the questioning, argumentative intellectual ferment of ancient Greece.

We are not suggesting that Greek culture was pervaded by atheism. On the contrary, it is difficult to find thinkers from, say, the fifth century BCE who totally denied the existence of any gods. Ancient Greece had its share of nonbelievers who tended to denounce or satirize popular religious beliefs, but they did not usually deny outright that the gods are real. The pre-Socratic philosopher Xenophanes (who led a very long life in the sixth and fifth centuries BCE) was one thinker who ridiculed anthropomorphic gods, but even he claimed that there is a supreme deity. A more radical view was that of the fifth century (BCE) sophist Protagoras, who rejected popular religious beliefs and expressed agnostic views about gods in general, but this was a rare exception. Only a small number of ancient Greek thinkers could arguably be classified as atheists – believing in no gods at all (Walters, 2010, pp. 24–25).

More important, we think, was the emergence of a body of thought devoted to examining the natural world and human phenomena (such as morality and political life) from a perspective that assigned little or no role to any god or gods. This continued into Roman times, and it left behind a rich intellectual legacy, even though only a small fraction of the philosophical texts remain. The various schools of Greek and Roman philosophy were populated, in most part, by individuals with some kind of god-belief, yet those same individuals typically showed worldly and humanistic, rather than religious, outlooks (Law, 2011, pp. 10–15).

Teaching and writing in the fourth and third centuries BCE, Epicurus developed a comprehensive naturalistic philosophy in which the universe and everything in it are made of minute, indestructible particles called "atoms." On this picture, all that exist are physical bodies and void. Even the gods are physical entities – seen as eternally detached and tranquil beings who have no concern for the affairs and problems of human beings.

Epicurus and his followers, most famously the Roman poet and philosopher Lucretius, who lived about 250 years later, also developed a naturalistic approach to ethical inquiry. For the Epicureans, we should judge people's conduct and character in terms of how much they promote a pleasant life. On this approach, dispositional capacities for justice, honesty, courage, self-control, prudence, and wisdom are instrumentally good, since without them it is not possible to live pleasurably, or in any sense happily. In passing, however, we should note that the Epicurean conception of pleasure was rather austere – the aim was not intensity of experience but, rather, the achievement of *aponia* and *ataraxia*, the absence of pain and mental distress. For this, it was best to adopt a rather simple, self-disciplined, and inexpensive way of life.

During the medieval period, intellectual and artistic endeavor in Europe were oriented toward and dominated by Christianity, and little philosophical dissent was tolerated. In a passage decrying the violence, poverty, illiteracy, and intellectual backwardness of the Middle Ages, Joachim Kahl emphasizes that it was a time when the Christian Church exercised enormous power and influence: "nothing could take place unless it was blessed by Holy Mother Church"; "the Christian spirit permeated and fashioned everything," whether in the private or public sphere, and including "the family, education, the economy and politics"; while "the popes were so powerful that they could name and depose emperors and kings at will" (Kahl, 1971, p. 194).

However, more liberal intellectual trends could be found in the Islamic world, particularly with Averroës in twelfth-century Spain (Law, 2011, p. 15). The Renaissance, which was partly inspired by a revival in classical learning, included a broadening of possibilities in intellectual inquiry and art – the latter becoming more naturalistic (in respect of pictorial realism) and less oriented to religion (Law, 2011, pp. 15–16). Nonetheless, atheistic views were almost unknown until the European Enlightenment, which spanned from the late seventeenth century to the end of the eighteenth, and were rare even then (Law, 2011, p. 18).

Beginning Atheism

But what is atheism? At the beginning of modernity, we see the term "atheist" and its cognates being used with little discrimination by current standards. We can turn to Michael J. Buckley for an instructive discussion of how ambiguous the terms really are. In antiquity, few people admitted to being atheists. The term was applied to various naturalists, skeptics, and others. In some cases, these thinkers debunked, or demythologized, specific gods, or denied divine involvement with the world – but they did not usually deny the existence of all deities (Buckley, 1987, pp. 4–6). Much later, when the word "atheist" came into English usage in the sixteenth century, it was again used to denote (and denounce) a wide range of people and doctrines. In a 1540 essay, appended to his translation (from Greek into Latin) of Plutarch's *On Superstition*, John Cheke evidently conceived of atheism as a denial of divine providence; in the following decades, the idea was stretched this way and that to cover many theologically heterodox ideas having little to do with each other (Buckley, 1987, pp. 9–10).

We doubt that philosophical atheism as it is understood today had any serious adherents in Europe until the late sixteenth or early seventeenth century, when some intellectuals moved toward a naturalistic worldview, influenced by a revival of Epicurean ideas (Wilson, 2008, pp. 15–38). Even in the milieu of intellectual libertines in Paris and other great cities, strict atheism was probably still rare.

However, we can see a transition taking place in the eighteenth century. One interesting figure here is Jean Meslier, a French priest who died in 1729, leaving behind a lengthy manuscript (see Meslier, 2009 [1729]) that argues against the existence of any god or gods, and derides all forms of religion. According to Kerry Walters, Meslier inspired anticlerical figures such as Voltaire, as well as outright atheists such as Denis Diderot and Baron d'Holbach, who were confident that reason could ultimately explain all phenomena without the need to invoke a god (Walters, 2010, pp. 26–27). Of these, Diderot is often regarded as European modernity's first significant exponent of atheism. Buckley describes him as making the first statement of a conviction that underpins Marxist humanism as well as positivist thought: "there is no god; the principle of everything is creative nature, matter in its self-activity eternally productive of all change and all design" (Buckley, 1987, p. 250).

During the Enlightenment, much in the way of established thinking came under challenge. New political ideas cast doubt on older concepts such as the divine right of kings. Many thinkers abandoned traditional Christianity for a more austere deism (with a more distant God), while a smaller number promoted unequivocal atheism. Enlightenment atheism was a product partly of the success of empirical science, which seemed to render supernatural explanations unnecessary, and partly of anticlericalism, especially in France, where there were widespread attitudes of rebellion against the fear, superstition, and obedience promoted by the Catholic Church (Walters, 2010, pp. 27–28).

David Hume may have been a deist, but he made an incomparable contribution to the rise of modern atheism in his *Dialogues Concerning Natural Religion*, first published in 1779, a few years after his death. Through the medium of a fictional debate among three characters – Cleanthes, Demea, and Philo – Hume cast doubt on arguments for the existence of God that had been used up to his own time. This book provided successive generations of atheistic philosophers with a valuable resource for their own arguments, and it is still frequently quoted and defended (and of course, often criticized) by academic philosophers of religion.

Though he claimed that we must presuppose God's existence as a requirement of practical reason, Immanuel Kant also subjected previous theistic arguments to withering scrutiny. In Chapter III of his monumental *Critique of Pure Reason* (1781), Kant demolishes the main arguments that had been adduced to that time. Between them, Hume and Kant dramatically placed philosophical theists on the defensive.

Since the Enlightenment, atheism has increasingly become a respectable, or even dominant, position in formal Western philosophy. In part, this relates to the work of philosophers such as Hume, Kant, Bentham, and Mill, who developed secular theories of ethics that rendered religious morality redundant. It also relates to the early success of science. By the beginning of the nineteenth century, science was describing our world and the universe in a new way, gaining some initial appreciation of the mind-boggling vastness of space and depth of time. The old worldview based on the Bible also came under serious challenge from another direction: textual-critical study of the biblical texts themselves revealed a collection of books whose provenance, history, and mode of composition were entirely different from what was claimed in traditional teachings of the Christian churches.

By the 1850s, even before the publication of Charles Darwin's *On the Origin of Species* in 1859, the steady, incremental processes of rational inquiry had rendered orthodox Christian faith untenable for many in the educated classes of Europe. By the later decades of the nineteenth century, humankind itself could be plausibly understood as the product of material causes, something that had emerged without any need for divine agency.

Thinkers such as Marx, Nietzsche, and Freud now rejected religious ideas. Even more people moved away from religion in the twentieth century, with many sophisticated religious thinkers adopting positions hard to distinguish from nonreligious ones. During the second half of the century, there was a collapse in religious belief in many countries, especially in Europe, though it is also true that highly conservative forms of religion remained entrenched, and politically influential, in many countries (Law, 2011, pp. 25–26).

In short, there has been a cultural shift in the last few hundred years. Just how this happened is the subject of Charles Taylor's monumental work *A Secular Age* (2007). Throughout, Taylor discusses "a move from a society where belief in God is unchallenged and indeed, unproblematic, to one in which it is understood to be one option among others, and frequently not the easiest to embrace" (2007, p. 3). Later, he asks the key question this way: "why was it virtually impossible not to believe in God in, say, 1500 in our Western society, while in 2000 many of us find this not only easy, but even inescapable?" (p. 25).

How Did We Become Secular?

Taylor (2007, pp. 25–27) suggests, we think quite plausibly, that three features of the social world in 1500 acted together to make atheism virtually unthinkable in the societies of Europe. First, the natural world was seen as testifying to divine purpose and action, both in its appearance of order and in "acts of God" such as plagues, disasters, and years of exceptional fertility. Second, the life of the kingdom as a whole, along with that of each of its constituent associations, was seen as somehow underpinned by God, with the functioning of all of these pervaded by ritual and worship. Third, there was a strong sense of living in what we can call an enchanted cosmos, full of miraculous agents and powers (such as demons, spirits, moral forces, and sacred objects). In addition, Taylor emphasizes that there was no fully developed purely humanist and naturalistic view available as an alternative to religion (2007, pp. 27–28).

Taylor attributes some of the changes in attitudes and beliefs to social and economic tendencies, such as urbanization, but he also blames latent tensions in Christian societies and latent problems within various theological positions. Though he accepts that science played a role in the disenchantment of the world, he tends to understate this as a crucial factor leading to the practical possibility of atheism. By contrast, we think it deserves much emphasis. We realize that it is difficult, even unrealistic, to proportion the roles of urbanization, science, internal theological developments, and the many other factors that must have contributed historically to the "thinkability" of atheism. Furthermore, many of these factors must have been mutually reinforcing. But the large role of science seems clear enough to us, and it is largely science that stands in the way of our thinking like early sixteenth-century Europeans, for whom God's existence was (seemingly) obvious.

Modern science took on a recognizable form in the sixteenth and seventeenth centuries, perhaps most dramatically in the work of astronomers such as Copernicus, Galileo, and Kepler, and in the extraordinary synthesis of early modern physics achieved by Newton. However, advances took place in many fields during this time, producing the sense of a comprehensive transformation in human knowledge. As this continued, the new breed of empirical investigators (who became known as "scientists" only in the nineteenth century) discovered more and more explanatory mechanisms of kinds that had previously eluded human efforts.

Increasingly, science offered the possibility that all the mysterious phenomena of nature could be explained without recourse to God – or to other aspects of the enchanted cosmos. The natural order could be explained in terms of underlying mechanisms that followed rationally discoverable laws, and even extraordinary events could be seen as the rare products of nature unfolding according to those same laws. Even if it did not disprove the existence of God, science did much to make atheism thinkable, and to encourage its philosophical beginnings in the Enlightenment.

Together with new moral and political ideas, science provided the resources for a naturalistic and humanistic view of the world. For scientifically informed philosophers and other thinkers, Christianity (of one form or other) was no longer the only game in town.

As the nineteenth century began, it had become far more thinkable, for educated Europeans, that the traditional religious conceptions of the world and our place in it might be wrong. According to Gavin Hyman, historians of that century generally agree that three developments especially contributed to a decline in religiosity (Hyman, 2010, p. 82). These were, first, moral considerations related to the perceived immorality of some theological doctrines, particularly doctrines associated with Heaven, Hell, and Jesus's substitutionary atonement for human sins; second, the rise of science and its apparent clash with theological claims; and third, the development of new approaches to biblical criticism and interpretation.

The moral concerns related to a cluster of arguably cruel or unjust doctrines, though it must have taken much in the way of social change for them to be widely seen in that way. Steven Pinker writes of a humanitarian revolution during the Enlightenment, with a far greater emphasis on compassion, distress at others' suffering, and new ideas of justice and equality (Pinker, 2011, pp. 129–188). However, exactly, we understand and explain this transformation, it surely undermined much of the old theology. This had emphasized torments closely associated with God's own actions, as when sinners are consigned to eternal and excruciating punishment. By the nineteenth century, many thoughtful people found such ideas a stumbling block to belief.

Hyman argues that four developments in the twentieth century may have helped alter the moral concerns about religion. The new emphasis was not so much on repellent doctrines relating to God's actions and character. Leaving that aside, how could a world that obviously contains much pain and suffering be reconciled with the existence of a theologically orthodox God who is supposed to be both all-powerful and loving (Hyman, 2010, pp. 129–132)?

One such development was a decline in literal belief in doctrines such as that of eternal hellfire – reducing one source of moral anxiety about Christian teachings. Second, there was an explosion in mass communications, making widely apparent the immense global burden of evil and suffering (which could no longer be explained plausibly in terms of individual sin and culpability or as part of a divinely ordained social and economic hierarchy). Ubiquitous evil and suffering inflicted on individuals across the world, via natural and social forces beyond their control, could not so plausibly be harmonized with ideas of a divinely ordained order of things. Third, the two world wars, the Holocaust, and other spectacles of mass killing produced widespread feelings of horror, accompanied by a sense of abandonment by God. Fourth, the development of formal academic philosophy took a path that led it to treat metaphysical and religious claims in a detached, analytical, and intellectually rigorous way. This sort of analysis tends to emphasize logical puzzles, such as the (admittedly ancient) puzzle about the source of evil in our world if there exists a being with both the power and the motivation to prevent it.

We should note, however, Hyman's claim that the various nineteenth-century developments were so damaging to religion precisely because a modern form of theism was vulnerable to critiques based on them – unlike, so the argument goes, premodern theologies (Hyman, 2010, p. 82). Likewise, Hyman suggests that the Problem of Evil is a problem only for a god seen in modern terms – as a powerful (indeed, all-powerful) agent who, nonetheless, is good in a recognizably human sense, involving the benevolent use of his power (Hyman, 2010, pp. 137–53). According to Hyman's approach, premodern orthodoxy did not regard God in such a way; thus there would have been no conflict between the existence of God and such all-too-obvious phenomena as suffering and cruelty. If we were to return to such a premodern understanding of God – an understanding such as Hyman locates in medieval theology – the problem would dissolve away, or at least take a very different form.

But how plausible is all this? We recommend a degree of skepticism. Consider, for example, the new approaches to biblical studies that did much to undermine the integrity and plausibility of the biblical texts. Hyman describes various mystical, allegorical, and typological approaches to interpretation that were used in ancient and medieval times, and then observes:

> If such approaches had been carried over from the medieval into the modern period, it is interesting to speculate as to whether the advent of biblical criticism would have had quite the disturbing impact that it did in fact have. (Hyman, 2010, p. 89)

It seems to us, however, that this exaggerates both the dominance of these approaches in earlier times and their eclipse in early modernity. As we have seen (Myth 37), St Augustine emphasized the importance of the literal biblical narrative. Although he was open to a variety of means of interpreting the Bible, he maintained that these should not conflict with an understanding of it as a record of historical truth. For Augustine, such exegeses may be permissible and valuable provided we also accept the literal record. Thus, in discussing various interpretations of the paradise of Eden, he concludes: "There is no prohibition against such exegesis, provided that we also believe in the truth of the story as a faithful record of historical fact" (Augustine, 2003, p. 535). Conversely, the rich heritage of modern biblical exegeses contains no shortage of allegorical and other meanings, in addition to the literal.

A similar argument applies to scientific discoveries that cast doubt on the biblical narrative as a faithful historical record. If no one had treated the Bible in that way in the first place, or if this had been merely an ephemeral theological fashion, the challenge from science might not have mattered so much. But there was a long tradition of regarding the Bible as historically correct – whatever other meanings could also be legitimately be ascribed to it – and it is likely that textual-historical findings to the contrary would have had a dramatic impact in any period of history. Even if some ancient and medieval theologians placed their primary emphasis on nonliteral meanings, the biblical texts gained much of their authority from a semblance of historical accuracy (a point that was, once again, well known to Augustine). Similarly, we doubt that Christianity would have maintained its intellectual credibility in the face of science if it had opted for an interpretation of God very different from the one that Hyman sees as "modern."

The medieval deity that Hyman describes, approvingly, was not "powerful" in the normal meaning of that word, which surely relates to its ability to accomplish various tasks, or "good" in a recognizably human sense. According to Hyman, this being was not thought of as having any attributes that we can understand straightforwardly. Instead, on the approach of theologians such as St Thomas Aquinas in the thirteenth century, God is a good, powerful, or wise being only by analogy with our ordinary understandings of words such as "good," "loving," "powerful," and "wise," making it difficult to falsify any claim about the attributes of this being. Thus God is not literally good, in the sense of human goodness, but possesses a quality that stands to him as ordinary goodness stands to us.

One difficulty with all this is why, unless we wish to take theologians and priests on trust, we should believe that God is "good," "loving," "powerful," or "wise" in such a mysterious sense. How is the analogy supposed to work, and what evidence could there be for such inchoate claims? Even worse, how intelligible are these claims, especially if we are going to say that *all* God's attributes are somehow analogical? Finally, how attractive would such claims be to ordinary people who would surely struggle even to understand them? We suspect that ordinary people in medieval times – and probably even most priests and theologians – pictured a rather less abstract and theoretical deity whose attributes they understood pretty much literally. Indeed, many ordinary people and clergy of the time may have held a considerably more anthropomorphic idea of God than prevails today, even among conservative Christians.

In the next section, we examine some of the classic arguments in favor of God's existence, showing why they are inconclusive at best. Before we get to that, however, we must acknowledge that high levels of belief in God persisted in Europe and other Western countries until quite recently. Though many intellectuals began to doubt the truth of Christianity during the eighteenth and nineteenth centuries, the percentage of the general population who retained some kind of allegiance to the Christian churches fell steeply only in the mid-twentieth century. The piling up of intellectual doubts and difficulties may have had a delayed effect, and may certainly have *allowed* this outcome to happen. It appears, however, that the eventual collapse of old certainties among ordinary people owes much to social factors, such as rising levels of affluence and personal security in postwar Europe.

For all that, it's important to obtain a sense of how inconclusive, or even frail, the classic theistic arguments really are, and why they offer little support to anyone who starts to doubt the words of theologians, priests, and holy books.

Credited to Jesus and Mo, www.jesusandmo.net

Classic Theistic Arguments

Many diverse arguments have been given for the existence of gods, particularly monotheistic gods such as the God of orthodox Christianity and other Abrahamic religions. A well-known and traditional classification speaks of ontological, cosmological, and teleological arguments, but some theistic arguments fall outside these categories.

We do not have the space to dissect the whole range of theistic arguments, though in earlier chapters we discussed some of them in passing (for example, we touched on the so-called moral arguments for the existence of God in Myth 20). In truth, it would take an entire book just to give a fair and adequate account of traditional kinds of ontological, cosmological, and teleological arguments. We provide a sketch of why these sorts of arguments have turned out to be inconclusive, and why they are likely to remain so. Some of the main criticisms explored here go back at least as far as Hume and Kant.

In fairness, readers might also wish to read some leading theistic philosophers, such as Richard Swinburne (2004) and Alvin Plantinga (2000, 2011), to see some of the arguments developed with remarkable ingenuity. Plantinga has also debated atheist philosopher Michael Tooley in their book *Knowledge of God* (2008) – this is written in a more technical philosophical register.

First, some distinctions, and here we follow the analysis in Graham Oppy's *Arguing About Gods* (2006). As described by Oppy, ontological arguments rely on a priori considerations: that is, they "start from definitions, or claims about the contents of conceptions or ideas, or claims about what is conceivable or logically possible, or allegedly analytic claims about the concept of existence, or the like" (Oppy, 2006, p. 2). If this is rather abstract, think about a typical ontological argument. It will begin with a definition of the concept of God, then attempt to show, without requiring any empirical evidence, that God (as defined) *actually exists*. Cosmological arguments begin with premises relating to very general structural features of the universe or ways of understanding it (Oppy, 2006, pp. 3, 97), while teleological arguments rely on more specific features of the universe that supposedly evidence intelligent design (Oppy, 2006, p. 3). Our aim here is to focus on the main kinds of ontological, cosmological, and teleological arguments – those most easily classified in such categories and most commonly advanced by theologians and philosophers of religion.

The usual kinds of ontological arguments fail to convince most people, even religious believers, and are perhaps the least likely to be advanced seriously by modern religious apologists. But they still have their proponents, and more logically sophisticated ontological arguments are constructed by each new generation of philosophers. Their relative lack of appeal is not surprising given the seemingly absolute distinction between an abstract concept and the instantiation of that concept in the real world that we live in.

Consider, for example, St Anselm's version of the argument from the eleventh century, which defines the concept of God along the lines of "a being than which no greater can be conceived (or thought)." On one reconstruction, the argument proceeds as follows:

1. There is, in the fool's understanding, a being than which none greater can be conceived.

2. If it exists in the fool's understanding, it can be thought by the fool to exist in reality as well.
3. Which would be greater.
4. Therefore, a being that exists only in the fool's understanding, and not also in reality, is not a being than which none greater can be conceived – such a being is one that exists in reality as well.
5. Therefore, the fool must admit that a being than which none greater can be conceived exists not only in the fool's understanding but in reality as well. (Compare Martin, 1990, p. 80; Oppy, 2006, pp. 72–73)

So someone who is inclined to be a "fool," and so denies the existence of God, ends up being forced to admit that God exists. The idea that drives all this is that a being with the property of existing in reality, as well as in our understanding, is "greater" than an otherwise identical being that has the property of existing *only* in our understanding. It seems to follow from this that, once we conceptualize God as a being than which none greater can be conceived, we must admit that God actually does exist.

When ontological arguments are formulated in ways that appear to be logically valid, they prove far too much (Oppy, 2006, pp. 92–93). After all, as Oppy points out, proponents of these arguments such as St Anselm could simply define the word "God" as "an existent perfect being" (Oppy, 2006, p. 92) – or even, we might add, "an existent-in-reality-not-just-our-thoughts perfect being" – which would seem to do the required job. An existent perfect being has the property of existing, so it follows that such a being actually exists. However, think what else this sort of argument would prove. We could demonstrate the existence of all sorts of arcane entities, such as an existent perfect unicorn, an existent perfect superhero, an existent Loch Ness monster (compare Martin, 1990, p. 85), and so on. Thus allow us to offer you the concept of an existent Loch Ness monster – and it quickly follows that this creature actually exists. Something must have gone wrong here.

Such a short way of establishing the existence of entities fails because existence is not an ordinary property like being 12-legged, purple, or nine inches long (or the combination of all three, like that thing currently crawling on your shoulder!). One way to look at this is to say that we first have a *concept* of something, with various properties that the "something" would have if it actually existed – and it is always a separate question whether or not there is actually an instance of the concept in the real world. Even if we do think of existence as a property of some kind, it must refer to something other than the real-world instantiation of a concept.

Is there *any* sense in which "existence" is a property? Well, you can, in a sense, *think of* a certain character in a fictional narrative as actually existing, and not as "existing" only in someone's thoughts. You might, at the same time, think of other characters in the narrative as merely dreams or illusions experienced by the first-mentioned character (and thus "existing" only in that character's thoughts). It does not follow that *any* of these fictional characters exists in reality, or, to put it another way, that the concepts of *any* of these characters are actually instantiated, even though it might be said that your concept of the first-mentioned character encodes a property of existing or being real. Let's grant that this is the sort of property that a concept can encode, but even if you possess this concept and think about this property, it does not follow that the concept is actually instantiated. For example, the governess in Henry James's 1898 novel *The Turn of the Screw* does not exist in the real world any more than do the ghosts which, within the fictional universe of *The Turn of the Screw*, she may be imagining.

Depending on how they are interpreted and formalized, ontological arguments may simply be invalid on their face, or they may fail because they use terms such as "exists" equivocally, failing to make these sorts of distinctions, or they may rely on dubious ideas such as that when I have a concept it is thereby actualized in a way (actualized in my understanding).

The situation gets more complicated if the property asserted of God (or some other imagined thing) is not "existence" but something that sounds grander such as "necessary existence" or "essential existence." To consider the first of these for a moment, it is not clear whether necessary existence is suspect as a property in precisely the same way as existence. Nonetheless, how could anything like God have the property of necessary existence, if that means *logically* necessary existence, or existence in every logically possible world? Is this a coherent property at all for beings and entities? What if I define "a necessarily existent Loch Ness monster" as a large and necessarily existent sea creature that inhabits the Scottish lake Loch Ness? Does it follow that any necessarily existent Loch Ness monsters actually exist in Loch Ness? Surely not.

This brief discussion should suffice to show why even the most ingenious ontological arguments have not convinced many philosophers. We doubt that these sorts of arguments have ever persuaded anyone to believe in God.

We think we've said enough for current purposes about why ontological arguments run into difficulties. In contrast, cosmological arguments, which rely on very general features of the universe, are more likely to command assent from people who read them or hear them from religious apologists.

Most typically, cosmological arguments attempt to prove a cause of the existence of the universe, or a first cause of all phenomena other than itself. But as Law points out, ultimate cosmological questions run into philosophical problems too. First, it is not clear that it is meaningful to ask, in effect, why there is something rather than nothing, as it raises a more radical question than, say, "Why is there nothing in my cup?" This is a kind of *absolute* nothing in which we are removing even the framework of space and time against which questions about such things as cups are asked (Law, 2011, pp. 31–32). Second, why does introducing a further thing, God, answer the question? Why stop with God (Law, 2011, p. 32)?

This leads us to a problem frequently noted by philosophers: why think that we *have* stopped with God, rather than with some *other* cause of the universe? Even if a cosmological argument were successful in proving a cause of the universe or a first cause of all phenomena other than itself, it would take more to show that this cause of the universe or first cause of all other phenomena was God (as described by, say, orthodox Jewish, Christian, or Islamic theologians), or any similar being. Indeed, it would not show, without a great deal more, that the cause of the universe, or the first cause of all other phenomena, possessed even the most *minimal* attributes that something requires to count as a god – we have in mind such attributes as consciousness, intellect, agency, and personality. Why might not this supreme cause, if we might call it that, be some phenomenon describable by physicists with no reference to any such attributes?

A contemporary version of the argument cosmological argument, popularized and elaborated by William Lane Craig, although based on the work of medieval Christian and Islamic theologians, takes this form:

1. Everything that begins to exist has a cause of its existence.
2. The universe began to exist.
3. The universe has a cause of its existence. (See, e.g., Craig and Sinnott-Armstrong, 2004, pp. 1–9)

Does this withstand critical scrutiny? Not in our view. The various transformations of matter and energy that we see in the everyday world in which we live – the world of cats and dogs and human beings, of cities and mountains, tables and chairs – do, indeed, follow a causal order, or so it appears. But it is not at all clear that we can extrapolate this to infer that the entire causal order that we see, going back to the Big Bang, is itself part of some *larger* causal order. We cannot know that. If it is not, the argument breaks down because the first premise is false. Given the limitations of our knowledge, the first premise is at least doubtful.

The second premise also has problems. We can look at mathematical models of the Big Bang and ask whether they really amount to a model in which "the universe began to exist" – bearing in mind that the overall universe is very different from any particular phenomenon that might be found within it. Physicists can get into fascinating arguments about whether, in the case of the universe itself, having a finite age (approximately 13.7 billion years) is the same as "beginning to exist." What, for example, was the earlier temporal order of things within which the universe can be said to have *begun* to do anything at all? Temporal order as we know it is, itself, a feature of the universe.

But we can set all that aside. Perhaps what we see as the universe *is* part of a larger causal order. If so, however, this is a larger causal order that we cannot easily find out anything about, though some physicists are currently attempting to do just that. If this larger order does exist, but we are unable to observe it directly, that creates a fascinating, challenging, and of course somewhat frustrating, situation for physicists. It does not, however, establish the existence of any agent, entity, or phenomenon in particular. More specifically, it does not demonstrate the existence of a particular intelligent being, such as the God described by orthodox theologians.

In this context, J.L. Mackie says, we think persuasively:

> We have no good ground for an *a priori* certainty that there could not have been a sheer unexplained beginning of things. But in so far as we find this improbable, it should cast doubt on the interpretation of the big bang as an absolute beginning of the material universe; rather, we should infer that it must have had some physical antecedents, even if the big bang has to be taken as a discontinuity so radical that we cannot explain it, because we can find no laws which we can extrapolate backwards through this discontinuity. (Mackie, 1982, pp. 92–93)

Teleological arguments, or arguments from design, use remarkable features of the natural world, for which God is then posited as the best explanation (Law, 2011, p. 35) or inferred in some other way. For example, William Paley produced elaborate arguments at the beginning of the nineteenth century, attempting to draw an inference from the functional intricacy of biological organs and organisms to the existence of a powerful intelligence that must have designed them. Paley regarded the inference as an inevitable one, and perhaps as just obviously correct (Oppy, 2006, p. 182), but why should it be?

He draws an analogy with a watch, where, in fact, the inference to a human artificer really is inevitable and correct, but this is because of a great deal of background factual information that we have about watches and their materials – for example, that refined metals are not found in nature, and nor are such things as cogwheels or smooth, clear glass, and that watches are, in any event, products of human artifice. By contrast, we do not have this sort of background knowledge about animals or their organs (such as a rabbit's heart) and we do not have a basis to draw the same inevitable, obviously correct, inference (Oppy, 2006, pp. 176–181).

That leave us with the intriguing question of how such functionally intricate things came to be. Should we posit design and artifice, even though we have no further evidence beyond their functional intricacy that animals and their organs are products of design and artifice? Or should we simply reserve judgment? Whatever might have been the best approach in Paley's day, the theory of biological evolution removes whatever force his argument might have had. That is, it gives the missing explanation as to how diverse, complex, functionally adaptive things such as animals might have come to exist. In that sense, biological science can be regarded as a nail in the coffin of this sort of design argument.

It is arguable, however, that the steady advance of other science and engineering fields has been even more compelling. As our knowledge has increased about what sorts of materials exist in nature, and why, it is possible to give an increasingly detailed and compelling explanation as to why we would recognize a watch, a laptop computer, or a rocket ship as the product of conscious and intelligent design, without being compelled to extend the analysis to such things as animals and their organs.

In passing, before turning to an issue that requires greater attention, we should note that some religious apologists and others employ scientific, or quasi-scientific, arguments against the unguided evolution over time of living species. We are thinking of intelligent design theorists, who see life as best explained via the operations of a designing intelligence, whether supernatural or merely alien (the broad hint is almost always that this intelligence must be God). In some cases, the arguments are based on a claimed irreducible complexity of certain biological systems. To put this in a rather quick and slippery way, the systems could not have evolved over time, but must have appeared all at once, to be functionally effective.

Such arguments have been rejected by mainstream science. Biologists have found no need for an additional element of involvement by an external intelligent agent in the evolutionary process. This is not the place to enter into the detail of the scientific response to intelligent design theory (interested readers might wish to begin with Coyne, 2009, pp. 136–143).

Let us, however, take further note of the slipperiness of "irreducible complexity." In part, this seems to refer to (1) the fact that the system, as it currently exists, will not function if you remove one of its components. But that is quite different from (2) the idea that the system could not have evolved gradually from some other system, perhaps something rather simpler, that lacked the same structure of components. Advocates of irreducible complexity often seem to conflate senses 1 and 2, but there is no reason in principle why a system that is irreducibly complex in sense 1 must *also* be, as it were, unevolvable – sense 2. The evolutionary process takes many paths, often indirect and, from the viewpoint of human engineers, wasteful or strange (see, for a start, Coyne, 2009, pp. 81–85; Dawkins, 2009, pp. 356–371). Thus Oppy is on strong ground when he ultimately dismisses arguments based on irreducible complexity:

> even if it is true that there are biological systems that are "irreducibly complex" in the sense that they are composed without remainder of parts each of which is indispensable for any level of functioning in the system in question, I see no reason at all why such systems could not evolve as the result of Darwinian evolution. Given the strong, independent evidence in favour of the claim that current organisms are the result of an extremely long chain of Darwinian evolution, we should not suppose that "irreducible complexity" poses a serious threat to "evolution by numerous, successive, slight modifications". (Oppy, 2006, p. 195)

Teleological arguments based on the functional complexity of living things no longer cut any ice. In recent decades, however, the most popular kind of teleological argument begins with a claim that the laws of nature and initial conditions of the universe must be very finely tuned in order for life to appear – making such a universe extraordinarily improbable as a result of mere chance, and leading to the inference that it was designed by a powerful intelligent agent such as God. Readers might wish to consult Plantinga's book, *Where the Conflict Really Lies* (2011, pp. 194–199) for one of the many accounts of the fine-tuning argument (and for extensive references to others).

In Plantinga's version, the argument clearly has a probabilistic aspect. It is based on the idea that the phenomenon of fine tuning is not improbable on the assumption that God exists – since God would want there to be life – while it is improbable that the constants would have the values that they do as a result of chance (Plantinga, 2011, p. 199). As Plantinga acknowledges, however, it is difficult to see just how the argument is supposed to work, and particularly how probability can be determined (or even understood) in a field of inquiry such as this (pp. 219–224).

Accordingly, he draws the conclusion that a fine-tuning argument gives "only mild support" to theism (p. 224). Thus it might do no more than raise the probability of God's existence from virtually zero to "merely" very unlikely.

But can it achieve even that much? How confident are we that fine-tuning is a genuine phenomenon? Even if it is, how likely is it that no naturalistic explanation will be found (as happened with the functional complexity of living organisms), in which case there is no reason to resort to a supernatural one? In his brief discussion of fine-tuning arguments, Stephen Law notes that some physicists question whether the universe really is fine-tuned for life, while others propose that there may be a multiverse – a vast ensemble of universes, perhaps governed by different laws – in which case the existence of some that are finely tuned for life is not especially improbable (Law, 2011, pp. 40–42; for science-based skepticism about the fine-tuning phenomenon see Stenger, 2008, pp. 144–154, 2011, 2012, pp. 173–186).

Some readers might think that arguing for the existence of a monstrous number of universes is an egregiously ad hoc step to avoid the conclusion that fine-tuning reveals the presence of a supernatural designer. That, however, would be a mistake. Consider again the question of whether our universe is part of some larger causal order that has brought it into being. While this cannot simply be assumed, as we saw in discussing the cosmological argument, it is not obviously implausible. If, however, there is some larger causal order that brought into being our entire universe, why would it *not* have the power to bring into being an indefinitely large number of other universes alongside ours? Why would something with that kind of causal power bring about exactly one universe?

In fact, various models are being developed and discussed by physicists, based on independent scientific considerations. Lawrence Krauss, a renowned theoretical physicist, makes the point strongly: "Almost every logical possibility we can imagine regarding extending the laws of physics as we know them, on small scales, into a more complete theory, suggests that, on large scales, our universe is not unique" (Krauss, 2012, p. 126). The models under discussion do not involve supernatural intelligent agents, but they do specify causal processes that could be expected to generate an indefinitely vast number of universes. That being so, and with the prospect of better models being developed in the future, Plantinga is correct not to place too much trust in fine-tuning arguments.

However, we should note that he appears to make an outright error at one point of his discussion. He acknowledges the possibility that our universe is part of a vast ensemble of universes. If that is so, only a tiny proportion of universes might be finely tuned for life as we know it to be possible – however, beings that are capable of understanding the problem would arise only in those universes. If this scenario is the correct one, then we see exactly what should be expected: evidence that our own universe is finely tuned for the possibility of life. Thus what science has discovered to date in no way stands as evidence that this is *not* the actual scenario. So far, so good. But here is what we consider an error.

Plantinga seems to think that there is some further question as to why *our* universe is one of the finely tuned ones (Plantinga, 2011, pp. 213–214). By analogy with a poker game, why have *we* drawn such a good hand? But rational, intelligent beings within an indefinitely vast ensemble of universes will *always* find themselves in universes where such beings could come into existence. Once it is stipulated for argument's sake that we live in this kind of multiverse, there is no further question as to why *our* particular universe is one of the fine-tuned ones. There is simply no possibility that we would have come into existence in any of the others.

There is nothing suspicious here that can be analogized to the poker game type of example. Think about it for a moment: it is not as if we already existed somewhere (in some supernatural realm?), then had the good luck to be "dealt" a fine-tuned universe.

Enough has been said to show the difficulty in constructing decisive ontological, cosmological, or teleological arguments. However, there is another side to all this that we have largely ignored until now: the difficulties that positively weigh *against* God as the cause or designer of the universe. Just how probable are theistic explanations of the existence, structure, or specific details of everything we see around us?

An obvious problem if we offer such an explanation is that God is supposed to be a disembodied, purely "spiritual" intellect. But why postulate something like *that* as the cause or designer of the universe? It is not as if we have experiences of other disembodied intellects, much less other disembodied intellects that are the causes or designers of natural phenomena, or of large ordered objects (if that's how we should regard the universe) – or of anything else. Moreover, we do not find large, ordered objects being created by infinite beings (such as God is said to be) or by *individual* beings (again, such as God is said to be). Rather, they are created by multiple finite beings. And when we examine the universe as a whole, as mentioned earlier, it does not possess the sorts of properties from which we would normally infer artifice – here it differs from such things as machines made of metals, plastics, and clear glass. Overall, everything we know about the universe makes it *prima facie most unlikely* that it was a product of artifice, let alone created and/or designed by an intelligent agent matching the traditional description of God (Martin, 1990, pp. 317–333).

It should be added that things did not have to turn out like this. For all our ancestors knew at the beginning of the scientific revolution, science might have discovered disembodied intellects – perhaps in such forms as demons, angels, and ancestor spirits – playing a causal role in the world around us. For example, the activity of evil spirits might have turned out to be a good explanation for mental illness. We might have found that certain very large, ordered objects are the creations of individual intelligent agents – perhaps even disembodied ones – and our best criteria for sorting out which things are artifacts might have turned out differently. As human beings explored the universe through scientific means, it might have remained an enchanted cosmos, brimming with all sorts of miraculous agents and powers, and we might have learned more about how they act and what they want. But of course, none of it happened that way.

Given how the universe actually looks, based on the path actually taken by science in the past four or five centuries, theistic hypotheses are implausible. Thus Oppy defends a view that we might, at the outset, rationally assign a very small probability to them:

> I do not see any reason to suppose that it is somehow "contrary to reason" to assign a *very* small prior probability to the hypothesis that our universe is the product of intelligent design. There is nothing in our experience that weighs against the claim that all intelligent designers are physically embodied agents who work with pre-existing physical materials; moreover, there are no details that we can supply to explain how there could be intelligent designers that are not physically embodied agents who work with pre-existing materials. Furthermore, we have plenty of evidence that consciousness and intelligence in our universe are reducible to neurological functioning. While these – and other similar – considerations are plausibly taken to be defeasible, it seems to me to be very hard to deny that non-theists can mount a serious defence of the claim that the prior probability that our universe is the product of intelligent design is very low indeed. (Oppy, 2006, p. 208)

Or, as J.L. Mackie puts it, "the very notion of a non-embodied spirit, let alone an infinite one, is intrinsically improbable in relation to our background knowledge, in that our experience reveals nothing of the sort" (Mackie, 1982, p. 100). Mackie also discusses the oddness of creation by such a being – a sort of creation that we never actually see:

> All our knowledge of intention-fulfilment is of embodied intentions being fulfilled indirectly by way of bodily changes and movements which are causally related to the intended result, and where the ability thus to fulfil

> intentions itself has a causal history, either of evolutionary development or of learning or both. Only by ignoring such key features do we get an analogue of the supposed divine action. (Mackie, 1982, p. 100, see also p. 149)

Perhaps the existence of our universe, with its apparent beginning a finite (though vast) number of years in the past, and its alleged fine-tuning for life, calls for some explanation. If so, however, nothing about our ordinary experience, in combination with our scientific knowledge, should push us in the direction of postulating some kind of powerful disembodied intellect that lurks behind the material order of things. As we understand more about how the phenomena of the world actually do come about, there is no reason to think that the logical stopping point should be something mental, such as a disembodied intellect.

There are further problems, if we are going to use a theistic hypothesis to explain general or particular features of the universe (this paragraph is loosely based on Law, 2011, pp. 43–46). What, for a start, is the nature of the hypothesized God? Can it even be described in a consistent way? If it is a timeless being, as often alleged of the orthodox Christian God, does this claim make sense at all, and how can such a being have desires, such as the desire to make a universe? Conversely, if God exists in time, did he always have the desire to make universes, in which case why is ours not infinitely old, and in any event is God the sort of being in whom desires of this sort can be expected to arise from time to time (isn't God also supposed to be *changeless*?)? And finally, if all this is meant to be understood in some nonliteral way (as Gavin Hyman might insist), what does it really mean, and how can something not meant literally have any explanatory power?

We seem to be owed a great deal before the God hypothesis becomes a coherent explanation of anything. Then there are other problems. If our universe really has been finely tuned for life, why was an omnipotent God unwilling or unable to make it more pervasively hospitable to living things? As Stenger asks pointedly, why is the universe actually so uncongenial to *human* life, if it was designed by a being who takes a special interest in us (2008, pp. 154–161)? Only a vanishingly tiny volume of space could possibly support human life, or seemingly any kind of intelligent life, without massive technological efforts.

And all this is before we start worrying about whether a God with certain properties (such as, perhaps, omnipotence and benevolence) seems a plausible explanation for any universe that contains so much obvious pain, suffering, and cruelty. We touched on this issue earlier, and will return to it in the following sections.

Credited to Jesus and Mo, www.jesusandmo.net

Religion and Science – Conflicting or Compatible?

At a number of points in this chapter, we have discussed aspects of the relationship between theistic religion and science, noting, in particular, how the success of science contributed to a disenchantment of the cosmos. As more phenomena were plausibly explained by entirely natural mechanisms, it increasingly became possible, even defensible, for educated Westerners to understand the world around them without reference to any supernatural powers or agents. This is just one way in which science tends to undermine the authority, and indeed the plausibility, of religion.

So we return to a question discussed rather briefly earlier in this book (Myth 41). Are religion and science compatible? That may depend on what is meant by "compatible," but we contend that it is misleading at best when Chris Mooney and Sheril Kirshenbaum (among others) claim that religion and science are perfectly compatible with each other. This position is, they say, the most tolerant and intellectually responsible on the religion and science question, and they praise two American science organizations, the National Academy of Sciences and the American Association for the Advancement of Science, for adopting it officially (Mooney and Kirshenbaum, 2009, p. 103). In part, they are impressed that systems of religious belief can be modified over time, steadily eliminating any direct inconsistencies with well-established scientific findings.

However, they are also impressed by the fact that many great scientists have been religious (Mooney and Kirshenbaum, 2009, pp. 100–101) and that many religious organizations and leaders "uphold the principle of compatibility" (p. 105). Indeed, it is true that many scientists, both historically and today, have been religious – so, short of their being disingenuous, this provides prima facie evidence for at least the psychological possibility of mixing science with religion. Alister McGrath – whose qualifications include a doctorate in molecular biology – is just one of many religious apologists who argue for the compatibility of science and religion by pointing to surveys that show a large number of contemporary scientists have religious – including theistic – beliefs (McGrath, 2004, pp. 110–111). At least in the United States, scientists tend to be considerably less religious than the general public (Ecklund, 2010, pp. 15–17), but many do find ways of reconciling their religious views with their science-based knowledge of the world and their own involvement in scientific practice. What should we make of this?

We do not deny that many people find it psychologically possible to commit themselves to a scientific view of the world (or even to practice in an area of scientific inquiry) while also being devoutly religious. Nor do we deny that systems of religious belief can, at least in principle, change over time to remove direct inconsistencies with scientific findings. However, it is an open question just how far any particular religion can do this in practice. In any event, we can grant such concessions while still insisting that science has tended to erode religious belief. How could it be otherwise if science has tended to cast doubt on the appearance of living in an enchanted cosmos – and if this appearance is one of the very things that formerly kept atheism off the table as a viable intellectual option?

Nonetheless, some authors claim that there is *never* a conflict between religious teachings and views of the world and its inhabitants (on the one hand) and (on the other hand) scientific knowledge about this same world and its inhabitants. For example, Madrid and Hensley pour scorn on the idea that science, as a way of investigating the natural world, could ever tell us anything about the existence of God (2010, pp. 27–30).

Hyman suggests that tensions between religion and science are unnecessary, and seems to think they would not have arisen historically if theologians had managed to retain medieval understandings of God, God's attributes, revelation, and other core Christian concepts, into the modern period. Thus he expresses dismay at Enlightenment-era attempts, by Isaac Newton and others, to sustain a total worldview integrating science and theology. He comments as follows on the relationship between religion and science around the eighteenth century and leading up to the discoveries of Darwin – a period when science was thought, at least by some major European thinkers, to ground both philosophy and theology:

> If this is so . . . it does cast some considerable light both on the nature of the earlier amity between science and religion and also on the process of its rapid collapse. For what it does suggest is that, however secure and entrenched the accord between science and religion appeared to be, it was in fact utterly precarious in the sense that it depended entirely on science not in any way contradicting religious teaching, something that could not be indefinitely guaranteed. (Hyman, 2010, p. 104)

Citing passages from Terry Eagleton and others, Hyman claims that theology and science operate on different levels and deal with different subjects. Unlike science, so the argument goes, theology deals with such questions as why anything exists in the first place and why we find our experience intelligible. And thus, Hyman thinks, there is now a generally recognized accord between science and religion (Hyman, 2010, pp. 117–123).

We will return to these issues, but first we must acknowledge that some very influential scientists have offered systematic approaches to reconciling religion and science. At the beginning of the scientific revolution, Galileo himself proposed a solution, which he elaborated most fully in a lengthy letter of 1615, addressed to the Grand Duchess Christina (Galilei, 1957 [1615], pp. 173–227). Science and religion can be reconciled, so he argued, by progressively reinterpreting Bible passages as and when they are ever contradicted by scientific discoveries.

According to Galileo, the Bible's words could not always be interpreted according to their plain grammatical meaning, as this would result in inconsistencies and theological errors, such as denial of God's omniscience. Rather, the choice of words had been accommodated in ancient times to the abilities of "rude and unlearned" common people, and must be interpreted by "wise expositors," who could also explain "the special reasons" for the actual wording (Galilei, 1957 [1615], pp. 181–182). On this approach, it was not surprising that the Bible did not always speak literally of the phenomena of physical nature, since such knowledge was essential neither for salvation nor for serving God. Accordingly, where what was discovered by science contradicted the literal words of the Bible it was preferable to seek an interpretation that was consistent with scientific knowledge.

Although Galileo's approach met with disfavor from the Roman Catholic Church – and indeed, the Church strove to suppress the printed edition of the letter to Christina – it was not without theological precedent. Galileo was able to find support in respected Church authorities, including St Thomas Aquinas and other Church Fathers. Throughout the letter to Christina, he quotes extensively from St Augustine's writings, particularly Augustine's monumental exposition of Genesis, *De Genesi ad literatum*. We should, however, recall that Augustine was theologically opposed to purely allegorical or symbolic exegeses. These were of value, he thought, only as long as the Bible was also considered a faithful historical record, as with the Genesis narrative of Adam and Eve (Augustine, 2003, p. 535).

Albert Einstein also thought that science and religion were compatible, though he was not a theist in any orthodox sense, and his reconciliation of religion and science depended on his particular definitions of both (see Myth 45). He conceived of science as a systematic attempt to explain and unify the phenomena of the perceived world (Einstein, 1954, p. 44). He believed that this was a relatively uncontroversial conception of the scientific enterprise, but we might well raise a complication. The observed phenomena are often unified only by positing entities and forces that cannot be observed directly. We might question whether, in principle, those entities and forces could not have resembled the unseen powers described by various religions. In that case the phenomena of the physical world would be unified by something that would normally be regarded as supernatural.

Einstein's views on religion did not find favor with most religious leaders and thinkers, and in this case he was well aware that his ideas were controversial (Jammer, 1999, pp. 91–107). For Einstein, religion relates to unselfish, or "superpersonal," values, objectives, and goals. It deals "with evaluations of human thought and action, and cannot speak of facts or the relationships among them" (Einstein, 1954, pp. 44–45). More specifically, it encourages certain ideals through such devices as symbolism and mythic narrative:

> Religion is concerned with man's attitude toward nature at large, with the establishing of ideals for the individual and communal life, and with mutual

> human relationship. These ideals religion attempts to attain by exerting an educational influence on tradition and through the development and promulgation of certain easily accessible thoughts and narratives (epics and myths) which are apt to influence evaluation and action along the lines of the accepted ideals. (Einstein, 1954, p. 50)

If science and religion are conceived like this, they might well never conflict, but that might not comfort the faithful! A problem for ideas such this is simply that many religious people refuse to accept them. Einstein's attempt at reconciliation requires an understanding of religion that subsumes it within moral philosophy and takes away its ability to make factual claims about the world (whether the world we perceive or an otherworldly order of things). Einstein denied religion the right to make such claims as that the statements made in the Bible are all absolutely true, thus intruding on the work of scientists such as Copernicus and Darwin (Einstein, 1954, p. 45). He thought, furthermore, that conflict was caused by the essentially primitive and intellectually untenable idea of God (Einstein, 1954, pp. 46–49). This is hardly a reconciliation of science with religion as it is usually understood in the Abrahamic traditions of monotheism.

For Einstein, science could provide knowledge of how religion's values could actually be obtained. Conversely, science required what he called a "faith" that the empirical world is comprehensible to us – that investigation of its workings will yield intelligible answers. He summed up this philosophy with the aphorism: "science without religion is lame, religion without science is blind" (Einstein, 1954, p. 46). There was a role in his view of the world for both science and religion, but only if they were understood in a specific way.

More recently, the Harvard paleontologist Stephen Jay Gould developed a similar approach. Gould's attempt to reconcile religion and science forms the central argument of his book *Rocks of Ages: Science and Religion in the Fullness of Life* (1999). Here he claims that there can be no conflict between science and religion so long as each sticks to (what Gould sees as) its proper place:

> Science tries to document the factual character of the natural world, and to develop theories that coordinate and explain these facts. Religion, on the other hand, operates in the equally important, but utterly different, realm of human purposes, meanings, and values – subjects that the factual domain of science might illuminate, but can never resolve. Similarly, while scientists must operate with ethical principles, some specific to their practice, the validity of these principles can never be inferred from the factual discoveries of science. (Gould, 1999, pp. 4–5)

Gould calls his "central principle of respectful noninterference" that of "nonoverlapping magisteria" (or NOMA), and he defines a "magisterium" as a "domain of authority in teaching" (Gould, 1999, p. 5). The principle of NOMA, therefore, is that religion and science are nonoverlapping domains of intellectual authority. Because they do not overlap, they cannot contradict each other, and hence can coexist in mutual respect. According to this view, we are entitled to tell religious leaders to keep out of such matters as the age of the earth, how it came into existence, and whether our species, *Homo sapiens*, evolved from earlier forms of life. However, so the idea goes, scientists should not challenge the authority of religion in the moral realm.

Gould maintains that science asks questions about the workings of the natural world, while religion asks questions about how we should live, find a sense of meaning in our lives, and so on. In effect, Gould conflates the religious realm with a broadly interpreted realm of ethical discussion. Thus, in his usage, (1) "religion" just is the domain of discussion about ethics (interpreted to include issues of value, "purpose," "meaning" and so on), the "ought" realm; and (2) science, which deals with the "is" realm, cannot impinge on this (broadly understood) ethical realm. That is because no number of claims about the natural world can add up to a claim about, say, how we should treat each other or about the meaning of life.

Notice, however, that Gould rules out conflict between science and religion, not so much by holding back the reach of science (though *Rocks of Ages* does contain an element of this), but by radically constraining the claims, true or false, that religion can make without going beyond the legitimate or essential boundaries for religion – or, alternatively, by radically redefining "religion," much as Einstein did.

Gould's NOMA principle makes religion invulnerable to some kinds of scientific criticism, but only by ruling out many religious claims as illegitimate in the first place. For example, Gould does not attack fundamentalist Christian beliefs in a relatively young earth merely on the basis that it is unreasonable to maintain them in the light of well-established scientific knowledge. Instead, he argues that it is illegitimate *in principle* to have any religious beliefs about matters of empirical fact. Unfortunately for Gould's analysis, however, most actual religions have not confined themselves to making "ought" statements or related statements about value, meaning, or purpose.

Religious organizations, leaders, teachers, and sacred texts have frequently put forward factual statements about the existence of supernatural beings, such as gods, nymphs, demons, and ancestral spirits. They have made claims about the dispositions and activities of these beings or have invoked overarching forces or principles, such as Moira, Karma, or the Tao. They have described the structure of the cosmos and depicted unseen places, such as Hades, Valhalla, Paradise, and Purgatory. They have posited deep components or aspects of the human makeup, such as the soul or *Atman*. However remote some of these may be from empirical investigation, such claims take the form of "is," not "ought," statements.

Furthermore, many religious truth-claims, taken at face value, are not just about supernatural beings, places, and so on, in isolation from the natural world. Rather, they involve interactions with the natural world that could leave traces behind and so be detectable to science. Historically, the various answers to "ought" questions offered by religious authorities have been entangled with, and informed by, beliefs about empirical matters. In some cases, scientific discoveries directly contradict the (evidently false) information provided by religious authorities. For example, the actual structure of the cosmos bears little resemblance to what is implied or explicitly described in any religious text.

Most notoriously, it is possible to calculate from the words of the Bible at least a rough idea of the age of the earth and the larger universe. As Gould points out (1998, pp. 94–96), there are sufficient gaps and ambiguities in the Bible's genealogies to stretch or contract the total age of the earth somewhat. Accordingly, we are not stuck with Bishop Ussher's precise answer (delivered in 1650) that it was created on the evening immediately before October 23, 4004 BCE. However, Ussher was massively in error, not merely "out" by a small margin, perhaps produced by (unconsciously?) fudging the data to get an overly neat result – the creation of the world just on 4000 years before the supposed birth of Jesus (Groves, 1996; Gould, 1998, pp. 80–98). Leaving aside such possibilities as a symbolic or allegorical interpretation of the seven days of Genesis, the Bible's gaps and ambiguities are not sufficient to allow for an answer of a different order of magnitude. Yet the age of the earth is now known to be billions of years (Dalrymple, 2001).

Should religious leaders now shut up about such things – well, *why* exactly? The view that they should do so is considered unacceptable by, for instance, conservative evangelical Christians. Indeed, the problem goes far wider:

> Gould's view that genuine religion does not conflict with science is tautological because he considered religions that do conflict with science, such as fundamentalist Protestantism, as not "genuine." And it is not only fundamentalist Protestants whose religion is not really "religion" by Gould's lights, but also the many Mormons, Jehovah's Witnesses, Orthodox Jews,

> Scientologists, Muslims, Hindus, and mainstream Protestants and Catholics who subscribe to creationist narratives. It is simply not kosher to delimit "religion" in a way that excludes a huge fraction of the world's believers. (Coyne, 2012, p. 2659)

At the same time, many secular thinkers will find another aspect of NOMA's proposition disturbing. If the principle were accepted, it would hand over an extremely important sphere of authority in teaching to religious doctrines, religious organizations, and religious leaders. Essentially it would surrender moral reflection to organized religion. While we empathize with Gould's attempt at getting religion out of his professional life (i.e., science), it is irresponsible of him to concede authority in matters of life's meaning and direction to religious authorities. There will remain crucial conflicts, for instance where scientific research and religious values clash. Just recall the most recent argument over embryonic stem cell research. Is Gould seriously suggesting that scientists have nothing to contribute to such debates, and that the normative decision on whether or not such research should be prohibited should be left to religious authorities?

Religious authorities' pronouncements on matters of ethics, derived as they are from the authority ascribed to their holy texts, are as baseless as their empirical pronouncements. Analytic philosophers, on the other hand, take it as one of the primary tasks of ethics to provide universal, reason-based answers to the question of how we ought to live our lives (e.g., Kant, 1993 [1785]; Sidgwick, 1874; Rachels and Rachels, 2010). Religious believers rely on divine authority. Martha Gill captures the difference between secular and religious approaches to morality quite nicely when she writes:

> Religious morality is not quite like other kinds of morality, because instead of consulting your sense of right and wrong, you're consulting the moral sense of an invisible being who takes sides depending on who believes in him the hardest. With God on your side, there is a certain feeling of moral immunity. Historically, then, it is unsurprising that leaders lucky enough to have divine guidance made grand, sweeping decisions with little concern for detail –decisions like taking on a "moral" war. (Gill, 2012)

Secular ethics aims to address two challenges meaningfully. It strives to provide us with practical guidance on how we should act in particular ethically challenging circumstances, and it must provide us with conceptual frameworks capable of justifying those answers. Religious ethics and secular ethics then will be able to address the first challenge. Both will be able to offer practical guidance with regard to what we ought to do, but only secular ethics is capable of providing justifications (reasons at a minimum). Religious ethics fails that second challenge. Reference to religious documents is no acceptable substitute for a reason-based argument or analysis. This is so because no convincing case has as yet been made for why we should accept the authority of the Bible, Qur'an, or similar texts. Some have pointed out that even if God existed, God also needed reasons for following particular causes of action when the choice between two or more courses of action was available, or else God's action would have been arbitrary. Arbitrariness does not go well with God's supposed omniscience and omnipotence as well as his general goodness. Secular ethics survives on the quality of its arguments and analyses alone.

Ethics must base its advice on *rational argument* rather than on a recourse to God or God's representatives saying so. As we have shown in earlier chapters, there are often significant divergences between the teachings of religious ethics (i.e., ethics based on the Bible, Qur'an, etc.) and reason-based ethics. Just take the issue of human sexuality as an example. Our sex lives are of great importance to religious leaders. They tell us that masturbation is a bad thing, multiple sexual partners are abhorrent (unless, perhaps, you are a traditional Muslim), homosexuality is abominable, and the list goes on. Their justifications rely on centuries-old scriptures that were driven by the cultural mores of their times. Arguments among theologians of liberal or conservative bents usually entail whether religious dictates that seem unreasonable in the twenty-first century can be explained away by reference to that ancient cultural context or whether they are still applicable to us. However, it is self-evident to them that our sex lives produce ethical problems. Compare that to a typical secular ethicist, Peter Singer. He notes in his bestselling *Practical Ethics* that "Ethics is not Primarily About Sex" (Singer, 2011, p. 1), and should concentrate on other things:

> We no longer think that morality, or ethics, is a set of prohibitions particularly concerned with sex.... Decisions about sex may involve considerations about honesty, concern for others, prudence, avoidance of harm to others and so on, but the same could be said of decisions about driving a car. (In fact, the moral issues raised by driving a car, both from an environmental and from a safety point of view, are much more serious than those raised by safe sex.) Accordingly, this book contains no discussion of sexual morality. (Singer, 2011, p. 2)

Similarly, women's reproductive rights are under continuous attack by religious authorities. They are mostly driven by unsubstantiated beliefs in the existence of what they call the "soul." Despite an uncontroversial lack of evidence for its existence, religious leaders continue ascribing infinite value to human embryos because of these beliefs. Unsurprisingly, abortion is then considered to be unethical, even when it is the result of rape. At the time of writing, this extremist Christian position had also become the official stance in the election platform of the Republican Party in the 2012 Presidential elections in the USA (GOP, 2012). The harmful societal impact of rendering authority over ethical issues to religious authorities in our daily lives is all too obvious and requires no further argument.

To put the matter bluntly, actual religions are not secular ethical philosophies dressed up with narratives and symbols. It may be difficult to define what a religion is, as we saw when considering the myth that atheism is a religion. However, religions have typically been far more encyclopedic explanatory systems than Gould acknowledges: among other things, they make sense of the world of human experience in terms of a supernatural realm and its workings. Thus they frequently make statements about humanity's place in the space-time universe – statements that often conflict with scientific statements about physical nature – and it would be naïve and ahistorical to claim that this somehow lies outside religion's legitimate or essential role. With the example of the Bible's creation narrative and the biblical genealogies, theological reinterpretations are possible, and not just of the first three chapters of Genesis. Nonetheless, it is wrong-headed to rule out the religious *legitimacy* of accepting the holy book's literal words.

Furthermore, even claims about supernatural entities and forces do not lie entirely outside of scientific investigation. Science already investigates very small, very distant, and very ancient events, drawing conclusions about mechanisms that are not directly observable. In doing so, it reasons about the effects of these events on present-day, medium-sized things that fall within our sensory range. Supernatural entities and forces, including gods, could be approached in the same way if enough information were offered as to how their activities are supposed to affect the world that we can observe. If they are said to act capriciously, that might, indeed, exempt them from scientific investigation (to this limited extent, we agree with Pennock, 2000, p. 195). However, many religions claim that the supernatural powers they describe acted on the observable world in specific ways on past occasions and/or that they continue to operate on the world in relatively consistent ways. In either case, we can look for evidence.

Thus we reject such attempted reconciliations of science and religion as those proposed by Einstein and Gould. In the real world, religion and science can and often do compete, and it is no use trying to define the problem away with a technical definition of either. It is not possible to draw a clear dividing line between science and religion, unless the latter retreats to a very thin position in which it posits no interaction between this world and a transcendent world – or adopts a position that its claims about a transcendent world are merely metaphors or allegories. Some religious groups might adopt this strategy, but there is no prospect of religion in general ever taking such a form.

The sorts of approaches advocated by Galileo and (to some extent) St Augustine may be more promising – where the words of a religious text come into conflict with sufficiently well-established science, the religious text should be reinterpreted to conform with scientific findings. History shows that theology has great resources for reinterpreting creeds and sacred texts. Let us grant, then, that the various religions can be adjusted over time, as required, to avoid making claims that are directly inconsistent with established scientific findings. However, this is not a true "no conflict" model. It is one in which conflicts are successively resolved in favor of science, as and when scientific findings become sufficiently well established.

Until an emerging scientific position is sufficiently established for religious doctrine to be modified, and until the modification takes place, there will be conflict. Furthermore, the conflict will last between science and any religious groups that refuse to make the required adjustments. In any particular case, many religious people are likely to resist modifying their beliefs to remove the inconsistencies. There can be different reasons for this, but one is that certain beliefs which are inconsistent with current science might strike these believers as core doctrines rather than matters of relative indifference.

Just think of the views of Christian fundamentalists, which exert much political and social influence in the United States. They subscribe to a theological system that includes the introduction of sin and corruption into the world at a specific point in historical time, God's covenant with the Jews, Jesus Christ's sacrificial atonement for sin, and an ultimate, world-cleansing victory of God over Satan. This system would fall apart if the narrative of a literal Garden of Eden were discarded. Integrated theological systems cannot be tampered with easily: in some cases this may make them resistant to change, while in others the forced changes may greatly alter what was originally in place. Incidentally, given how integral this worldview is to true believers' understanding of the world, it is understandable why they should be reluctant to change their views even in the face of overwhelming evidence.

Moreover, Galileo's proposal leaves a more general problem unresolved. If an actual religion's more general claims were *true*, there is no compelling reason why it should not be authoritative on matters to do with the functioning of the empirical world. And for all our ancestors knew, say in 1500 or 1600, Christian theology possessed just that kind of authority. For all they knew, science might have had a future in discovering all sorts of amazing powers and agents playing a causal role in the world around us.

After all, if a god or angel or other cognitively superior being inspired the *true* religion's poets and prophets, or dictated actual text for inclusion in its holy books, the god or angel (or whatever) could easily have avoided talk of agents and powers that do not exist (such as evil spirits). At the same time, it could have revealed such facts as the evolutionary origin of human beings, the true age of the earth, the fact that it revolves around the sun, and that it is approximately spherical and rotates on its axis. As Stenger points out, holy books could even contain cryptic (at the time of composition) but clear (at the time of fulfillment) prophecies about future advances – though nothing of the kind actually exists (Stenger, 2008, p. 176).

There is no reason in principle why a true religion with genuinely supernatural origins could not have correct and authoritative teachings on all these things. Accordingly, there is no reason in principle why a true religion could not have teaching authority that extends to empirical matters. This is worth dwelling on for a moment. Coyne is one author who quite rightly emphasizes the different methodologies adopted by religion and science, leading him to see a methodological incompatibility between them (2012, p. 2656). While he is correct to make this point, it *could have been* that the methods of religion, or at least the true religion, give the same results as science.

It could have turned out that science routinely *confirms* what theology had already discovered, or at least never finds anything contrary to it. Notwithstanding the different methodologies used, this would tend to support the authority of the theology in its original form. Unfortunately for religious apologists of various kinds, this has not proved to be the case (as Coyne also points out: 2012, pp. 2656–2657). When religion and science produce quite different results, with their respective methodologies *not* converging on the same truths from different directions, we have to wonder why – and this tends to discredit religion. And if theologians associated with a particular religion keep altering doctrines to conform to the findings of science, we might well wonder how divinely inspired their system of doctrine was in the first place.

Even if a particular religious system is modified so as to conform to all the well-established findings of *current* science, can its adherents be sure that it will be immune to the findings of *future* science? Well, if the religion is true, future science will never falsify it, but how realistic is that, given the experience so far? As Stenger reminds us, scientists will still be "open to change tomorrow, next week, or whenever new evidence is found" (Stenger, 2012, p. 29). Will the religious system be just as open to change? And if it does keep updating its theological claims to conform to new scientific findings, this starts to looks ad hoc.

As we've seen, Galileo's approach was to claim that the Bible's words were fitted for the relatively primitive people for whom it was first written. Thus it contains scientific errors if its words are interpreted in their plainest sense. But this becomes an increasingly less plausible explanation as the pervasiveness and nature of the errors become apparent. Surely the Bible could have been written in a way that did not require *so much* reinterpretation in the light of science, and surely even primitive people could have understood such ideas as the actual order of creation and that human beings arose over a vast sequence of time (perhaps with divine guidance of the process, if that had actually been the case).

In a recent debate with Daniel C. Dennett, Plantinga argued that religion and science are "compatible," but his approach actually illustrates the problems for any "no conflict" model. Plantinga argued for two points. His stronger claim was that biological evolution and philosophical naturalism are actually in conflict: we disagree with this, and will return to it, but here he at least makes an interesting case. However, his notion of the compatibility between science and religion, the other point that he argued for, was a surprisingly weak one. For the sake of argument, we are even prepared to grant this weak form of compatibility. It is simply that contemporary science cannot *entirely rule out* a divine role in guiding the process of biological evolution. Note, however, that this idea of compatibility is so weak that Plantinga will regard science and religion as "compatible" even if science provides evidence against religion, or if it makes religion less plausible to someone who is neutral or unsure about religious claims (see Dennett and Plantinga, 2011, pp. 3–16).

Can this really be seen as a no conflict model? It should not give solace to authors such as Gould, who want to claim that science and religion, properly understood, do not, or cannot, come into conflict. It leaves in place the direct inconsistencies that arise over time between science and religion, together with the fact that some of these persist if religious organizations refuse to modify their doctrines. More importantly, it does not detract from the more general tendency for science to undermine the credibility of religion in numerous ways.

Contrary to models that attempt to separate science and religion, these two "magisteria" come into contact, often overlap, and can compete.

Credited to Jesus and Mo, www.jesusandmo.net

To put it mildly, science does not leave theology untouched. Rather, scientific evidence leaves its mark on theological understandings and on what arguments are used for and against the existence of God. Consider an example that we have already touched upon: the theodicy problem, or the Problem of Evil.

Theodicy and the Problem of Evil

Very much has been written about this, and it is another topic to which we could devote an entire book. In the end, the issue is why such things as pain, suffering, and cruelty coexist with a being who is powerful enough to prevent them and presumably motivated to do so – especially if that being is actually the *creator* of the world we see around us. In his *Dialogues Concerning Natural Religion*, Hume has one character, Philo, make this point with some force (1779, Part X).

You might respond in various ways. For example, you might conclude that it remains possible, in some sense, that there is a solution to the Problem of Evil. You could insist on that, however, while still being puzzled as to what the solution *could possibly be*. In the absence of a solution that actually appears at all plausible, you might then consider it simplest and most intellectually honest to doubt the existence of any all-powerful, all-benevolent creator. That strikes us as a very reasonable response, at least until someone provides a compelling argument *in favor* of this being's existence.

But what does science have to do with this? Does it make the Problem of Evil worse in any way? After all, the problem is an ancient one, and its essential elements do not depend on any recent empirical findings. Nonetheless, we do think that science has made things harder for anyone who proposes to justify the ways of God to the rest of us. For a start, we now have a greatly expanded knowledge of the suffering in the animal world. As we survey the vast abundance of this, inflicted over millions of years on so many vulnerable living things, it may not seem believable that a loving deity would have remotely adequate reasons to permit it all.

Furthermore, science rules out a literal reading of Genesis, a reading in which Adam and Eve were actual people who sinned of their own free will at the beginning of history, disobeying God at a particular time in an actual place. Instead, evolutionary theory reveals human beings as one outcome of a process with roots deep in time. More generally, the scientific picture entails that suffering came into the world long before human beings or any acts of free will that they could carry out. An entire approach to the Problem of Evil is thus incompatible with current science.

That does not mean that evolutionary theory eliminates all theological approaches to the problem. It does not – as Plantinga points out, theologians might argue that evil is ultimately for the best in some sense, or that it originates from the actions of Satan and other evil beings that long predate the evolution of *Homo sapiens* (Dennett and Plantinga, 2011, p. 13; Plantinga, 2011, pp. 58–59). But how plausible is any of this in a scientifically disenchanted cosmos? As to Satan and his minions, much of the motivation for believing in such beings has been lost. We have not discovered the presence of devils, demons, or evil spirits operating in the world, and it is not good enough for Plantinga to say, "Some may snort with derision at this suggestion; it is none the worse for that" (2011, p. 59). Alas, suggestions about evil, disembodied intellects steering events in horrible directions are now highly implausible. In 1500, things did not seem that way; in the intervening period, however, our broader picture of the world in space and time has changed drastically. Today, appeals to the possibility of evil, disembodied intellects at work fouling things up quite rightly meet with the derision that Plantinga mentions.

Evolutionary theory and other aspects of the scientific picture greatly alter our understanding of how the world came to be as we see it. Thus McGrath notes that evolutionary theory shattered certain views of the divine creation, but he adds that it did not eliminate *every* possible theological approach. He has in mind the view that God made the world make itself, that is, gave a kind of autonomy to nature so that matter would develop life and eventually consciousness (McGrath, 2004, p. 105). Such views are increasingly popular with theologians, and they come with a built-in answer to the Problem of Evil that we will consider in a moment. However, these strategies have obvious weaknesses, and they show how evolutionary science puts theology under intellectual pressure.

For one thing, theologians who accept that the earth is billions of years old, and suggest that the events described in the early chapters of Genesis are best read as a metaphor, gain a new problem if they wish to hang on to notions of human exceptionalism, particularly the idea that we (but not other animals) possess immortal souls.

But do they gain new resources for dealing with the Problem of Evil? One approach is to blame various natural evils on evolution itself – on the clumsy processes of mutation, survival, and adaptation, which produce imperfect, often cruel results. That way, we can claim that these natural evils are not God's specific design, seemingly letting him off the hook. This is, for example, the main argument running through Francisco J. Ayala's book, *Darwin's Gift to Science and Religion* (2007; see also Avise, 2010). But an all-powerful, all-knowing deity must surely have foreseen the dire consequences, at least in a general way. It would not need to use such clumsy methods; and if it were benevolent, why would it not prefer to envisage and create a universe specifically designed to be free of the evils? An omnipotent and omniscient being could have chosen the outcome it wanted, then brought it about, with no functional imperfections, in a blink of time or in a timeframe of mere days and nights, such as described in the opening verses of Genesis. As far as we can see, then, God remains on the hook.

Some theologians attempt to reverse this, saying, as John Haught does, that there would be something stultifying about a finished and perfect universe: "Only a still unfinished universe – such as the one that geology, cosmology, and biology have been revealing to us over the past two centuries – could provide the setting for human freedom and creativity" (Haught, 2008, p. 106). But it is by no means self evident that we, or our equivalents, could not be free and creative in a universe that was created without the kind of engineering flaws and suffering that we actually see around us. An answer to this will presumably be that the autonomy of nature is a great good in the way that has often been claimed of human free will. But our own free will – whatever, exactly it amounts to – may well seem like a great good on independent grounds, perhaps because we don't want to be puppets in the hands of another being. Whether or not we possess some kind of free will, the idea that the autonomy of nature is an additional good appears very dubious.

Ask yourself: how many theologians would be arguing along these lines, praising an unfinished universe that is made to make itself, if evolutionary theory had not prevailed? It seems clear enough here that science is pushing theology in a particular direction, and the outcome is a specific and controversial theological stance. A source of contradiction is removed between science and any religious system that takes this stance, but not between science and a religion that rejects it. Thus, even if science is compatible with the resulting theological approach, this is not a compatibility with religion as such. The reality is quite a bit more complicated – and it should, we think, be troubling to the religious.

Prior to the scientific revolution that got underway in the sixteenth and seventeenth centuries, human beings possessed little knowledge of the cosmos except on human scales. Human efforts had achieved relatively little in understanding very distant phenomena such as the sun, planets, and stars, very small phenomena such as the composition of our bodies, or very ancient phenomena that existed before human records began. Religious texts offered information about the overall history and structure of the cosmos, and about unseen phenomena such as gods, demons, Heaven, and Hell. These texts proved not, however, to be reliable sources of knowledge about the cosmos on nonhuman scales.

As the scientific revolution proceeded, science discovered much about the structure and development of the cosmos, and about our place in it. Although the scientific picture is far from complete, and will likely never be complete, science has become our best guide to the overall reality of space and time within which we are situated. As its investigations of the cosmos have continued, it has failed to discover such phenomena as ghosts, ancestor spirits, and demons.

The cosmos no longer seems enchanted, and new scientific discoveries can take away much of the motivation for taking religion seriously. For example, mental illnesses and other afflictions once attributed to the work of demons or evil spirits are now explained in very different ways. These beings might still exist, as it is difficult (or impossible) to disprove their existence once and for all, but it all becomes less plausible. Again, evolutionary theory offers an explanation for the intricate functional adaptation displayed by the world's varied life forms, undermining the need to believe that these were specially created by God. Modern understandings of human and animal reproduction have superseded ideas that required the involvement of a supernatural intelligence. All in all, we live in a world very different from what the world religions once seemed to describe.

There are fields where science has not yet delivered answers to difficult questions, such as how life originally arose from nonliving matter. But even here, the relative track records of science and religion to date suggest that there is likely to be a purely naturalistic answer, and that answers found in religious texts need not, and indeed cannot, be relied upon. In any case, it seems intellectually shallow for the religious to concede that one of their great unsolved questions has been resolved by science, only to point to new questions that the scientific approach has given rise to. It's the theological equivalent to shifting the goal posts in a soccer match. Regardless of this, the lack of a scientific answer to a particular question at any given point in time provides no rationale for the existence, or the need of a belief in the existence, of a being such as God.

We have shown that – and why – religion and science are not straightforwardly compatible, and that a simple claim of "no conflict" between them is glib and misleading. This analysis cannot be refuted by pointing to religious scientists and saying that they find no incompatibility between their scientific training and practice, on one hand, and their religious beliefs (whatever these actually are) on the other. Any useful discussion of these issues needs to get into the actual arguments about how religion and science, and their respective methods and truth-claims, compare with each other, and how they have related to each other over time. The actual position is not simple, and we do not advocate a simple-minded view of it. Nonetheless, it is fair to say that science has done serious damage to the rational credibility of religion.

Where does the conflict really lie?

Science and religion cannot be quarantined from each other, but whether religious apologists find science a hindrance or a help will depend on the actual arguments. For example, we discussed fine-tuning arguments for the existence of God without simply assuming that they are irrelevant to debates between atheists and theists.

Many apologists for religion argue that there is a deep consonance between theistic religion and science. It is often suggested, in fact, that Christianity provided uniquely fertile ground for the rise of modern science – see, for example, the arguments of Dinesh D'Souza (2007, pp. 83–99) and Alvin Plantinga (2011, pp. 265–303). This raises complex issues for historians, and we cannot settle the details. If there is any grain of truth in the argument, however, it cannot be that religion in general conduces to the rise of science.

Indeed, Christianity can take little if any credit for the scientific revolution: for hundreds of years, the Christian churches had a pervasive influence throughout European society and across the enormous terrain of the Byzantine Empire, with no dramatic advances in scientific knowledge. Indeed, there was a considerable tradition within ancient and medieval Christianity of opposition to natural philosophy (and hence anything resembling science), seeing it as distracting or even idolatrous (Gaukroger, 2006, pp. 57–59, 151). Conversely, some impressive advances in technology and the empirical understanding of nature took place in classical antiquity long before Christianity established itself (Carrier, 2010b, pp. 400–404). The scientific revolution, which ultimately gave us an astonishingly new picture of the universe, arose in particular places within Europe, influenced by the reclamation of much pagan learning – particularly the materialist philosophy of the Epicureans.

Perhaps it can be argued that certain theological approaches, emphasizing God as a lawgiver, and thus the regularity of nature, were conducive to science, though Stephen Gaukroger's magisterial study of the rise of modern science (Gaukroger, 2006) lends little support to this. We doubt that medieval and Renaissance theology were more supportive to science than the assumptions of ancient rationalists, who were quite familiar with the idea of natural, regular, though largely hidden, mechanisms producing observed phenomena. As events turned out, a number of intellectual tendencies converged in the seventeenth century to influence the early progress of science. Among them were the revival of interest in ancient atomist theories, along with a new emphasis on the possibility of improving the world through technological means. Though the ancient Epicureans were content to conjecture about a number of possible mechanisms behind the events we observe, the Epicurean revivalists of the early modern era sensed that the atomic theory offered a promising framework within which to obtain useful knowledge (Wilson, 2008, pp. 64–70). This was not an especially Christian idea, though atomism had to be rationalized along lines that were acceptable in a still-Christian society.

For the sake of argument let us grant that certain tendencies growing out of late medieval Christian theology favored the rise of science, once they were blended with atomist philosophy and early modern ideas of technological meliorism. Even if this were so, this is logically consistent with the idea that science, in turn, undermines religion (in all the ways we've discussed). It could even be suggested that whatever theological tendencies favored science thereby created long-term problems for religion.

Gaukroger has advanced a somewhat more subtle and plausible thesis about the relationship between Christianity and early science. The idea is not that Christian theology provided the impetus for sixteenth and seventeenth-century science, but that it must be given some credit for the *consolidation* of science in Europe in the late seventeenth century and thereafter, bearing in mind that the development of scientific inquiry in other times, places, and cultures had tended to be fragmented and stop-start, with long periods of stagnation (Gaukroger, 2006, pp. 20–22). Gaukroger claims that the natural philosophy of the scientific revolution was attractive to many thinkers in the seventeenth and eighteenth centuries precisely because it appeared to show promise for the renewal of natural theology (2006, p. 23).

We doubt that even this much weaker thesis has been demonstrated convincingly. It is true that some theological exponents, especially in the UK, attempted to include scientific ideas in their metaphysical systems, that others attempted to reconcile scientific theories of the formation of the earth with the Genesis account of creation and the biblical chronology of history, and that there was a widespread view that scientific discoveries could be used as a source of evidence for God (Gaukroger, 2006, pp. 493–505). Some strains of theology thus accommodated and drew upon science, but we see little reason to regard this largely British phenomenon as central to the unprecedented consolidation of science. Surely part of the reason can be found in the strong arguments that were developed by Galileo and others, based on close observations with scientific instruments, the development of increasingly precise experimental apparatus, and the imaginative and rigorous use of mathematics. A careful reading of events in the seventeenth century, in particular, shows the extraordinary density of the interrelationships among theorists, hypotheses, and observations, as the new breed of natural philosophers vied with each other, criticized each other's ideas, and built on each other's work.

One interesting question might be why orthodox Christian theology did not prove to be a formidable barrier to all this. After all, there had been considerable theological resistance to natural philosophy, and, as Gaukroger points out, "Christianity . . . had traditionally laid claim to universal competence in all matters of understanding the world and our place in it, most notably in its Augustinian version" (Gaukroger, 2010, p. 54). Yet, despite the execution of Giordano Bruno, burned at the stake in 1600 for numerous sins of heresy in the eyes of the Church, and notwithstanding the persecution of Galileo soon afterwards, Christianity did little in the second half of the seventeenth century to *hinder* scientific inquiry. Given Christian theology's long-standing intellectual hegemony in Europe, it could doubtless have done much to prevent the consolidation of science in the late seventeenth and early eighteenth centuries, or what Gaukroger refers to as science's ability to establish itself "as a permanent and integral feature of Western intellectual life" (2010, p. 11).

As Gaukroger reminds us, it was widely understood that scientific theories would not be acceptable to the culture of Europe unless they were compatible with common assumptions about morality, humanity's place in the world, and the general claims of religion (Gaukroger 2010, pp. 12–13). Putting this another way, early modern science might have been greeted with a destructive hostility if scientists had said or done too much that rocked the theological boat. In the upshot, however, they did not do so: to some extent, seventeenth-century scientists avoided heresy by carefully defining their field of inquiry as the natural world (while drawing a sharp boundary with the supernatural world), and to some extent they produced theories that ultimately appealed to the actions of God, as we find in the enormously fruitful work of Sir Isaac Newton.

All this shows early modern science accommodating itself to Christianity, while certain theologians did, in turn, welcome science's discoveries as a resource for theology. But to some extent, Christianity had already lost much of its intellectual hegemony and political power for totally different reasons. Partly this was a consequence of the disastrous Thirty Years' War (1618–1648), which turned many seventeenth- and eighteenth-century intellectuals and statesmen away from insistence on a comprehensive orthodoxy. Partly, perhaps, it was because of extensive contact with cultures in the New World and the Far East: this was a mind-broadening experience for many thoughtful Europeans, and it tended to undermine absolutism and certainty. There is much to say about how Christianity increasingly lost its intellectual authority through the seventeenth century and beyond, and why it was increasingly less in a position to hinder the advance of science.

While some strains of early modern theology were hospitable to science, especially in the UK in the late seventeenth century – that much should be conceded – it is common for religious apologists to go much further. Thus we frequently see arguments that science is incompatible with a *rejection* of religion. One popular variant is that we cannot reliably obtain true beliefs if we are solely the products of a material process such as evolution. Thus we must be something more, something with connections to an otherworldly or supernatural realm. As D'Souza puts it, "evolution selects only for reproduction and survival, not for truth." He suggests that ideas could be useful for our survival without being true, and that a useful lie will be preferable from that viewpoint to "a truth that plays no role in genetic self-perpetuation" (D'Souza, 2007, p. 247). Lennox is one of many other Christian apologists to argue along the same lines, and he cites several other thinkers (religious and otherwise) in an effort to bolster his position (2011, pp. 52–55).

Perhaps the most elaborate version of this argument is that of Plantinga, which might, for now, be considered the state of the art. In his 2011 book, *Where the Conflict Really Lies*, he also offers a useful footnote in which he cites a couple of precursors (see, e.g., Lewis, 1960, pp. 9–37), as well as summarizing his own previous (and rather frequent) expositions of the argument (see Plantinga, 2011, p. 310). His essential point is that we could not expect our cognitive faculties to be reliable if they were the product of a purely naturalistic process of biological evolution. Thus, if you think that philosophical naturalism and Darwinian evolutionary theory are both true, you should not trust your own ability to draw conclusions about such things – placing you in an invidious situation. Conversely, if you believe that we are God's creations (perhaps through a process of evolution that God has guided in some way) you can be confident that our cognitive faculties are largely reliable. This is because God has created us in his own image with a capacity to obtain knowledge of the world.

Accordingly, so the argument continues, we can embrace a form of evolution that includes an element of divine guidance, but should reject philosophical naturalism and adopt a view of the world in which we have been created in the image of God (Plantinga, 2011, pp. 309–350). On such an approach, we cannot engage in science – or, seemingly in any rational argument at all – unless we first presume the existence of God. We must either abandon all trust in our own cognitive faculties or adopt the idea that God exists and has created us in his image.

The key premise that Plantinga needs to support is that there is only a low probability that our cognitive faculties would be reliable if we were the products of a completely naturalistic evolutionary process. This is supposedly because such a process would only shape us to engage in *behaviors* that tend to maximize our reproductive fitness (our ability to pass our genes down to the next generation). According to Plantinga, fitness-enhancing behaviors do not depend on the possession of *true beliefs* or of cognitive faculties that tend to produce them. On the contrary, he suggests, evolution might have shaped us with innate beliefs that are actually false – though they might be fitness-enhancing ones, since they might lead us to behave in ways that conduce to passing on our genes.

What should best be said about such arguments? First, we need to distinguish between, on the one hand, having perfect or highly reliable cognitive faculties and, on the other hand, having cognitive faculties about as reliable as ours actually are. It is the latter that needs to be explained. The point here is that these faculties cannot be described as *highly* reliable: they are effective in some ways, but, as is well known, they often mislead us and require correction. Human senses can be deceived in numerous ways, as has been demonstrated, in the case of our eyesight, by the scientific study of optical illusions.

We have an intuitive grasp of many things that relate to our survival and reproductive prospects as social animals. It is difficult to see how we could have that much ability to perceive the world and reason about it unless our senses and brains had some basic reliability in getting true data about the world. So we appear to have some general capacity to obtain knowledge of our situations. However, we seem to falter when confronted by problems that are more remote from our social interactions and require more abstract reasoning. Our ability to derive logically correct answers appears to depend on the subject matter of problems that confront us, and not just on their inherent difficulty (Cosmides and Tooby, 1992).

Indeed, our commonsense beliefs about many matters are quite wrong, and can only be corrected with great difficulty. It is, for example, trite to point out that people who have not been taught otherwise start with a folk physics and astronomy that are mainly false (Kuhn, 1957, pp. 42–44; Rosenberg, 2011, pp. 166–168). The folk astronomy part of this has the earth at the center of things, with astronomical bodies, such as the sun and the stars, revolving around it. During the sixteenth and seventeenth centuries, observation, imagination, reason, and cooperation moved quite slowly to correct what "naturally" seems to strike people as the case. As a generalization, moreover, we seem to be prepared to believe all sorts of things that are not well-evidenced, such as ill-founded conspiracy theories and urban myths. Rosenberg puts this strongly, but not implausibly: "Mother Nature selected for people who see plots everywhere: conspiracy theorists" (2011, p. 13).

Atheists and religious people should agree, furthermore, that entire cultures can develop views of the world that are fundamentally wrong. As we've discussed, most atheists are philosophical naturalists, and thus reject claims about gods, ghosts, demons, evil spirits, astral influences, and so on.

But religious people *also* reject most of these claims – namely the ones made by other religions or by heretics in their own religious traditions. We can all agree that – again as a generalization – human beings are prone to believe erroneous things, not least about the supernatural.

Why all this confusion and error if human beings are made in the image of a rational and omniscient being such as God? Whether or not we are made in God's image, why did he not give us more perfect perceptions and cognition? This is a question that Descartes wrestled with in his Fourth Meditation (1996 [1641]), and in debate with other thinkers of his time, but it has never been satisfactorily answered. Perhaps a theological explanation can be attempted here, based on the corrupting power of sin and the notion that we have fallen from grace. But prima facie, it is actually the theist who needs to give some explanation as to why our senses, memories, and reasoning capacities are not more reliable than they are. Theologians are faced with a problem if their systems imagine us as beings who were created by an omniscient, omnipotent, and benevolent God – and even more so if we are in some sense created *in the image* of that God.

Conversely, why is there any problem about evolution producing beings with cognitive faculties about as reliable as ours actually are? Surely we'd expect a process such as biological evolution to produce creatures with imperfect, but largely reliable, cognitive faculties. After all, as Plantinga concedes (2011, p. 335), a gazelle won't last long (much less reproduce) if it imagines lions to be harmless, friendly pussycats; something similar applies to the reproductive prospects of a human rock climber who imagines that it's safe to jump from a two-hundred-foot cliff. In both human experience and the wider domain of living things, it seems clear enough that there is a reproductive advantage in possessing faculties that tend to form true beliefs.

In a key passage in *Where the Conflict Really Lies*, Plantinga attempts to rebut this. If there is no God in charge of things, and if some form of materialism about the mind is true, then having (or being able to form) true beliefs will not confer such an advantage at all (2011, pp. 335–339). This takes him into some interesting territory, but we submit that the main line of argument is untenable. We can draw some comfort from the fact that another leading theistic philosopher, Richard Swinburne, agrees with us, thinking that this particular argument from Plantinga offers no further good reason to embrace theism (Swinburne, 2004, pp. 350–354).

Plantinga thinks that in a godless and materialist universe we must regard a belief such as "lions are dangerous" as some kind of neurological structure in the brain of the creature that has the belief. Let's grant this.

But he then argues that what makes a gazelle run when it sees a lion is not the truth of the proposition "lions are dangerous" but only the physical structure of the gazelle's brain. Thus, he thinks, the reliability of the gazelle's cognitive faculties in producing true beliefs such as "lions are dangerous" plays no part in saving the life of a gazelle that flees lions. It follows that (in such a godless and materialist world) there is no reproductive value in having cognitive faculties that reliably produce true beliefs. Accordingly, such faculties would not have evolved.

With all respect to Plantinga, however, this is hopeless. It may be the physical structure of the gazelle's brain that produces certain nerve impulses, and so is immediately efficacious in causing the gazelle to flee. Note, however, that the gazelle's brain has a physical structure that models features of the world such as "lions are dangerous," as a result of various facts about the world including the fact that lions *really are dangerous to gazelles*. A gazelle might have an innate aversion to lions, or it might have cognitive faculties that enable it to form correct beliefs about lions. Either way, it will react differently, when it encounters a lion on the savannah, from a hapless gazelle that sees lions as friendly pussycats – and, of course, differently from a gazelle that fails to register the existence of a nearby lion at all.

Irrespective of how instinctive might be a gazelle's aversion to lions in particular, a gazelle with reliable faculties will produce the requisite physical structures in its brain to model salient aspects of the world – equating lions with danger. Such a gazelle will be more likely to survive the various hazards it encounters than a not-so-smart rival, and so have the opportunity to outbreed it. There is an obvious evolutionary explanation for why gazelles will evolve cognitive faculties sufficient to solve a wide range of survival problems, and why superior cognitive faculties might often have survival value.

Given the ways human beings characteristically behave, often engaging in intricate forms of cooperation as well as in-group competition, it makes perfectly good sense that evolution would select for various kinds of general problem solving and learning abilities, as well as for heuristics that might have been especially useful in our ancestral environment. More than gazelles, we have evolved to learn new truths about our environment, but that ability to learn is itself adaptive.

Swinburne points out that metaphysical beliefs are remote from beliefs about the mundane world, such as beliefs that lions are dangerous or the belief that a particular watering hole is good to drink from. This makes false metaphysical beliefs less dangerous to hold than false mundane beliefs, at least in a large class of cases. Indeed, false metaphysical beliefs might even have survival value if, for example, they are the only ones that are not persecuted in a particular society. However, Swinburne also makes the point that there is no clear dividing line between mundane and metaphysical beliefs or any ultimate difference in the criteria that we use to investigate their truth (2004, pp. 253–254).

Much the same applies if we compare mundane beliefs with beliefs about the causal mechanisms (perhaps distant, small, or lost in time) investigated by science. While it might be more *difficult* coming to true conclusions about scientific claims than about mundane events that we experience more directly, we have no reason to distrust the criteria that we use, which are continuous with those that we rely upon in everyday experience. Swinburne's suggestion is that we possess the needed cognitive capacities to form true beliefs over time even on metaphysical issues. Of course, many other factors may tell against this, such as wishful thinking, loyalties, or strong intuitions about beliefs into which we've been socialized.

Still, it appears quite possible for naturally evolved beings like us to work on our beliefs relating to matters remote from direct perception and ordinary experience – and to make intellectual progress. Indeed, look at all the progress we've actually made in physics, biology, chemistry, and elsewhere. There's no good philosophical reason why God had to help us out. In sum, naturalistic processes could give us all the reliability in selecting true beliefs that we actually have. Plantinga notwithstanding, it is theists who are forced to explain why their god or gods created us with cognitive and perceptual weaknesses that we need to correct for.

Conclusion – the Reasonableness of Atheism

Most of us have little inclination to believe in the extraordinary beings worshiped in other cultures, or in the strange narratives of their various motivations and exploits. We may, however, feel more charitable toward religious beliefs into which we were socialized as children, or at least those with which we grew up, so that they seem familiar, perhaps faintly plausible, even if we were never explicitly taught that they are *true*. If we grew up with Christian ideas around us, we may need to step back a little to obtain the same sense of estrangement from Christianity as we have from, say, pagan mythology, or the gods of Hinduism, or even the teachings of Islam.

The larger case for atheism depends, in part, on the specifics of the case against various religious beliefs. Some Christians – though we don't say all – may find they have little inclination to adopt some other religion once they start to doubt the inspired status of the Bible, the coherence or justice of the doctrine of substitutionary atonement, the plausibility of traditional religious morality, or the prospect of ever satisfactorily reconciling God's power and benevolence with the obvious presence of pain, suffering, and cruelty in our world. A full-scale case for atheism, intended to persuade a believing Christian, would proceed on all these fronts, showing the many difficulties that confront traditional kinds of Christianity. It is not just one set of problems that can make a religion like Christianity seem unbelievable to atheists: it's the convergence of many things.

Thus we recommend books, such as those edited by John W. Loftus (2010, 2011), that tackle the difficulties from multiple perspectives. These are valuable reading for people who find that they doubt their familiar religious beliefs – and now contemplate the next step.

Meanwhile, we have not attempted to present the last word in the intellectual debate between theism and atheism. There is far more to say, and we look forward to future opportunities to articulate some it. In this chapter, however, we've provided some historical background about atheism, sketched why traditional demonstrations of God's existence tend to be so unconvincing, especially in the light of modern science, and told some of the story of how science has undermined religion. There are unavoidable tensions between the emerging scientific picture of the world, the universe, and ourselves (on one hand) and (on the other hand) traditional religious, and especially Christian, understandings.

We have not definitively proved that there is no theologically orthodox creator and designer, but we have explained why the (supposedly) rational justifications for belief in this being's existence should leave nonbelievers unimpressed. In the absence of strong, independent evidence for such a being, believers might do well to examine why they are so credulous. Apart from a certain comfort with the idea – perhaps the product of socialization or plain, ordinary cultural familiarity – do you *really* have a basis to go on believing in this unseen, disembodied, otherworldly intellect?

Deep skepticism about the existence of God seems reasonable to us, and no truly persuasive argument has ever been advanced *for* the existence of such a strange being. If such an argument ever becomes available, we might be swayed to accept that this being exists, while lamenting that its full motivations are so opaque to mortal men and women. As things stand, however, we should conclude that no such deity is looking over us. We submit that it is most honest and reasonable to be atheists.

International Atheist and Related Organizations

This is a selective list of important and active organizations throughout the world, but there are doubtless many that we have missed, and we acknowledge a weighting toward the United States of America and other English-speaking countries. For readers living outside those countries, one good starting point might to be to contact Atheist Alliance International or the International Humanist and Ethical Union, since their affiliates include many national organizations that represent the views and interests of atheists.

In all cases, we provide postal addresses and websites. The latter generally include more detailed information about contacts, activities, and affiliated or related groups.

American Atheists
PO Box 158
Cranford, NJ 07016
USA
http://www.atheists.org/

American Humanist Association
1777 T Street NW
Washington, DC 20009
USA
http://www.americanhumanist.org/

Ateistisk Selskab (Danish Atheist Society)
Gammel Kongevej 1
1610 København V
Denmark
http://www.ateist.dk/

Atheism UK
BM Atheism UK
London, WC1N 3XX
UK
http://www.atheismuk.com/

Atheist Alliance of America
1777 T Street NW
Washington, DC 20009–7125
USA
http://atheistallianceamerica.org/

Atheist Alliance International
1777 T Street NW
Washington, DC 20009–7125
USA
http://www.atheistalliance.org/

Atheist Foundation of Australia
Private Mail Bag 6
Maitland, SA 5573
Australia
http://www.atheistfoundation.org.au/

Atheist Ireland
7 Dargle Road
Drumcondra
Dublin 9
Republic of Ireland
http://www.atheist.ie/

Black Atheists of America
PO Box 4024
Garden City, NY 11531
USA
http://blackatheistsofamerica.org/

British Humanist Association
1 Gower Street
London, WC1E 6HD
UK
http://www.humanism.org.uk/

Center for Inquiry
PO Box 741
Amherst, NY 14226
USA
http://www.centerforinquiry.net/

Centre for Inquiry Canada
2 College Street, Unit 214
Toronto, M5G 1K3
Canada
http://www.cficanada.ca/

Council of Ex-Muslims of Britain
BM Box 2387
London, WC1N 3XX
UK
http://ex-muslim.org.uk/

Council for Secular Humanism
PO Box 664
Amherst, NY 14226
USA
http://www.secularhumanism.org

Freedom from Religion Foundation
PO Box 750
Madison, WI 53701
USA
http://ffrf.org/

Free Society Institute
PO Box 39323
Capricorn, Cape Town 7948
South Africa
http://fsi.org.za/

Humanist Association of Ottawa
981 Lola Street,
Ottawa, ON, K1K 3P4
Canada
http://ottawa.humanists.net/

Humanists' Association (India)
P-2, Block B,
Lake Town,
Kolkata - 700 089
West Bengal
India
http://www.humanistassociation.org/

International Humanist and Ethical Union
1 Gower Street
London, WC1E 6HD
UK
http://www.iheu.org/

International League of Non-Religious and Atheists
Steinbach 19
51789 Lindlar
Federal Republic of Germany
http://www.ibka.org/

James Randi Educational Foundation
7095 Hollywood Blvd. No. 1170
Los Angeles, CA 90028
USA
http://www.randi.org/site/

Military Association of Atheists and Freethinkers
1380 Monroe St NW PMB 505
Washington, DC 20010
USA
http://www.militaryatheists.org/

National Secular Society
25 Red Lion Square
London, WC1R 4RL
UK
http://www.secularism.org.uk/

Norwegian Humanist Association
Human-Etisk Forbund
PO Box 6744, St. Olavsplass, 0130 Oslo
Norway
http://www.human.no/Servicemeny/English/

Rationalist Association
Merchants House
5–7 Southwark Street
London, SE1 1RQ
UK
http://newhumanist.org.uk/ra

Rationalist Society of Australia
PO Box 1312
Hawksburn, VIC 3142
Australia
http://www.rationalist.com.au/

Richard Dawkins Foundation for Reason and Science (UK)
PO Box 866
Oxford, OX1 9NQ
UK
http://www.richarddawkinsfoundation.org/

Richard Dawkins Foundation for Reason and Science (US)
11605 Meridian Market View
Unit 124 PMB 381
Falcon, CO 80831
USA
http://richarddawkins.net/

Science and Rationalists Association of India
P-2, Block B,
Lake Town,
Kolkata - 700 089
West Bengal
India
http://www.srai.org/

Secular Coalition for America
1012 14th St. NW #205
Washington, DC 20005
USA
http://secular.org/

Skeptics Society
PO Box 338
Altadena, CA 91001
USA
http://www.skeptic.com/

References

Abernethy, B. 2004. Bob Abernethy (PBS) interviews Chaplain Joseph Angotti. *PBS*, October 22. http://www.pbs.org/wnet/religionandethics/week808/profile.html (accessed March 28, 2013).

Abramovich, D. 2009. Celebrity atheists expose their hypocrisy. *The Sydney Morning Herald*, October 26. http://www.smh.com.au/opinion/contributors/celebrity-atheists-expose-their-hypocrisy-20091026-hevx.html#ixzz1KpXxRMKX (accessed March 28, 2013).

Ahdar, R. and Leigh, I. 2005. *Religious Freedom in the Liberal State*. Oxford: Oxford University Press.

Aikin, S.F. and Talisse, R.B. 2011. *Reasonable Atheism: A Moral Case for Respectful Disbelief*. Amherst, NY: Prometheus.

Alexander, D. 1991. Interview with Gene Roddenberry: writer, producer, philosopher, humanist. *The Humanist*, March/April. http://67.104.146.36/english/STAR_TREK/humanistinterview/humanist.html (accessed March 28, 2013).

Amnesty International. 2012. Indonesia: Atheist imprisonment a setback for freedom of expression. June 14. http://www.amnesty.org/en/library/asset/ASA21/021/2012/en/a8cc2dde-5390-41f8-a786-1cf0a2fa5862/asa210212012en.pdf (accessed March 28, 2013).

Angier, N. 2001. Confessions of an atheist. *New York Times*, January 14, Section 6, p. 34, Column 3.

Answerbag. 2010. Do atheists hate all religions equally or just Christians? November 9. http://www.answerbag.com/q_view/2347200 (accessed March 28, 2013).

Antony, L.M. 2007. For the love of reason, in *Philosophers Without Gods: Meditations on Atheism and the Secular Life* (ed. L.M. Antony). Oxford: Oxford University Press, pp. 41–58.

Anwar, Y. 2012. Highly religious people are less motivated by compassion than are non-believers. April 30. http://newscenter.berkeley.edu/2012/04/30/religionandgenerosity/ (accessed March 28, 2013).

Ardelt, M. and Koenig, C.S. 2006. The role of religion for hospice patients and relatively healthy older adults. *Research on Aging*, 28, 184–215.

Aristotle. 1999. *Nicomachean Ethics*, 2nd edn (trans. T.H. Irwin). Indianapolis: Hackett.

Augustine. 2003. *Concerning the City of God Against the Pagans* (trans. H. Bettenson). London: Penguin.

Avise, J.C. 2010 Footprints of nonsentient design inside the human genome. *Proceedings of the National Academy of Science*,107, 8969–8976.

Ayala, F.J. 2007. *Darwin's Gift to Science and Religion*. Washington, DC: Joseph Henry Press.

Ayer, A.J. 1988. What I saw when I was dead. *National Review*, 40(20), 38–40.

Baggini, J. 2003. *Atheism: A Very Short Introduction*. Oxford: Oxford University Press.

Baggini, J. and Pym, M. 2005. End of life: the humanist view. *Lancet*, 366, 1235–1237.

Baier, K. 2000 [1957]. The meaning of life (inaugural lecture), in *The Meaning of Life*, 2nd edn (ed. E.D. Klemke). Oxford: Oxford University Press, pp. 81–117.

Bailey, Kay 2012. Secularism fuels immorality. *The Gleaner*, May 1. http://jamaica-gleaner.com/gleaner/20120501/letters/letters5.html (accessed March 28, 2013).

Barker, D. 2008. *Godless: How an Evangelical Preacher Became One of America's Leading Atheists*. Berkeley, CA: Ulysses Press.

Bartels, A. and Zeki, S. 2004. The neural correlates of maternal and romantic love. *NeuroImage*, 21, 1155–1166.

BBC News. 2012. Row over Indonesia atheist Facebook post. January 20. http://www.bbc.co.uk/news/world-asia-16644141 (accessed March 28, 2013).

Bekkers, R. and Schuyt, T. 2008. And who is your neighbor? Explaining denominational differences in charitable giving and volunteering in the Netherlands. *Review of Religious Research*, 50 (1), 74–96.

Bekkers, R. and Wiepking, P. 2011. Who gives? A literature review of predictors of charitable giving. Forthcoming in *Voluntary Sector Review*. http://www.pamala.nl/papers/BekkersWiepking_VSR_2011.pdf (accessed March 28, 2013).

Benatar, D. 2006. What's God got to do with it? Atheism and religious practice. *Ratio*, 19, 383–400.

Benedict XVI. 2007. *Encyclical Letter Spe Salvi of the Supreme Pontiff Benedict XVI to the Bishops, Priests, and the Deaconsmen and Women Religious and all the Lay Faithful on Christian Hope*. Vatican: Libreria Editrice Vaticana.

Benfer, A. 2009. And the Rand played on. *Mother Jones*, July/August. http://www.motherjones.com/media/2009/07/and-rand-played (accessed March 28, 2013).

Benson, O. and Stangroom, J. 2009. *Does God Hate Women?* London: Continuum.

Berkeley Parents Network. 2009. Jewish families and Christian holidays. http://parents.berkeley.edu/advice/holidays/jewish-santa.html (accessed March 28, 2013).

Blackford, R. 2012. *Freedom of Religion and the Secular State*. Oxford: Wiley-Blackwell.

Blackford, R. and Schüklenk, U. (eds). 2009. *50 Voices of Disbelief: Why We Are Atheists*. Oxford: Wiley-Blackwell.

Boswell, J. 1971. *Boswell in Extremes: 1776–1778* (ed. C.McC. Weis and F.A. Pottle). London: Heinemann.

Boswell, J. 1980. *Life of Johnson* (ed. R.W. Chapman, revised J.D. Fleeman). Oxford: Oxford University Press.

Boudry, M., Blancke, S., and Braeckman, J. 2010. How not to attack intelligent design creationism: philosophical misconceptions about methodological naturalism. *Foundations of Science*, 15 (3), 227–244.

Boys, D. 2011. New atheists: no sense of humor or no sense?, November 24. http://www.canadafreepress.com/index.php/article/42674 (accessed March 28, 2013).

Brandes, S. 2006. *Skulls to the Living – Bread to the Dead. The Day of the Dead in Mexico and Beyond*. Oxford: Blackwell.

Branigan, T. 2004a. Tale of rape at the temple sparks riot at theatre. *The Guardian*, December 20. http://www.guardian.co.uk/uk/2004/dec/20/arts.religion (accessed March 28, 2013).

Branigan, T. 2004b. Stars sign letter in support of playwright in hiding. *The Guardian*, December 23. http://www.guardian.co.uk/uk/2004/dec/23/arts.religion (accessed March 28, 2013).

Brian, D. 2005. *The Unexpected Einstein: The Real Man Behind the Icon*. Hoboken, NJ: John Wiley & Sons, Inc.

Brights. 2012a. Vision statement. http://www.the-brights.net/vision/ (accessed March 28, 2013).

Brights. 2012b. Word talk. http://www.the-brights.net/vision/word.html (accessed March 28, 2013).

Brink, D.O. 2007. The autonomy of ethics, in *The Cambridge Companion to Atheism* (ed. M. Martin). Cambridge, UK: Cambridge University Press, pp. 149–165.

British Humanist Association. 2011. New survey evidence: census religion question "fatally flawed." http://www.humanism.org.uk/news/view/771 (accessed March 28, 2013).

Britten, N. 2004. Sikhs storm theatre in protest over play. *The Telegraph*, December 20. http://www.telegraph.co.uk/news/uknews/1479426/Sikhs-storm-theatre-in-protest-over-play.html (accessed March 28, 2013).

Bruce, S. 2001. Christianity in Britain, *R. I. P. Sociology of Religion*, 62, 191–203.
Buchanan, A. 2011. *Beyond Humanity? The Ethics of Biomedical Enhancement*. Oxford: Oxford University Press.
Buckley, M.J. 1987. *At the Origins of Modern Atheism*. New Haven, CT: Yale University Press.
Bullock, A. 1962. *Hitler: A Study in Tyranny*. New York: Random House.
Bullock, A. 1991. *Hitler and Stalin: Parallel Lives*. New York: HarperCollins.
Camus, A. 1975. *The Myth of Sisyphus* (trans. J. O'Brien). London: Penguin.
Carrier, R. 2002. The end of Pascal's wager: only nontheists go to Heaven. http://www.infidels.org/library/modern/richard_carrier/heaven.html (accessed March 28, 2013).
Carrier, R.C. 2003. Hitler's Table Talk: troubling finds. *German Studies Review*, 26, 561–576.
Carrier, R. 2009. *Not the Impossible Faith: Why Christianity Didn't Need a Miracle to Succeed*. Lulu.com.
Carrier, R. 2010a. Why the Resurrection is unbelievable, in *The Christian Delusion: Why Faith Fails* (ed. J.W. Loftus). Amherst, NY: Prometheus, pp. 291–315.
Carrier, R. 2010b. Christianity was not responsible for modern science, in *The Christian Delusion: Why Faith Fails* (ed. J.W. Loftus). Amherst, NY: Prometheus, pp. 396–419.
Carrier, R. 2012a. Ehrman on Jesus: a failure of facts and logic. Freethought Blogs. April 19. http://freethoughtblogs.com/carrier/archives/1026 (accessed March 28, 2013).
Carrier, R. 2012b. Proving history. Freethought Blogs. February 8. http://freethoughtblogs.com/carrier/archives/255 (accessed March 28, 2013).
Carrier, R. 2012c. *Proving History: Bayes's Theorem and the Quest for the Historical Jesus*. Amherst, NY: Prometheus.
Catechism of the Catholic Church. n.d. Vatican official website. http://www.vatican.va/archive/ENG0015/_P85.HTM (accessed March 20, 2013).
CBC. 2008. Belief in God a "product of human weaknesses": Einstein letter *CBC News*, May 13. http://www.cbc.ca/news/world/story/2008/05/13/einstein-religion.html (accessed March 28, 2013).
Cherry, M and Matsumura, M. 1998/9. 10 myths about secular humanism. http://www.secularhumanism.org/index.php?section=library&page=cherry1_18_1 (accessed March 28, 2013).
Christianity Today. 2007. The new intolerance: fear mongering among elite atheists is not a pretty sight. *Christianity Today*, January 25. http://www.christianitytoday.com/ct/2007/february/17.24.html (accessed March 28, 2013).
Christina, G. 2011. High school student stands up against prayer at public school and is ostracized, demeaned and threatened. *AlterNet*, May 25, 2011. http://www.alternet.org/belief/151086/high_school_student_stands_up_against_prayer_at_public_school_and_is_ostracized%2C_demeaned_and_threatened/ (accessed March 28, 2013).

Cimino, R. and Smith, C. 2007. Secular humanism and atheism beyond progressive secularism. *Sociology of Religion*, 68, 407–427.

Clark, R.W. 1985. *The Survival of Charles Darwin: A Biography of a Man and an Idea*. New York: Weidenfeld and Nicholson.

Cline, A. n.d. Atheism & Satan: do atheists worship Satan? Do atheists serve Satan? http://atheism.about.com/od/atheismmyths/a/AtheismSatan.htm (accessed March 28, 2013).

Cliteur, P. 2010. *The Secular Outlook: In Defense of Moral and Political Secularism*. Oxford: Wiley-Blackwell.

CNN. 2008. Presidential election exit polls. http://www.cnn.com/ELECTION/2008/results/polls/#val=USP00p2 (accessed March 28, 2011)

Cohen, J., Landeghem, P. van, Carpentier, N. and Deliens, L. 2012. Different trends in euthanasia acceptance across Europe. A study of 13 western and 10 central and eastern European countries, 1981–2008. *European Journal of Public Health*, DOI:10.1093/eurpub/cks186: e1-3.

Converse, R.W. 2003. *Atheism as a Positive Force*. New York: Algora.

Cornell, K. 2009a. Interview with a local atheist: Sari Nelson. April 28. http://www.examiner.com/atheism-in-dallas/interview-with-a-local-atheist-sari-nelson (accessed March 28, 2013).

Cornell, K. 2009b. For the record, atheists do not worship Satan. http://www.examiner.com/atheism-in-dallas/for-the-record-atheists-do-not-worship-satan (accessed March 28, 2013).

Cosmides, L. and Tooby, J. 1992. Cognitive adaptations for social exchange, in *The Adapted Mind: Evolutionary Psychology and the Generation of Culture* (ed. J.H. Barkow, L. Cosmides, and J. Tooby). New York: Oxford University Press, pp.163–228.

Coyne, J.A. 2009. *Why Evolution is True*. New York: Viking.

Coyne, J.A. 2012. Science, religion, and society: the problem of evolution in America. *Evolution* 66 (8), 2654–2663.

Craig, W.L. 1985a. Contemporary scholarship and the historical evidence for the Resurrection of Jesus Christ. *Truth* 1: 89–95. http://www.leaderu.com/truth/1truth22.html (accessed March 28, 2013).

Craig, W.L. 1985b. The historicity of the empty tomb of Jesus. *New Testament Studies* 31: 39–67. http://www.leaderu.com/offices/billcraig/docs/tomb2.html (accessed March 28, 2013).

Craig, W.L. and Sinnott-Armstrong, W. 2004. *God? A Debate Between a Christian and an Atheist*. Oxford: Oxford University Press.

Crimp, S. and Richardson, J. 2008. *Why We Left Islam: Former Muslims Speak Out*. Los Angeles, CA: WND Books.

Dacey, A. 2008. *The Secular Conscience: Why Religion Belongs in Public Life*. Amherst, NY: Prometheus.

Dalrymple, G.B. 2001. The age of the earth in the twentieth century: a problem (mostly) solved. *Special Publications, Geological Society of London*,190 (1), 205–221.

Darwin, C. 1859. *On the Origin of Species by Means of Natural Selection, Or the Preservation of Favoured Races in the Struggle for Life*. London: John Murray.

Davis, D.H. 2005. Is atheism a religion? Recent judicial perspectives on the constitutional meaning of "religion." *Journal of Church and State*, 47, 707–723.

Dawkins, R. 2003a. The future looks bright. *The Guardian*, June 21. http://www.guardian.co.uk/books/2003/jun/21/society.richarddawkins (accessed March 28, 2013).

Dawkins, R. 2003b. Religion be damned. *Wired*, October. http://www.wired.com/wired/archive/11.10/view.html?pg=2 (accessed March 28, 2013).

Dawkins, R. 2006. *The God Delusion*. London: Bantam.

Dawkins, R. 2009. *The Greatest Show on Earth: The Evidence for Evolution*. London: Bantam.

Debunking Atheists. 2008. http://debunkingatheists.blogspot.ca/2008/07/do-atheists-have-sense-of-humor.html (accessed March 28, 2013).

Demar, G. 2006. The soulless atheist. *American Vision*, November 2008. http://americanvision.org/1099/soulless-atheist/ (accessed March 28, 2013).

Dennett, D.C. 2003. The bright stuff. *New York Times*, July 12. http://www.edge.org/3rd_culture/bright/bright_index.html (accessed March 28, 2013).

Dennett, D.C. 2006. *Breaking the Spell: Religion as a Natural Phenomenon*. New York: Viking.

Dennett, D.C., and Plantinga, A. 2011. *Science and Religion: Are They Compatible?* Oxford: Oxford University Press.

Descartes, R. 1996 [1641]. *Meditations on First Philosophy* (trans. and ed. J. Cottingham). Cambridge, UK: Cambridge University Press.

Deschner, K. 1986–2008. *Kriminalgeschichte des Christentums* (9 vols). Reinbek: Rowohlt.

D'Souza, D. 2007. *What's So Great About Christianity*. Washington, DC: Regnery.

Durant, W. 1992 [1950]. *The Age of Faith*. Norwalk, CT: Easton Press.

Dworkin, G. 1988. *The Theory and Practice of Autonomy*. Cambridge, UK: Cambridge University Press.

Ecklund, E.H. 2010. *Science vs. Religion: What Scientists Really Think*. Oxford: Oxford University Press.

Edgell, P., Gerteis, J., and Hartmann, D. 2006. Atheists as "other": moral boundaries and cultural membership in American society. *American Sociological Review*, 71, 211–234.

Edis, T. 2007. *An Illusion of Harmony: Science and Religion in Islam*. Boston: Prometheus.

Edmondson, D, Park, C.L., Chaudoir, S.R., and Wortmann, J.H. 2008. Death without God: religious struggle, death concerns, and depression in the terminally ill. *Psychological Science*, 19, 754–758.

Edwards, P. 2000 [1966]. The meaning and value of life, in *The Meaning of Life*, 2nd edn (ed. E.D. Klemke). Oxford: Oxford University Press, pp.118–140.

Ehrman, B. 2012. *Did Jesus Exist? The Historical Argument for Jesus of Nazareth*. New York: HarperCollins.

Einstein, A. 1954. *Ideas and Opinions*. New York: Crown.

Exline, J.J., Park, C.L., Smyth, J.M., and Carey, M.P. 2011. Anger toward God: Social-cognitive predictors, prevalence, and links with adjustment to bereavement and cancer. *Journal of Personality and Social Psychology*, 100, 129–148.

Fernandes, P. 2009. *The Atheist Delusion*. Brentwood, TN: Xulon Press.

Field, M. 2012. Ruling: Jesus doesn't heal cancer. May 1. http://www.stuff.co.nz/national/6835139/Jesus-doesn-t-cure-cancer-ruling (accessed March 28, 2013).

Flew, A. 1995. The terrors of Islam. *Atheist Notes*, No. 6. http://www.libertarian.co.uk/lapubs/athen/athen006.pdf (accessed March 18, 2013).

Flew, A. and Varghese, R.A. 2007. *There is a God: How the World's Most Notorious Atheist Changed His Mind*. New York: HarperCollins.

Fortin, Jacob. 2009. Christians have no sense of humor. December 17. http://www.thegoodatheist.net/2009/12/17/christians-have-no-sense-of-humor/ (accessed March 28, 2013).

Fox, K.C. and Keck, A. 2004. *Einstein A to Z*. Hoboken, NJ: John Wiley & Sons, Inc.

Frame, T. 2009. *Losing My Religion: Unbelief in Australia*. Sydney: University of New South Wales Press.

Galilei, G. 1957. *Discoveries and Opinions of Galileo: Including The Starry Messenger, 1610, Letters on Sunspots, 1613, Letters to the Grand Duchess Christina, 1615, and, excerpts from The Assayer, 1623* (trans. S. Drake). New York: Doubleday.

Gallup Politics. 2012. In U.S., 46% hold creationist view of human origins. http://www.gallup.com/poll/155003/Hold-Creationist-View-Human-Origins.aspx (accessed March 28, 2012).

Gaukroger, S. 2006. *The Emergence of a Scientific Culture: Science and the Shaping of Modernity, 1210–1685*. Oxford: Oxford University Press.

Gaukroger, S. 2010. *The Collapse of Mechanism and the Rise of Sensibility: Science and the Shaping of Modernity*, 1680–1760. Oxford: Oxford University Press.

Garner, R. 1994. *Beyond Morality*. Philadelphia: Temple University Press.

Geissbuehler, S. 2002. No religion, no (political) values? Political attitudes of atheists in comparison. *Journal for the Study of Religions and Ideologies*, 2, 114–122.

Gervais, W.M., Shariff, A.F., and Norenzayan, A. 2011. Do you believe in atheists? Distrust is central to anti-atheist prejudice. *Journal of Personality and Social Psychology*, 101, 1189–1206.

Ghosh, P. 2009. Why I am NOT a theist, in *50 Voices of Disbelief: Why We Are Atheists* (ed. R. Blackford and U. Schüklenk). Oxford: Wiley-Blackwell, pp. 263–269.

Gill, M. 2012. How God corrupts creatures great and small. *New Statesman*, September 6. http://www.newstatesman.com/blogs/martha-gill/2012/09/how-god-corrupts-creatures-great-and-small (accessed March 28, 2013).

Glover, J. 1977. *Causing Death and Saving Lives*. Harmondsworth, UK: Penguin.

Glover, J. 1999. *Humanity: A Moral History of the Twentieth Century*. London: Pimlico.

Godfrey, M. 2010. Atheists are believers who hate God, says Anglican Archbishop Peter Jensen. http://www.heraldsun.com.au/news/breaking-news/atheists-are-believers-who-hate-god-says-anglican-archbishop-peter-jensen/story-e6frf7jx-1225848925206 (accessed March 28, 2013).

Golgowski, N. 2012. Private jets, 13 mansions and a $100,000 mobile home just for the dogs: Televangelists "defrauded tens of million (sic) of dollars from Christian network." *Daily Mail*, March 23. http://www.dailymail.co.uk/news/article-2119493/Private-jets-13-mansions-100-000-mobile-home-just-dogs-Televangelists-defrauded-tens-million-dollars-Christian-network.html (accessed March 28, 2013).

Goodstein, L. 2010. Basic religion test stumps many Americans. *The New York Times*, September 28. http://www.nytimes.com/2010/09/28/us/28religion.html (accessed March 28, 2013).

GOP. 2012. We believe in America: 2012 Republican platform. http://www.gop.com/wp-content/uploads/2012/08/2012GOPPlatform.pdf (accessed March 28, 2013).

Gould, S.J. 1998. *Questioning the Millennium: A Rationalist's Guide to a Precisely Arbitrary Countdown*. London: Vintage.

Gould, S.J. 1999. *Rocks of Ages: Science and Religion in the Fullness of Life*. New York: Ballantine.

Grayling, A.C. 2009. *To Set Prometheus Free: Essays on Religion, Reason and Humanity*. London: Oberon.

Groves, C. 1996. From Ussher to slusher; from archbish to Gish; or, not in a million years... *Archaeology in Oceania*, 31, 145–151.

Guthrie, S.E. 2007. Anthropological theories of religion, in *The Cambridge Companion to Atheism* (ed. M. Martin). Cambridge, UK: Cambridge University Press, pp. 283–299.

Hájek, A. 2011. Pascal's wager, in *The Stanford Encyclopedia of Philosophy* (ed. E.N. Zalta). http://plato.stanford.edu/archives/sum2011/entries/pascal-wager (accessed March 29, 2013).

Haldeman, J. 2009. Atheist out of the foxhole, in *50 Voices of Disbelief: Why We Are Atheists* (ed. R. Blackford and U. Schüklenk). Oxford: Wiley-Blackwell, pp. 187–190.

Harman, G. 1977. *The Nature of Morality: An Introduction to Ethics*. New York: Oxford University Press.

Harris, S. 2004. *The End of Faith: Religion, Terror, and the Future of Reason*. New York: W.W. Norton.

Harris, S. 2006a. *Letter to a Christian Nation*. New York: Knopf.

Harris, S. 2006b. The case against faith. *Newsweek*, November 13. http://www.samharris.org/site/full_text/the-case-against-faith/ (accessed March 29, 2013)

Harvey, P. 1961. Bar atheism from schools. *The Evening Independent*, December 14.

Haught, J.F. 2008. *God and the New Atheism: A Critical Response to Dawkins, Harris and Hitchens*. Louisville, KY: Westminster John Knox Press.

Hedges, C. 2008. *I Don't Believe in Atheists*. New York: Free Press, 2008.

Hepburn, R.W. 2000 [1965]. Questions about the meaning of life, in *The Meaning of Life*, 2nd edn (ed. E.D. Klemke). Oxford: Oxford University Press, pp. 261–276.

Hitchens, C. 1997. *The Missionary Position: Mother Teresa in Theory and Practice*. New York and London: Verso.

Hitchens, C. 2006. The caged virgin: Holland's shameful treatment of Ayaan Hirsi Ali. *Slate*, May 8. http://www.slate.com/articles/news_and_politics/fighting_words/2006/05/the_caged_virgin.html (accessed March 29, 2013).

Hitchens, C. 2007. *God Is Not Great: How Religion Poisons Everything*. New York: Twelve Books.

Hitchens, C. 2010. Pray for me? Christopher Hitchens? *Washington Post*, September 20. http://onfaith.washingtonpost.com/onfaith/guestvoices/2010/09/pray_for_me_christopher_hitchens.html (accessed March 29, 2013)

Hitler, A. 1941. *Mein Kampf: Complete and Unabridged*. New York: Yernal and Hitchcock.

Hitler, A. 1953. *Hitler's Table Talk 1941–1944* (trans. N. Cameron and R.H. Stevens, ed. H.R. Trevor-Roper). London: Weidenfeld and Nicolson.

Huckabee, M. 2012. Atheists don't have a good sense of humor. April 12. http://www.youtube.com/watch?v=nU4i9HgZGaM (accessed March 13, 2013)

Hume, D. 2010 [1777]. *On Miracles*, in *Essays and Treatises vol. 2: An Enquiry Concerning Human Understanding, a Dissertation on the Passions, an Enquiry Concerning the Principles of Morals, and the Natural History of Religion*. http://www.bartleby.com/37/3/14.html (accessed March 22, 2013).

Hume, D. 1779. *Dialogues Concerning Natural Religion*. http://www.gutenberg.org/ebooks/4583 (accessed March 26, 2013).

Hutton, R. 1989. *Charles II: King of England, Scotland, and Ireland*. Oxford: Oxford University Press.

Hyman, G. 2010. *A Short History of Atheism*. London: I.B. Tauris.

Jacoby, S. 2004. *Freethinkers: A History of American Secularism*. New York: Henry Holt.

James, W. 1982 [1902]. *The Varieties of Religious Experience: A Study in Human Nature*. London: Penguin.

Jammer, M. 1999. *Einstein and Religion: Physics and Theology*. Princeton, NJ: Princeton University Press.

Jensen, P. Intelligence squared debate: Why atheists are like flat-earthers. September 12, 2011. http://www.abc.net.au/religion/articles/2011/09/12/3315313.htm (accessed March 29, 2013).

Jim the evolution cruncher. 2012. Why do atheists hate Christ so much? *Yahoo answers*, April 30. http://answers.yahoo.com/question/index?qid=20081122040019AATNM3R (accessed March 29, 2013).

Johansson-Stenman, O. 2008. Who are the trustworthy, we think? *Journal of Economic Behavior & Organization*, 68, 456–465.

John Paul II. 1998. Fides et ratio: to the bishops of the Catholic Church on the relationship between faith and reason. http://www.vatican.va/edocs/ENG0216/_INDEX.HTM (accessed March 29, 2013).

Joyce, R. 2001. *The Myth of Morality*. Cambridge, UK: Cambridge University Press.

Joyner, R. 2012. Our prayers regrow amputated limbs. September 4. http://www.youtube.com/watch?v=PmH1YggCQ7Y&list=UUMXqRHe8n1TX5iDvkLS62rw&index=4&feature=plcp (accessed March 29, 2013)

Kahl, J. 1971. The *Misery of Christianity: A Plea for a Humanity without God* (trans. N.D. Smith). London: Penguin.

Kaminer, W. 2011. Sectarianism, deism, and the Ground Zero cross. *The Atlantic*, August 1. http://www.theatlantic.com/national/archive/2011/08/sectarianism-deism-and-the-ground-zero-cross/242867/ (accessed March 29, 2013).

Kant, I. 1781. *Critique of Pure Reason*. http://www.gutenberg.org/ebooks/4280 (accessed March 22, 2013).

Kant, I. 1996 [1784]. *Practical Philosophy* (trans. and ed. M.J. Gregor). Cambridge, UK: Cambridge University Press.

Kant, I. 1993 [1785]. *Groundwork for the Metaphysics of Morals* (trans. J.W. Ellington). Indianapolis: Hackett.

Kant, I. 1997 [1788]. *Critique of Practical Reason* (trans. and ed. M.J. Gregor). Cambridge, UK: Cambridge University Press.

Keltner, D. and Haidt, J. 2003. Approaching awe, a moral, spiritual, and aesthetic emotion. *Psychology*, 17 (2), 297–314.

Kernohan, A. 2006. *A Guide for the Godless – The Secular Path to Meaning*. Dalhousie University, Department of Philosophy, Halifax. http://myweb.dal.ca/kernohan/godless (accessed March 29, 2013)

Keysar, A. 2007. Who are America's atheists and agnostics?, in *Secularism and Secularity: Contemporary International Perspectives* (ed. B.A. Kosmin and A. Keysar). Hartford, CT: Institute for the Study of Secularism in Society and Culture, pp. 33–40.

Kirsch, J. 2004. *God Against the Gods: The History of the War Between Monotheism and Polytheism*. New York: Penguin.

Kitcher, P. 2007. *Living with Darwin: Evolution, Design, and the Future of Faith*. Oxford: Oxford University Press.

Krauss, L.M. 2012. *A Universe from Nothing: Why There Is Something Rather Than Nothing*. New York: Free Press.

Kuhn, T.S, 1957. *The Copernican Revolution: Planetary Astronomy in the Development of Western Thought*. Cambridge, MA: Harvard University Press.

Kuhse, H. 1987. *The Sanctity of Life Doctrine in Medicine: A Critique*. Oxford: Clarendon Press.

Law, S. 2011. *Humanism: A Very Short Introduction*. Oxford: Oxford University Press.

Lawley, B. 2009. The atheist antidote. http://www.youtube.com/watch?v=asC4xSVt7SY&feature=related (accessed March 29, 2013).

Lee, R.T. 2004. Exposing the atheist. http://www.tencommandments.org/heathens2.html (accessed March 29, 2013).

Leibniz, G.W. 1951 [1710]. *Theodicy: Essays on the Goodness of God, the Freedom of Man and the Origin of Evil* (ed. A. Farrer, trans. E.M. Huggard). London: Routledge and Kegan Paul. http://www.gutenberg.org/files/17147/17147-h/17147-h.htm (accessed March 29, 2013).

Lennox, J.C. 2011. *Gunning for God: Why the New Atheists are Missing the Target*. Oxford: Lion Books.

Lewis, C.S. 1952. *Mere Christianity*, revised and amplified edn. London: Geoffrey Bles.

Lewis, C.S. 1960. *Miracles: A Preliminary Study*. London: Fontana.

Locke, J. 1983 [1689]. *A Letter Concerning Toleration*. Indianapolis: Hackett Publications. http://press-pubs.uchicago.edu/founders/documents/amendI_assemblys7.html (accessed March 29, 2013).

Loftus, J.W. (ed.). 2010. *The Christian Delusion: Why Faith Fails*. Amherst, NY: Prometheus.

Loftus, J.W. (ed.). 2011. *The End of Christianity*. Amherst, NY: Prometheus.

Loftus, J.W. 2012a. *Why I Became an Atheist: A Former Preacher Rejects Christianity*, revised and expanded edn. Amherst, NY: Prometheus.

Loftus, J.W. 2012b. An interview with Richard Carrier about his book, *Proving History*. http://debunkingchristianity.blogspot.ca/2012/02/interview-with-richard-carrier-about.html (accessed March 29, 2013)

Lowenstein, R. 1995. *Buffett: The Making of an American Capitalist*. New York: Random House.

Luther, M. 2004 [1543]. *The Jews and Their Lies* (abridged translation of *Von den Jüden und iren Lügen*). York, SC: Liberty Bell Publications.

MAAF (Military Association of Atheists and Freethinkers). 2012. Atheists in foxholes, in cockpits and on ships. http://www.militaryatheists.org/expaif.html (accessed March 29, 2013).

Macdonald, S. 2007. *Propaganda and Information Warfare in the Twenty-first Century: Altered Images and Deception Operations*. London: Taylor and Francis.

Mackie, J.L. 1977. *Ethics: Inventing Right and Wrong*. New York: Viking.

Mackie, J.L. 1982. *The Miracle of Theism: Arguments for and against the Existence of God*. Oxford: Oxford University Press.

Madrid, P. and Hensley, K. 2010. *The Godless Delusion: A Catholic Challenge to Modern Atheism*. Huntington, IN: Our Saturday Visitor Publishing.

Marsden, G.M. 1980. *Fundamentalism and American Culture*. Oxford: Oxford University Press.

Martin, M. 1990. *Atheism: A Philosophical Justification*. Philadelphia: Temple University Press.

Martin, M. 1996. Are there really no atheists? http://www.infidels.org/library/modern/michael_martin/no_atheists.html (accessed March 29, 2013).

Martin, M. 2002. *Atheism, Morality, and Meaning*. Amherst, NY: Prometheus.

Martin, M. 2007. Atheism and religion, in *The Cambridge Companion to Atheism* (ed. M. Martin). Cambridge, UK: Cambridge University Press, pp. 217–232.

Marx, K. 1970 [1844]. *A Contribution to the Critique of Hegel's Philosophy of Right* (trans. and ed. J. O'Malley). Cambridge, UK: Cambridge University Press.

McDonald, G., Wearing, S., and Ponting, J. 2009. The nature of peak experience in wilderness. *The Humanistic Psychologist*, 37(4), 370–385.

McGrath, A. 2004. *The Twilight of Atheism: The Rise and Fall of Disbelief in the Modern World*. London: Bider.

McGrath, A. and Collicutt McGrath, J. 2007. *The Dawkins Delusion? Atheist Fundamentalism and the Denial of the Divine*. London: Society for the Promotion of Christian Knowledge.

McGrath, A. 2011. *Why God Won't Go Away: Engaging with the New Atheism*. London: Society for the Promotion of Christian Knowledge.

McLean's. 2010. Do atheists care less? Those who attend religious services are more charitable and more eager to volunteer. *McLean's*, May 6 http://www2.macleans.ca/2010/05/06/do-atheists-care-less/ (accessed March 29, 2013).

Mercier, A. 2009. Religious belief and self-deception, in *50 Voices of Disbelief: Why We Are Atheists* (ed. R. Blackford and U. Schüklenk). Oxford: Wiley-Blackwell, pp. 41–47.

Meslier, J. 2009 [1729]. *Testament: Memoir of the Thoughts and Sentiments of Jean Meslier*. Amherst, NY: Prometheus.

Metz, T. 2003. The immortality requirement for life's meaning. *Ratio*, 16, 161–177.

Micklethwait, J. and Wooldridge, A. 2009. *God is Back: How the Global Revival of Faith is Changing the World*. New York: Penguin.

Mill, J.S. 1979 [1863]. *Utilitarianism*. Indianapolis: Hackett Publishers.

Mill, J.S. 1996 [1904]. On nature. In *The Utility of Religion and Theism*. London: Watts and Co, pp. 7–33. http://www.lancs.ac.uk/users/philosophy/texts/mill_on.htm (accessed March 29, 2013).

Mochon, D., Norton, M.L., and Ariely, D. 2011. Who benefits from religion? *Social Indicators Research*, 101, 1–15.

Montaigne, M.E. de. 1580. Essays (trans. J. Florio 1603). https://scholarsbank.uoregon.edu/xmlui/bitstream/handle/1794/766/montaigne.pdf?sequence=1 (accessed March 29, 2013).

Mooney, C. and Kirshenbaum, S. 2009. *Unscientific America: How Scientific Illiteracy Threatens Out Future*. Philadelphia: Basic Books.

Moore, J. 1994. *The Darwin Legend*. Ada, MI: Baker Publishing Group.

Mosbergen, D. 2012. Dalai Lama tells his Facebook friends that "religion is no longer adequate." *Huffington Post*, September 13. http://www.huffingtonpost.com/2012/09/13/dalai-lama-facebook-religion-is-no-longer-adequate-science_n_1880805.html (accessed March 29, 2013).

Namazie, M. 2009. When the Hezbollah came to my school, in *50 Voices of Disbelief: Why We Are Atheists* (ed. R. Blackford and U. Schüklenk). Oxford: Wiley-Blackwell, pp. 270–273.

Neill, A. and Ridley, A. 2010. Religious music for godless ears. *Mind*, 119, 999–1023.

Nicolet, S. and Tresch, A. 2008. When church attendance is not enough: For a two-dimensional typology of religiosity in studies of political behaviour. *Staff Presentation*. November. http://www.unige.ch/ses/spo/Membres/Enseignants/Tresch/Recherches/staff_nicolet_tresch_final.pdf (accessed March 29, 2013).

Niebuhr, R. 1981 [1955]. The self and its search for ultimate meaning, in *The Meaning of Life*, 1st edn (ed. E.D. Klemke). New York: Oxford University Press, pp. 41–52.

Nielsen, K. 2000 [1964]. Linguistic philosophy and "the meaning of life," in *The Meaning of Life*, 2nd edn (ed. E.D. Klemke). New York: Oxford University Press, pp. 233–256.

Nietzsche Chronicle. 1885. Compiled by M. Brown, Dartmouth College. http://www.dartmouth.edu/˜fnchron/1885.html (accessed March 29, 2013).

No More Hornets (2007). http://nomorehornets.blogspot.ca/2007/05/atheist-jokes.html (accessed March 29, 2013).

Nye, B. 2012. Creationism is not appropriate for children. August 23. http://www.youtube.com/watch?v=gHbYJfwFgOU (accessed March 29, 2013).

O'Brien, S. 2004. American Morning. 9:30 am EST. November 9. Aired on CNN. Transcript at http://transcripts.cnn.com/TRANSCRIPTS/0411/09/ltm.06.html (accessed March 29, 2013).

Odone, C. 2011. The intolerant atheists will never be happy. *The Telegraph*, April 18. http://blogs.telegraph.co.uk/news/cristinaodone/100084211/the-intolerant-atheists-will-never-be-happy/ (accessed March 29, 2013).

Onfray, M. 2007. *In Defense of Atheism: The Case against Christianity, Judaism and Islam*. Toronto: Viking.

Oppenheimer, M. 2011. A Place on the right for a few godless conservatives. *New York Times*, February 18. http://www.nytimes.com/2011/02/19/us/19beliefs.html?_r=1&ref=atheism (accessed March 29, 2013).

Oppy, G. 1990. On Rescher on Pascal's wager. *International Journal for Philosophy of Religion*, 30, 159–68.

Oppy, G. 2006. *Arguing About Gods*. Cambridge, UK: Cambridge University Press.

Overbye, D. 2008. Einstein letter on God sells for $404,000, *New York Times*, May 17 http://www.nytimes.com/2008/05/17/science/17einsteinw.html (accessed March 29, 2013).

Pascal, B. 1910. *Pascal's Pensées* (trans. W.F. Trotter). http://freedownloadb.com/pdf/pens-es-online-christian-library-virtual-theological-4414951.html (accessed March 29, 2013).

Pearce, M. 2012. U.S. Rep. Paul Broun: Evolution a lie "from the pit of hell." *Los Angeles Times* October 7. http://www.latimes.com/news/nation/nationnow/la-na-nn-paul-broun-evolution-hell-20121007,0,4628858.story (accessed March 29, 2013).

Pennock, R.T. 2000. *Tower of Babel: The Evidence against the New Creationism*. Cambridge, MA: MIT Press.

Persona Humana. 1975. Vatican official website. http://www.vatican.va/roman_curia/congregations/cfaith/documents/rc_con_cfaith_doc_19751229_persona-humana_en.html (accessed March 20, 2013).

Pew Research Center. 2010. Religion among the millennials. http://pewforum.org/Age/Religion-Among-the-Millennials.aspx (accessed March 29, 2013).

Pew Research Center. 2012. Extract from American Values Survey question data base. http://www.people-press.org/values-questions/q41d/i-never-doubt-the-existence-of-god/#total (accessed March 29, 2013).

Pinker, S. 2011. *The Better Angels of Our Nature*. New York: Viking.

Plantinga, A. 2000. *Warranted Christian Belief*. New York: Oxford University Press.

Plantinga, A. 2008. Evolution vs naturalism: why they are like oil and water. *Books and Culture: A Christian Review*, July 1, 2008. http://www.ctlibrary.com/bc/2008/julaug/11.37.html (accessed March 29, 2013).

Plantinga, A. 2011. *Where the Conflict Really Lies: Science, Religion, and Naturalism*. Oxford: Oxford University Press.

Plantinga, A. and Tooley, M. 2008. *Knowledge of God*. Oxford: Wiley-Blackwell.

Popper, K.R. 1963. *Conjectures and Refutations: The Growth of Scientific Knowledge*. London: Routledge.

Prinz, J. 2007. *The Emotional Construction of Morals*. Oxford: Oxford University Press.

Pugmire, D. 2006. The secular reception of religious music. *Philosophy*, 81, 65–79.

Rachels, J. 1971. God and human attitudes. *Religious Studies*, 7, 325–337.

Rachels, J. and Rachels, S. 2010. *The Elements of Moral Philosophy*, 6th edn. Boston: MacMillan.

Ramakrishna, G. 1981. Some loud thinking about the Bhagavadgita, in *Marxism and Indology* (ed. D. Chattopadhyaya). Calcutta: K.P. Bagchi & Co., pp. 216–221.

Ravenhill, M. 2008. God is behind some of our greatest art. *The Guardian*, April 14. http://www.guardian.co.uk/stage/theatreblog/2008/apr/14/godisbehindsomeofourgrea (accessed March 29, 2013).

Regan, T. 2004. *The Case for Animal Rights: With A New Preface*. Berkeley: University of California Press.

Reitan, E. 2009. *Is God a Delusion? A Reply to Religion's Cultured Despisers*. Oxford: Wiley-Blackwell.

Resnicoff, A.E. 2004. On becoming our own worst enemy. *Christian Science Monitor*, June 28. http://www.csmonitor.com/2004/0628/p09s02-coop.html (accessed March 29, 2013).

Reuters. 2011. Islamic bloc drops 12-year U.N. drive to ban defamation of religion. http://blogs.reuters.com/faithworld/2011/03/24/islamic-bloc-drops-12-year-u-n-drive-to-ban-defamation-of-religion/ (accessed March 29, 2013).

Rey, G. 2007. Meta-atheism: religious avowal as self-deception, in *Philosophers Without Gods: Meditations on Atheism and the Secular Life* (ed. L.M. Antony). Oxford: Oxford University Press, pp. 243–265.

Ridge, M. 2010. Moral non-naturalism, in *The Stanford Encyclopedia of Philosophy* (ed. E.N. Zalta). http://plato.stanford.edu/archives/spr2010/entries/moral-non-naturalism (accessed March 29, 2013).

Riley-Smith, J. 1999. *The Oxford History of the Crusades*. Oxford: Oxford University Press.

R.M. 2012. Growing disbelief. *The Economist*, August 22. http://www.economist.com/blogs/democracyinamerica/2012/08/atheism?spc=scode&spv=xm&ah=9d7f7ab945510a56fa6d37c30b6f1709 (accessed March 29, 2013).

Romano, L. 2004. Bush's guard service in question: Democrats say president shirked his duty in 1972. *Washington Post*, February 3, A08.

Rosenberg, Alex 2011. *The Atheist's Guide to Reality: Enjoying Life Without Illusions*. New York: W.W. Norton.

Rosenberg, Alfred 1930. *Der Mythus des 20. Jahrhunderts. Eine Wertung der seelisch-geistigen Gestaltenkämpfe unserer Zeit*. Munich: Hoheneichen-Verlag.

Rousseau, J.-J. 1987 [1762]. *The Social Contract* (trans. M. Cranston). Harmondsworth, UK: Penguin.

Rowe, W.L. 1979. The problem of evil and some varieties of atheism. *American Philosophical Quarterly*, 16, 335–341.

Rowland, T. 2011. Intelligence squared debate: atheists are fundamentally wrong about the human. September 12, 2011. http://www.abc.net.au/religion/articles/2011/09/12/3315307.htm (accessed March 29, 2013).

Rummel, R.J. 1994. *Death By Government*. New Brunswick, NJ: Transaction Publishers.

Rushdie, S. 2012. *Joseph Anton: A Memoir*. New York: Random House.

Russell, B. 2000 [1903]. A free man's worship, in *The Meaning of Life*, 2nd edn (ed. E.M. Klemke). New York: Oxford University Press, pp. 71–77.

Ruthven, M. 2005. *Fundamentalism: The Search for Meaning*. Oxford: Oxford University Press.

Ruthven, M. 2007. *Fundamentalism: A Very Short Introduction*. Oxford: Oxford University Press.

Sagan, C. 1996. *Billions and Billions: Thoughts on Life and Death at the Brink of the Millennium*. New York: Ballantine.

Schlesinger, R. 2009. Poll on birthers: most Southerners, Republicans question Obama citizenship. *USA News and World Report* July 31, 2009. http://www.usnews.com/opinion/blogs/robert-schlesinger/2009/07/31/poll-on-birthers-most-southerners-republicans-question-obama-citizenship (accessed March 29, 2013).

Schopenhauer, A. 1995 [1860]. *On the Basis of Morality* (trans. E.F.J. Payne). Indianapolis, IN: Hackett.

Schüklenk, U. 2009. Human self-determination, medical progress and God, in *50 Voices of Disbelief: Why We Are Atheists* (ed. R. Blackford and U. Schüklenk). Oxford: Wiley-Blackwell, pp. 321–331.

Schüklenk, U., van Delden, J.J.M., Downie, J. *et al.* 2011. End-of-life decision-making in Canada: the report by the Royal Society of Canada expert panel on end-of-life decision-making. *Bioethics*, 25 (SI), 1–73.

Sciabarra, C.M. 1995. *Ayn Rand: The Russian Radical*. University Park, PA: Pennsylvania State University Press.

Selim, J. 2004. Useless body parts – what do we need sinuses for anyway? *Discover*. http://discovermagazine.com/2004/jun/useless-body-parts/article_view?b_start:int=1&-C (accessed March 29, 2013).

Severson, L. 2012. Godless chaplains. *PBS*, April 20. http://www.pbs.org/wnet/religionandethics/episodes/april-20-2012/godless-chaplains/10814/ (accessed March 29, 2013).

Short, P. 2005. *Pol Pot: Anatomy of a Nightmare*. New York: Henry Holt & Co.

Sidgwick, H. 1981 [1874]. *The Methods of Ethics*. Indianapolis, IN: Hackett.

Singer, P. 1976. *Animal Liberation: A New Ethics for Our Treatment of Animals*. London: Cape.

Singer, P. 1981. *The Expanding Circle: Ethics and Sociobiology*. Oxford: Oxford University Press.

Singer, P. 2006. What should a billionaire give and what should you? New York Times (Magazine) December 17. http://www.nytimes.com/2006/12/17/magazine/17charity.t.html?pagewanted=all&_r=0 (accessed March 29, 2013).

Singer, P. 2011. *Practical Ethics*, 3rd edn. Cambridge, UK: Cambridge University Press.

Sinnott-Armstrong, W. 2009. *Morality Without God?* Oxford: Oxford University Press.

Sjølie, M.L. 2010. The Danish cartoonist who survived an axe attack. *The Guardian*, January 5, G2, p. 12.

Smith, B. 2011a. Christian apologist calls atheists' war on Christmas misguided. *Christian Post*, December 13. http://www.christianpost.com/news/christian-apologist-calls-atheists-war-on-christmas-misguided-64763/ (accessed March 29, 2013).

Smith, B. 2011b. Atheists up charity giving; good without God? *The Christian Post*, December 28. http://www.christianpost.com/news/atheists-up-charity-giving-good-without-god-65929/ (accessed March 29, 2013).

Smith, G.H. 1979. *Atheism: The Case Against God*. Buffalo, NY: Prometheus.

Smith, K. 2012. Against homeopathy: a utilitarian perspective. *Bioethics*, 26, 398–409.

Sowle Cahill, L. 1990. Can theology have a role in "public" bioethics discourse? *Hastings Center Report* 20 (4 suppl.), 10–14.

Speer, A. 1970. *Inside the Third Reich: Memoirs* (trans. R. and C. Winston). London: Weidenfeld and Nicolson Touchstone.

Spiegel, J.S. 2010. *The Making of an Atheist: How Immorality Leads to Unbelief*. Chicago: Moody Publishing.

Stenger, V.J. 2008. *God: The Failed Hypothesis – How Science Shows That God Does Not Exist*. Amherst, NY: Prometheus.

Stenger, V.J. 2011. *The Fallacy of Fine-Tuning: Why The Universe Is Not Designed For Us*. Amherst, NY: Prometheus.

Stenger, V.J. 2012. *God and the Folly of Faith: The Incompatibility of Science and Religion*. Amherst, NY: Prometheus.

Stephens, S. 2011. The unbearable lightness of atheism. September 12, 2011. http://www.abc.net.au/religion/articles/2011/09/13/3316962.htm (accessed March 29, 2013).

Swenson, D.F. 2000 [1949]. The dignity of human life, in *The Meaning of Life*, 2nd edn (ed. E.D. Klemke). Oxford: Oxford University Press, pp. 20–30.

Swinburne, R. 2004. *The Existence of God*, 2nd edn. Oxford: Oxford University Press.

Tao Yang, D. 2008. China's agricultural crisis and famine of 1959–1961: A survey and comparison to Soviet famines. *Comparative Economic Studies*, 50, 1–29.

Taylor, C. 2007. *A Secular Age*. Cambridge, MA: Harvard University Press.

Thibaut, G. 1962 [1904]. (trans.) *Vedanta-Sutras with the Commentary by Sankaracarya*, vol. I. Delhi: Motilal Banarsidass.

Thiry, P.H., Baron D'Holbach. 2006 [1770]. *Good Sense Without God: Or Freethoughts Opposed to Supernatural Ideas*. Teddington, UK: Echo Library.

Todd, L. 2008. Why I celebrate Christmas, by the world's most famous atheist. *Daily Mail* (London), December 23. http://www.dailymail.co.uk/debate/article-1100842/Why-I-celebrate-Christmas-worlds-famous-atheist.html (accessed March 29, 2013).

Tooley, M. 2009. Helping people to think critically about their religious beliefs, in *50 Voices of Disbelief: Why We Are Atheists* (ed. R. Blackford and U. Schüklenk). Oxford: Wiley-Blackwell, pp. 310–322.

Turnbull, L. 2010. World Relief rejects job applicant over his faith. *Seattle Times*, March 9. http://seattletimes.nwsource.com/html/localnews/2011301098_worldrelief10m.html (accessed March 29, 2013).

Upshur, R. 2009. Cold comfort, in *50 Voices of Disbelief: Why We Are Atheists* (ed. R. Blackford and U. Schüklenk). Oxford: Wiley-Blackwell, pp. 177–181.

Vaidyanathan, B., Hill, J.P., and Smith, C. 2011. Religion and charitable financial giving to religious and secular causes: does political ideology matter? *Journal for the Scientific Study of Religion*, 50, 450–469.

Van Til, C. 1969. *A Christian Theory of Knowledge*. Phillipsburg, NJ: Presbyterian and Reformed Publishing.

Vincent, L. 2007. Over there and over there. *World (magazine)*, June 9. http://www.worldmag.com/articles/13025 (accessed March 29, 2013).

Voltaire. 2005 [1759]. *Candide: Or Optimism* (trans. T. Cuffe). London: Penguin.

Walters, K. 2010. *Atheism: A Guide for the Perplexed*. New York: Continuum.

Warraq, I. 2003. *Leaving Islam: Apostates Speak Out*. Amherst, NY: Prometheus Books.

Warren, M.A. 1998. Abortion, in *A Companion to Bioethics* (ed. H. Kuhse and P. Singer). Oxford: Blackwell, 127–134.

Watchtower Society. 2013. Do all good people go to Heaven? Watchtower Online Library http://wol.jw.org/en/wol/d/r1/lp-e/2010082 (accessed March 13, 2013).

Weber, S.R., Pargamant, K.I. Kinuk, M.E., *et al.* 2012. Psychological distress among religious nonbelievers: a systematic review. *Journal of Religion and Health*, 51, 72–86.

White, M. 2012. *The Great Big Book of Horrible Things: The Definitive Chronicle of History's 100 Worst Atrocities*. New York: W.W. Norton.

White, S. 2011. Christmas and religion: dealing with Christianity as an atheist parent. *Huffington Post*, May 12. http://www.huffingtonpost.ca/2011/12/05/christmas-religion-kids_n_1128115.html (accessed March 29, 2013).

Wiepking, P. and Bekkers, R. 2009. Explaining differences in charitable giving in Europe, in *Nederland in Vergelijkend Perspectief* (ed. H. Ganzenboom and M. Wittenberg). Tweede Nederlandse Workshop European Social Survey. Den Haag: DANS, pp. 185–191.

Wilkinson, P.J. and Coleman, P.G. 2010. Strong beliefs and coping in old age: a case-based comparison of atheism and religious faith. *Ageing and Society*, 30 (2), 337–361.

Williams, E. 2012. Atheism, religion more alike than different. *The Gleaner*, April 22. http://jamaica-gleaner.com/gleaner/20120422/letters/letters1.html (accessed March 29, 2013).

Williams, K. and Harvey, D. 2001. Transcendent experience in forest environments. *Journal of Environmental Psychology*, 21 (3), 249–260.

Wilson, C. 2008. *Epicureanism at the Origins of Modernity*. New York: Oxford University Press.

Wohlgennant, R. 1987. Has the question about the meaning of life any meaning?, in *Life and Meaning: A Reader* (ed. O. Hanfling). Oxford: Blackwell, pp. 34–38.

Wolf, F.O. 2009. A voice of disbelief in a different key, in *50 Voices of Disbelief: Why We Are Atheists* (ed. R. Blackford and U. Schüklenk). Oxford: Wiley-Blackwell, pp. 236–251.

Woodruff, P. 2001. *Reverence: Renewing a Forgotten Virtue*. Oxford: Oxford University Press.

Wright, R. 2009. *The Evolution of God*. New York: Little, Brown.

Wright, R. 2012. Creationists versus evolutionists: An American story. *The Atlantic*, June 11. http://www.theatlantic.com/national/archive/2012/06/creationists-vs-evolutionists-an-american-story/258384/ (accessed March 29, 2013).

Zecchino, L. and Schabner, D. 2009. Radio legend Paul Harvey dies. *ABC News* March 01. http://abcnews.go.com/Entertainment/story?id=6982226&page=1 (accessed March 25, 2013).

Zuckerman, P. 2007. Contemporary numbers and patterns, in *The Cambridge Companion to Atheism* (ed. M. Martin). Cambridge, UK: Cambridge University Press, pp. 47–65.

Index